AN AUCTIONEER'S LOT

TRIUMPHS & DISASTERS AT CHRISTIE'S

Charles Hindlip

Third Millennium
Publishing

FOR FIONA

_____

First published in Great Britain in 2016 by Third Millennium Publishing,
an imprint of Profile Books Ltd.

3 Holford Yard
Bevin Way
London WC1X 9HD
United Kingdom
www.tmbooks.com

A CIP catalogue record for this book is available from
The British Library.

ISBN 978 1 908990 81 5

Project Manager: Eleanor Tollfree
Design: Jon Allan
Production: Simon Shelmerdine

Reprographics by Studio Fasoli, Italy
Printed and bound in Italy by Printer Trento srl

Author's Acknowledgements

I am particularly grateful to Jacob Rothschild for writing the foreword to this book and to Sarah Riddell for persuading me to write it. Sarah introduced me to my long-suffering publishers, Third Millennium: Peter Jones, Patrick Taylor, Matt Wilson and Eleanor Tollfree. Thank you all.

Victoria von Preussen gave me the title for the book. Anne Mace and Heather McConville typed out my scribbles and meanderings and corrected and revised them with enormous enthusiasm, and Anne has also wrestled tirelessly with the Sisyphean task of the illustrations.

To all the clients, too numerous to mention here, who consigned lots for sale over the forty years I worked in Christie's; especially David Beaufort, Spenny Northampton, Charles Butter and his family, Julian and Robert Byng, Debbie Brice and her brother John Loeb, David Cholmondeley, Vivien Duffield, Hubert de Givenchy, Nahed Ojjeh, Juliet Tadgell, Richard Stanley and the Longleat Trustees.

To Charlotte Fraser for the Sunflowers (the last version), and George and Maria Embiricos for the first version with three blooms. My godmother Peg Margadale and so many members of the Morrison family are particularly missed, as is my godfather, George Burns. So too is Betty Looram, who, in entrusting me with her sale, did more for me than she will ever know.

To Neil MacGregor, who, as director of the National Gallery, was always wonderful to work with, even if we were on opposing sides.

To Philip Niarchos and Rupert Burgess, Director of the Niarchos Collections, and their curator, David Oakey, for permission to use images of lots both bought and sold and for their generous help over illustrations.

My thanks go to Matthew Hollow for his photography. To the following institutions which have all been prompt and generous with their help: in London, the Bridgeman Art Library and particularly John Moelwyn-Hughes, the National Gallery, the Tate, the National Portrait Gallery, the British Museum, the V&A and the Royal Collection Trust; the National Gallery of Scotland, Edinburgh; the Musée des Beaux-Arts, Strasbourg; the Rijksmuseum, Amsterdam; the Prussian Palaces and Gardens Foundation Berlin-Brandenburg; DACS; the Scala archives, Milan; the Norton Simon Museum, Pasadena, California; the Getty's Open Content Program, Los Angeles, California; the Yale Center for British Art, New Haven, Connecticut; the Iris & B. Gerald Cantor Center for Visual Arts, Stanford University, Stanford, California; the National Gallery of Art, Washington; the Metropolitan Museum of Art, New York; Harvard Art Museums, Cambridge, Massachusetts; the Wadsworth Atheneum, Hartford, Connecticut; the Mondrian Trust; the National Gallery of Canada, Ottawa; and the Miho Museum, Japan.

To the Directors and staff at Christie's, in particular to Christie's archivist Lynda McLeod and the archives department, Charles Cator, Rania Konstantinidou, Orlando Rock, Noël Annesley, John Lumley, Anthony Phillips and most especially to Francis Russell for his suggestions and help over both facts and photographs. Also to Christie's in-house lawyer Martin Wilson for checking the text (I hope he really did!). Thanks to Sotheby's and its archivist, Joanna Ling. Now he has left, I can admit my debt to Henry Wyndham and to Lucinda French and, of course, to Mark Poltimore, who remains at Sotheby's.

I would also like to thank David Ker, Simon Dickinson and James Roundell for their help and moral encouragement post-Christie's and to Nick Hemming-Brown and the staff at Dickinson's.

Thanks to John Richardson, to Julia Mount for her advice, Christopher Balfour, John Julius Norwich, Charles Beddington and Johnny van Haeften for finding the Swythamley catalogue of his dead ancestor's dead animals. Thanks to David Dawson, Eric de Rothschild and Humphrey Butler.

To those who buy this book, I hope you enjoy it as much as I enjoyed writing it and, lastly, to my children, who will probably never read it, as they must be bored to tears by my subjecting them to endless snippets from it over the last twelve months.

Contents

Foreword

In 1888 George Redford, the author of two monumental volumes on the history of art sales, wrote:

> Christie's is not a mere picture market. It has wide relations with art and deserves to be named among the art institutions of this country.

His words remain as valid this year as Christie's celebrates its 250th anniversary. It is an amazing history of survival and renaissance, not least during the crucial forty or so years when the author of this book contributed so hugely to Christie's success, in a period during which the art market changed so radically.

Charlie Hindlip tells us the stories of the great sales with humour and insights benefiting from his close relationships with the great historical families of this country who own so many treasures. Many of these most desirable works of art were to cross the Atlantic where our author had also established excellent relationships. In telling us the stories of these sales, however modest he may be, he cannot but illustrate his incredible knowledge, connoisseurship and passionate enthusiasm across an astonishing range: paintings, drawings, furniture, silver, tapestries, carpets, books, manuscripts, clocks, watches, musical instruments and porcelain are all examples.

The firm as it is today has changed over the last forty years from being a relatively small family company reliant on its relationships with the British aristocracy to becoming a powerful force in the global art market with its emphasis on contemporary works of art. Charlie Hindlip was deeply involved in this process from the day he joined Christie's to when he became Chairman in 1986. Before then Christie's had become a public company and had established its presence in the USA. The USA was soon to overtake London and its sales but the 1980s were difficult years financially and saw the collapse in the price of Christie's shares in 1987. Throughout this period, Charlie's good nature, good sense, humour and optimism, combined with his passion and enthusiasm for works of art, were crucial in enabling Christie's to transform itself.

Charlie ends his book by quoting from his hero Hilaire Belloc:

> From quiet homes and first beginning,
> Out to the undiscovered ends,
> There's nothing worth the wear of winning,
> But laughter and the love of friends.

Charlie indeed won and he won with the laughter and the love of many friends.

The Lord Rothschild, OM, GBE

With John Lumley and James Roundell after the sale of Van Gogh's *Sunflowers*, 30 March 1987.

Chapter 1

Early drawing, Eton; the Coldstream Guards; a start at Christie's

This book is about selling pictures and works of art, and a few other things as well. The paintings were sold mainly by Christie's during the forty years I worked there and also at Christie's rival, Sotheby's. I must, I suppose, give a very brief explanation of how I became involved in the art world in the first place. It certainly was not, as one ex-colleague of mine claimed of himself, because by the age of six the later works of Picasso made him feel physically sick. I had no such sensibilities.

I was, however, at a young age, intrigued by drawing. I was introduced to it by my grandfather, Colonel Malcolm Borwick, DSO, MFH, who was primarily interested in breeding foxhounds and then in hunting them. He was also by definition interested in foxes and, although he never pretended to be a draughtsman, he taught me to draw them. Here is the fox he taught me to draw at his desk, in the smoking room of the house in Northamptonshire where I was born. That was pretty much the extent of my formal training in fine art.

I did give drawing a try at Eton where I spent six remarkably undistinguished years. There was nothing wrong with the years – just me. But my efforts at learning to draw were stillborn because the senior art master, Wilfrid Blunt – a charming man, good draughtsman and fine teacher, who ended up curating the Watts Gallery near Godalming – had decided it was impossible to teach drawing to Etonians. He gave up, resting on the laurels of his one success, Rory McEwen, whom he taught to draw the most beautiful tulips. (I do not want a flood of letters telling me that I have forgotten about Howard Hodgkin – I know he was an Old Etonian.)

Wilfrid Blunt's No. 2 was called Thomas. I cannot remember his Christian name. We always called him 'Oily'. 'Oily' Thomas approached me in the drawing schools where I was struggling with a still life of a vase. Someone had made off with the flowers. He said something vaguely complimentary and asked me what I was interested in. 'Canaletto, sir,' I replied. 'Oh, a terrible artist!' he said. That was it. I never went back.

I did, though, return to the drawing schools much later wearing another hat when, as a young officer in the Coldstream Guards, I was sent to examine members of the school cadet corps who were trying to pass their Certificate A Part 2, a sort of military GCSE. This surreal experience reduced me to tears of laughter so that I

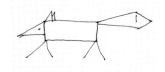

TOP TO BOTTOM

My grandfather, Colonel Malcolm Borwick, DSO, MFH

Charles Hindlip. **Fox**

OPPOSITE

Anthony Van Dyck. **Portrait of the Abbé Scaglia**, 1634

Giovanni Antonio Canal (Canaletto).
Capriccio view of Eton College,
*c.*1754

had to run and hide in the drawing schools which abutted the parade ground. In terms of influence, the parade ground clearly won, as there are a great many more generals and field marshals from that seat of learning by the Thames than ever there were famous artists.

I struggled through Eton, went to France for a bit, developed a passion for the chateaux of the Loire and pretty much everything French, and then joined the Coldstream Guards in the summer of 1959. I completed a three-year short service commission which I thoroughly enjoyed. The Coldstream is a wonderful regiment in which I was proud to serve, but I never showed a real aptitude for soldiering and so decided to pester Christie's to give me a job.

My part in the history of Christie's starts with Augustus John's *Self-Portrait* which was sold on 20 July 1962 shortly before 1pm. I.O. Chance was Chairman of Christie's and the auctioneer. He had conducted the sale with great aplomb and achieved a considerable success with the sale of John's studio. He left the rostrum, walked up to his club, White's, where he had a good lunch, came back to King Street and interviewed me. I had met him before but only for a couple of seemingly unpromising discussions. On this occasion, though, he was in a particularly good frame of mind. I think had Quasimodo applied for a job that day he probably would have got one! He agreed to take me on a year's trial and asked me if I wanted to be paid. I did. He picked up the telephone and rang someone who for the next twelve months would be the centre of my working universe – Ridley Cromwell Leadbeater, who was in charge of Christie's Front Counter. 'What are the boys paid now, Leadbeater?' he asked. '£6 a week, sir.' 'Is that all right with you, Allsopp?' asked the Chairman. 'Yes, sir,' I replied – not true but I thought it probably was not the right moment to say so.

**Ridley Leadbeater
at the Front Counter**

I went back to my battalion for a few days, confident that I had made a wise move and that I had a job, albeit only on a trial basis, with a salary barely one-third of what I was being paid to march up and down the Mall. But it was a new beginning and I can honestly say that that first year on the Front Counter was among the happiest of my life.

I may have been happy, but Christie's per se was not. It was suffering from an almost total eclipse by its rival, Sotheby's. Most people reading this today will be accustomed to an art world dominated by Christie's and Sotheby's who fight tooth and claw over every single lot coming on to the market; where chief executives or whatever they are called can be summarily dismissed like football managers if turnover falls more than a couple of percentage points; where prices of works of art at other auction houses seldom, if ever, reach those achieved by Sotheby's or Christie's; and where dealers, however big (and in some cases, like Gagosian, they are enormous), only occasionally compete.

Were this book to have been written in 1928, the situation would have been quite different. That year, on 17 and 18 May, Christie's held a sale of paintings from the collection of the late Sir George Holford which made £416,917. In the foreword to the first Christie's review, *Christie's Season 1928*, A.C.R. Carter, the renowned saleroom correspondent of the *Daily Telegraph*, wrote thus:

> In less than 'forty years on', as they sing at Harrow, Christie's will be commemorating the bicentenary of its foundation, for it was on 'Fryday, Dec. 5, 1766,' according to the earliest catalogue in the archives, that James Christie, the 'onlie begetter' of the famous house, held his first public sale in Pall Mall. It is not my purpose here to re-write the stirring chronicles of the greatest firm of art auctioneers in that city which is admitted to be the most important clearing-house in the world of art, but when I survey in retrospect

the remarkable events in the season of 1927–8, I begin to wonder what will be the expanded dimensions of the bidding at Christie's art sales in 1966.

OPPOSITE

Augustus John. **Self-Portrait**, *c.*1940

Well, it did not quite turn out the way A.C.R. Carter expected. Although the art market continued to flourish with Christie's continuing to dominate it, that dominance, firmly established by James Christie himself, was to be of a very short duration. The sale of the Holford Collection in 1928 was to be the market's high-water mark, with the world plunging into economic chaos and Wall Street crashing the following year.

The most expensive picture at the Holford sale (which was to prove the largest ever) was Rembrandt's *Man with a Torah*, which made 48,000 guineas, but the best picture, by general consent, was Van Dyck's *Portrait of the Abbé Scaglia*. It was knocked down with a single bid to 'Berry' for 30,000 guineas. William Berry, later first Viscount Camrose, was the proprietor of the *Daily Telegraph* and had come to the sale out of curiosity. I believe he had thought this beautiful Van Dyck would sell for much more; he had not seriously thought that his single bid from the back of the room to Christie's Senior Partner, Lance Hannen, would result in him buying this masterpiece. But it did.

The art market survived the Wall Street Crash for a couple of years before it, too, collapsed, seeing only a brief revival just before the Second World War engulfed it again. One day someone will write a really good history of the firm from the late eighteenth to the early twentieth centuries, illustrating its amazing achievements during that period. It was a remarkable story, soon to draw to a close.

Chapter 2

Christie's and Sotheby's early sales compared; Christie's Front Counter

Sotheby's emerged from the Second World War in a much stronger position than Christie's. Although obviously I was not there, this volte-face appears to have taken the then Directors of Christie's by surprise, almost as if they were sleepwalking.

Christie's position had not been helped by the fact that their headquarters in King Street had received a direct hit from six incendiary bombs on the night of 16–17 April 1941, but that was not the real reason. The Directors did not see what Peter Wilson at Sotheby's, in particular, saw in the late 1950s, that the art market was fundamentally changing. The accepted dominance of old master pictures was on the decline, and the era of impressionist, post-impressionist and modern pictures was about to replace it. Obviously this did not happen overnight, but there was one sale, held shortly after my first interview with I.O. Chance, which gave a clear indication that times were changing. This was of course the Goldschmidt sale which took place on 15 October 1958. The executors of the estate offered the paintings both to Christie's and to Sotheby's. There has always been conjecture over why Sotheby's rather than Christie's were given the sale.

The Berkeley Castle silver service by Jacques Roettiers, late 1730s

OPPOSITE

Nicolas de Largillière. **La Belle Strasbourgeoise**, 1703

There is a good account of the approaches made by the two firms in John Herbert's book *Inside Christie's*. This places the blame fairly and squarely on the shoulders of Sir Alec Martin, Christie's Managing Director, who, without question, had failed to see the writing on the wall. Sotheby's had sold some good impressionist pictures in the two or three years beforehand, but the Goldschmidt sale was by any standards exceptional, including as it did Cézanne's *Garçon au gilet rouge*, Edouard Manet's *Manet par lui-même* and Van Gogh's *Jardin du poète*, and it established Sotheby's as the leading auctioneer, a position that was not to be challenged until the 1980s.

In the same year as the Goldschmidt sale, Sotheby's sold the Duke of Westminster's Rubens for £275,000. Great old masters were still just more valuable than the best paintings by the great impressionists but while the supply of impressionist pictures for the following fifty years would be plentiful, the supply of old master pictures would be ever diminishing. Sotheby's predominance continued with the auction house frequently in the headlines and not just for pictures: in 1960, the Berkeley silver dinner service by the French goldsmith Jacques Roettiers, made a staggering sum of £207,000 and was bought by John Partridge for Stavros Niarchos.

It was against this background that I was given my job, and in the letter that I.O. Chance wrote to my father confirming that he would take me on for a year's trial, he included a slightly discouraging sentence: 'I see little hope for a boy of his age in the firm at the moment.' He could of course have been alluding to my very limited qualifications for employment by Christie's, but he might also have been airing his subconscious feeling that there was little hope for the continued existence of Christie's.

I have referred to my old Chairman up to this point as I.O. Chance. He was christened Ivan Oswald and, always a stickler for correct form, insisted on being addressed on paper as I.O. or Ivan, but he did not particularly like either. At a young age, he had been nicknamed Peter by his mother. He preferred it and to those at Christie's he was either I.O.C. or Peter. In future, I will refer to him by his informal name.

Christie's problems were unknown to me. I was embarking on my first proper job, I was pleased to have it, I was very excited by the prospects, and I did not understand how dire the circumstances were. As a private company Christie's did not have to publish its accounts, but it had barely made a profit since the 1930s and by now, in 1962, it was on the verge of bankruptcy. It was still, though, a fascinating place to work and I am going to try to describe what happened during the forty years I was there. I am

Monday 1st October
ORIENTAL PORCELAIN, JADES AND BRONZES

Tuesday 2nd October
PRINTS AND DRAWINGS BY OLD MASTERS

Wednesday 3rd October
FINE SILVER

Thursday 4th October
OAK AND EARLY WALNUT FURNITURE, PEWTER
AND A RARE BATTERIE DE CUISINE

Friday 5th October
FINE OLD MASTER PAINTINGS

Sales announcements

certainly not, however, going to go into the politics of the business, some of the strange practices of the auction rooms, and the stranger people who practised them.

All that, in any case, was years away. The job in hand was performing the daily tasks set by Mr Leadbeater: opening up the Front Counter every morning and stencilling the announcement of the sales for the following week.

This task had to be done with old plastic stencilling and black indelible ink. One mistake, and it was all to be done again – quite a challenge for a seasoned dyslexic like myself. After this came entering yesterday's receipts in the day book and taking round the Directors' post. Only the six Directors were allowed to write letters in their own names, everyone else had to write: 'Dear Sir … Yours faithfully, Christie's' and have the letter signed off by a Director. Consequently, except on rare occasions, no one except the Directors received letters. All correspondence addressed to Christie's or Christie, Manson & Woods would be opened and placed in a tray for the relevant department to collect from the post room by 10.30am, or by 8.30am on Tuesdays when the Directors met and the post room reverted to its true function, the firm's boardroom.

This happy routine was in a world where Sotheby's had sold all the major works of art in almost every category. During the 1961–2 season, they had posted a turnover of £8,836,000 compared with Christie's £3,500,000. In the foreword to that year's *Christie's Review*, the writer – almost certainly the Chairman – commented that for the first time since the Second World War there was a marked shortage of fine French furniture, detailing the total of that department's sales at £101,000. Frank Davies, *The Times*'s saleroom correspondent, writing in *Sotheby's Review*, records 'many notable pieces of 18th-century French furniture'. Those coming from Lord Powis alone made in excess of £50,000.

An even greater imbalance existed with old master pictures. The sale of Augustus John's studio, the highlight of Christie's season, made just under £100,000 while Sotheby's sold Rembrandt's *St Bartholomew* from the collection of W.M.P. Kincaid-Lennox of the 'real' Downton – Downton Castle in Hereford – for £190,000. Even though it was not a spectacular season for old masters, there were many other good pictures at Sotheby's too.

Sotheby's also outclassed Christie's meagre offerings in 1961–2 in the field of impressionist and modern paintings, with the sales of pictures from the collection of Sir Alexander Korda, the famous film director, and the no-less-impressive collection of the writer Somerset Maugham. Korda's collection included a wonderful Monet of members of the painter's family on the river which made £56,000, and the star of the collection, Van Gogh's *Still Life of Oranges and Lemons with Blue Gloves*, which fetched £80,000. Maugham's double-sided Picasso also made £80,000.

Vincent van Gogh. **Still Life of Oranges and Lemons with Blue Gloves**, 1889

The best that Christie's could do in my first autumn was to sell the Heywood-Lonsdale *Dido and Aeneas in Carthage* by Claude – a beautiful picture which was recently exhibited in the Ashmolean Museum in Oxford – for 52,000 guineas. It was joined by a few other good old masters, but this time the foreword in *Christie's Review of the Year* bewails their shortage. This was true at Christie's but hardly so at Sotheby's, who sold Largillière's ravishing *La Belle Strasbourgeoise* for £145,000. A Raphael from the same owner, Mrs Fitzgerald, went for £95,000; a remarkably good group of Dutch pictures from a Dutch collector, J.C.H. Heldring, including a masterpiece by Pieter Saenredam, *Interior of S. Bavo's, Haarlem*, made £36,000; and pictures from Col. William Stirling of Keir, including works by Zurbarán, Murillo and Pietro Longhi, did well. No shortage there! Sotheby's turnover increased to just short of £11 million, widening the gap with Christie's, who increased theirs by a modest £25,000 to £3,750,000; but that was neither the high point for Sotheby's nor the low-water mark for Christie's.

Claude Lorrain. **Dido and Aeneas in Carthage**, 1676

BELOW

A Meissen figure of Harlequin by J.J. Kändler, c.1740

The most attractive collection of the year in fact came from René Fribourg, the New York collector principally of porcelain but also of some good pictures and furniture, which Peter Chance really felt he was going to get for Christie's: he had holidayed with the Fribourgs the previous year. However, it was not to be. The collection went to Sotheby's and made exceptional prices. One particular lot, a figure of a Harlequin by J. J. Kändler, which sold for £9,000, somehow seemed to typify the collection. I went to Sotheby's and viewed it with a very disconsolate Chairman.

A bigger blow was to come on 11 June 1963 with the sale of 'The Highly Important Collection of French Impressionist Paintings formed by the late William A. Cargill of Carruth, Bridge of Weir, Scotland'. This was the first time I had been to a sale at Sotheby's. For an aspiring member of Christie's Picture Department it was a painful evening. But it was a fascinating one, too, with beautiful pictures and stunning results. Two lots particularly impressed me: the Degas pastel *Danseuse basculant (danseuse verte)* and Monet's *Pont du chemin de fer à Argenteuil*.

OPPOSITE

Edgar Degas. **Danseuse basculant (Danseuse verte)**, 1877-9

The evening also laid bare for me the myth which was propagated at Christie's, that Peter Wilson was not a good auctioneer. The reverse was true. No one I have ever subsequently seen could rival his ability to quieten an excited saleroom with skilful use of silence and a pause for dramatic effect which almost invariably attracted another bid. These pauses helped him to raise £1,043,590 for the evening's work.

The following year saw the gloom punctuated by Christie's selling much better pictures. We negotiated, on behalf of Lord Derby, Rembrandt's great *Belshazzar's Feast* in lieu of tax for a gross price of £750,000, net of £150,000. We also sold by private treaty, on behalf of the Throckmorton family, Largillière's portrait of *Sir Robert Throckmorton*, which was a worthy rival to Sotheby's *Belle Strasbourgeoise*. We sold at auction, in rather complicated circumstances and for 62,000 guineas, the portrait of Sir Robert's sister, *Elizabeth Throckmorton, Canoness of the Order of the Dames Augustines Anglaises* by the same artist.

There were a number of other good things, including a little Pieter Bruegel the Elder, *Two Soldiers Playing Musical Instruments*, now in the Frick. David Carritt, Christie's new old master expert, identified it as having belonged to King Charles I when Prince of Wales. On the reverse was a brand, a crowned *CP*; Carritt realised that *CP* stood not, as had been believed, for Choiseul-Praslin but for Carolus Princeps. Also included in the sale were three not bad pictures which I managed to extract from East Germany; I was given a bonus for my efforts.

David Bathurst's position as Head of the Impressionist and Modern Picture Department bore fruit and that year we had a sale which, if it did not rival Sotheby's, at least put us on the map with a portrait of the writer, painter and caricaturist André Rouveyre by Modigliani; a good Vuillard pastel, *Le Salon, le soir à Vaucresson*; a Boisgeloup Picasso, *Figures et plante*; and an important early Monet, *La Pointe de la Hève, Honfleur*, painted in 1864, which was the first to draw attention to his name at the Paris Salon of 1865. It made 20,000 guineas.

But anything we could do, they could do better. Sotheby's turnover that year, 1964, increased to £13,251,000, more than three times Christie's turnover of £4,300,000. What was, in a way, worse, was that Sotheby's had no particularly large or spectacular consignments that season. They just had a wealth of works of art in every field, seemingly from all over the world. Looking through their review, the *Ivory Hammer*, the picture that I would most like to have taken home would definitely have been Pissarro's *La Barrière du chemin de fer aux pâtis près de Pontoise*, which made £32,000 and now belongs to an old friend of mine, sadly not a seller.

Chapter 3

Christie's secure the Cook and Northwick collections; failure with Sickert; trip to America; the Barnes Foundation; the Lehman Collection and the Frick

Sotheby's sales continued like hammer blows to rain down on Christie's corporate head. We lost our last remaining record, furniture, which had been for the Llangattock Oeben table. It was replaced in the public's esteem by Lord Rosebery's spectacular Roentgen commode, which made £63,000. I went to Sotheby's with Peter Chance to look at it. It was another sale that he had hoped to get. The commode was bought by that redoubtable couple Jack and Belle Linsky, who made their considerable fortune from two remarkably simple inventions: the staple remover which Jack Linsky's company Swingline sold with the stapler – 'so you won't have to look all over the place for one' – and (less obvious but I believe even more profitable) a sunken screw in the old telephone dial.

Sunken was almost Christie's sad state, but at the eleventh hour fate came to the rescue. It was always said, both at Christie's and Sotheby's, that these firms' best friends were death and divorce, closely followed by fast women and slow horses, and cards and dice that, like slow horses, did not win. The first turn of fate, just in time to save Christie's, was sad but not unexpected: the death of Captain Edward George Spencer-Churchill of Northwick Park. George Churchill disliked both horses and women and never married. Christie's other great benefactor in this time of need was the seven-times-married Francis Cook. Both men had inherited substantial portions of what had been two of the greatest collections in Britain and both had a genuine interest in works of art. Churchill was from boyhood a passionate collector, and Cook was a painter, albeit not a very successful one. Captain George was a loyal friend of Christie's, Cook possibly less so although his last wife, Brenda, was very loyal to Christie's and subsequently to me. That, though, was where the similarities ended.

While all this excitement was going on, with the triumphant smiles at Sotheby's and the stiff upper lips at Christie's, I had been working away in the warehouse, having been promoted to the junior position in the Picture Department in the summer of 1963. Even before I had officially become a member of the Department, I had been told to deal with a rather intriguing picture. A client had consigned a painting by

OPPOSITE

Edouard Manet. **The Railway**, 1873

Walter Sickert of HM King Edward VIII during that brief time when he was in fact king in 1936. He was depicted, probably for the last time, in the uniform of the Welsh Guards, whose colonel he had been as Prince of Wales. As I had only just left the brigade of guards myself, I was asked if I would get in touch with Welsh Guards' regimental headquarters and see if they would be interested either in bidding on the picture or buying it privately before the sale. The price was, from memory, £800. I was very enthusiastic about the picture but no one was interested. Someone asked me: 'Why would we want the picture?' How could they not want it? I thought, and had I had the room to hang it, I would have tried to buy it myself. It remained unsold. It is now regarded as one of Sickert's most important late paintings and the fact that it was painted from a photograph adds to rather than detracts from that interest, as it links Sickert's work even more closely to his mentor, Degas. Looking again at the troubled features of the King, I regret even more that I did not buy it. The first of many failures!

That autumn I was selected, along with Brian Sewell and the lovely Julia Lucas, now the wife of Ferdinand Mount and mother of *The Spectator*'s Harry Mount, to go on a National Art-Collections Fund trip to the east coast of America. All three of us were very excited as none of us had ever been to the US before.

We made landfall in Boston and the first port of call was the Museum of Fine Art. This first American museum bowled me over. The great staircase was hung with late Monets of the Seine. The galleries were filled with endless wonderful pictures;

my favourite, Degas's *At the Races*, featured a carriage intriguingly offset to the right of the composition. It is an image that will always remain with me. We also saw splendid old masters at the Isabella Stewart Gardner Museum and were received at the Somerset Club. If English clubs could be stuffy and old-fashioned, nothing could be as archaic as the Somerset Club, which appeared to have been last decorated by an elderly relation of Edith Wharton and had not been touched since. I loved it. I hope it's still the same today. We also went to the Fogg Art Museum at Harvard, where I first saw Ingres's sketch *Study for 'Roger Freeing Angelica'*. Many years later, Stavros Niarchos told me he thought it was the sexiest picture he had ever seen and asked me to find out if it would ever be for sale. It was not, but I see what he means.

We made our way south on our Greyhound bus, stopping at the Wadsworth Atheneum in Hartford, Connecticut and met death on the way in the shape of the haunting *Old Man and Death* by Wright of Derby. We nearly did meet death later on the trip, driving over a red light on the way to see Jefferson's incomparable Monticello, but before that we stopped in Baltimore to see the Walters Art Museum and spent a day and a half in Washington. I was again entranced, this time by the National Gallery: the collection was so well displayed in John Russell Pope's splendid white marble temple. The only thing I found upsetting about it was that the most popular picture was Salvador Dalí's *Crucifixion*, where Mary Magdalene is depicted as the artist's wife, which I thought ticked all the wrong boxes. A much more uplifting note was provided by Manet's little girl clutching the railings in the picture entitled *The Railway*. The patriot in me resented the presence of the superb Raphael, *St George and the Dragon*, given to Henry VII by the Duke of Urbino on his receiving the Order of the Garter, currently shown on St George's left leg. The picture had travelled variously from Charles I to Pierre Crozat, to Catherine II and then to Andrew W. Mellon who bought it for the museum. We also went to the Phillips

LEFT TO RIGHT

Edgar Degas. **At the Races in the Countryside**, 1869

Jean-Auguste-Dominique Ingres. **Study for 'Roger Freeing Angelica'**, 1818

Collection, where I fell in love with Renoir's *Déjeuner des canotiers*, and headed off again to Williamsburg and down the James River to the southern point of our trip: Charlottesville, Virginia and Monticello.

On the way back, we stopped in Philadelphia where I had two excitements. The first was to be asked to tea by Henry McIlhenny to look at the collection of paintings in his house in Rittenhouse Square. He was very kind but told me he regarded auctioneers as crows on telegraph poles waiting for a message that someone had died. I couldn't argue with this, but more about his remarkable collection later. We also visited the Barnes Foundation. Not all of our party (I think there were about sixty of us) was allowed in and there was a ballot. I was lucky enough to get one of the tickets. During my first hour, looking at what must surely be the greatest collection of nineteenth- and early twentieth-century paintings ever put together, I heard two of the elderly members of our group asking the guards whether they could possibly see a catalogue or at least a list of the pictures. One of the guards said (in an American accent), 'Ma'am, we expect people who come here to know what they are looking at.' Undaunted, one of them replied (this time in an English accent), 'My good man, were the pictures better lit, we might be able to see what we are looking at!'

The way the Barnes Foundations's art collection was then displayed was completely eccentric, with less-than-brilliant Dutch pictures close hung next to stunning Renoirs and Van Goghs, interspersed with pieces of ironwork of dubious origin and, as the two old ladies observed, very badly lit. After an hour of intense viewing, I decided I would go out into the garden, dressed in its best fall colours, and contemplate what I wished to go back and study for the second time. I went round the garden, came back and was told to go away – there was no readmission.

The following day we arrived in New York and the first of many treats was a cocktail party at the Frick, where I met the then director, Professor Harry Greer. In the course of the conversation I told him about the Barnes Foundation and he said, 'My word, you are lucky! I have never managed to see the pictures.' 'Surely someone in your position can go any time he wants?' I said. 'No,' he explained, 'Quite the reverse is true. I did once get an appointment to see the pictures and I was greeted by Dr Barnes at the door, who took one look at me and said, very disagreeably, "Young man, I don't like your hat!" I removed it and apologised and he said, "I told you I don't like your hat and no one wearing a hat like yours will ever get to see my pictures. Good day, sir."' There are many stories like this of Dr Barnes, who was eventually killed being driven by his chauffeur through a red light: such was his mania for punctuality that he did not allow such minor details as traffic signals to interfere. The chauffeur survived and, with Barnes's widow, continued to exercise the doctor's perverse wishes from beyond the grave. As most readers will probably now realise, the Barnes has been reformed, the pictures rehung, and the visiting

Henri Matisse. **Le Madras Rouge**, 1907

arrangements and the welcome improved. It is thoroughly worth a visit to see its 181 Renoirs, 69 Cézannes, 59 Matisses (many painted *in situ*), 46 Picassos, 16 Modiglianis and 7 Van Goghs.

Fascinating though my visit to the Barnes Foundation was, nothing up to that point could compare with the Frick and, to this day, a visit there always raises the spirits. There is one picture, a popular favourite, Giovanni Bellini's *St Francis in the Desert*, sometimes called *St Francis in the Garden* (which once belonged to Thomas Holloway, the founder of Holloway College), which I will talk about in a later chapter but illustrate here. It is one of the most beautiful pictures in the whole museum and that is saying quite a lot. The Frick, though, is well known to anybody who knows New

ABOVE

Giovanni Bellini. **St Francis in the Desert**, *c.* 1476–8

LEFT

Giovanni di Paolo. **Creation of the World and the Expulsion from Paradise**, 1445

York and loves works of art. What I was privileged to see the following day no longer exists in the form it did then. It is almost in its entirety in the Metropolitan Museum, not lost but not quite so special as it was. I am referring to the collection of Robert Lehman, then still housed at West 54th Street.

New York was and is full of superlatives but few could compete with the Lehman Collection as it then was. The main room contained El Greco's *St Jerome as Scholar* over the mantelpiece, Rembrandt's *Portrait of Gérard de Lairesse*, Holbein's *Erasmus of Rotterdam*, El Greco's *Christ Carrying the Cross* and a Frans Hals. In the other room there was the Maître de Moulins's enchanting *Suzanne de Bourbon*, a major Petrus Cristus, then known as *The Legend of St Eligius*, Memling's stunning *Portrait of a Young Man* and Ingres's *Princesse de Broglie* – almost as good as *La Comtesse d'Haussenville* in the Frick. But the pictures that entranced me the most were Degas's *Chez la modiste* and one of the smallest pictures in the collection (but surely one of the most beautiful), Giovanni di Paolo's *Creation of the World and the Expulsion from Paradise*, which shows the world as an extraordinary, circular rainbow.

That same day, Brian Sewell and I went together (we had introductions) to the apartment of Judge Irwin Untermyer, which was remarkable in its way for the amazing English furniture and silver, but slightly depressing if you liked pictures: there were none. The panelled walls of the apartment were covered in early needlework and it was here that I learnt something about America's view of heredity. Judge Untermyer admitted that the gifts from his parents formed the basis of the collection, but when I said how wonderful it would be to be one of his children, he asked, rather crossly, why? And I said, because they would be getting all this. 'They won't get anything,' he said. He was right; it too all went to the Metropolitan. I don't think Judge Untermyer liked people very much; he certainly gave that impression to Brian and me. That experience was probably the only thing about our trip to America which I did not enjoy.

When, the following year, I was offered the opportunity to work in New York, I grabbed it with both hands. I still always get a lift from the Frick, and I get the same lift from driving over the Triborough Bridge and seeing again New York's incomparable skyline.

The Northwick saga had, in fact, started before our trip and continued after it. On our return, we joined the rest of the Picture Department, already ensconced at Northwick.

Chapter 4

The Northwick Collection in more detail; Sir Francis Cook and Rembrandt's *Titus*; the Harewood desk

The Northwick Collection was formed, in the main, by John, second Lord Northwick and housed originally at Northwick Park, Gloucestershire. This large, rambling house had been bought by Sir John Rushout, first Lord Northwick, the head of a Flemish banking family who had come to England in the seventeenth century (the baronetcy dates from 1661). The house had been remodelled from a design, reputedly by Lord Burlington, around 1730. Despite the addition of a picture gallery in 1832, it had not proved big enough to house what was to become one of the largest collections of paintings in the country. As a young man, John Rushout had lived in Rome and travelled and collected extensively throughout Europe. On his father's death in 1800, he finally returned home to live at Northwick but, finding the house, even with its enlargements, still inadequate for his ever-growing collection, he also bought Thirlestane House in Cheltenham. John, second Lord Northwick never married and on his death in 1859 it was discovered that he had not made a will.

OPPOSITE

Sandro Botticelli. **Portrait of a Young Man**, c.1480-5

His nephew, George, third Lord Northwick, offered to buy out the remaining heirs in order to keep the collection intact. Sadly, his very handsome offer of £80,000 was refused and sales took place at Northwick and Thirlestane House which lasted for some twenty-two days and totalled £91,000. The sales were conducted, ironically, not by Christie's but by Phillips and attracted huge interest. The third Lord Northwick, frustrated by his relations, did his best, but in a rather haphazard way, to buy as much as he could of the collection, in the end securing about one-third of it. The results were intriguing in that, not for the first or the last time, popular fashion came up with some strange surprises. The most expensive picture was Daniel Maclise's *Robin Hood and His Merry Men Entertaining Richard the Lionheart in the Forest of Sherwood*, which cost him 1,370 guineas, whereas the beautiful *Portrait of a Young Man* by Botticelli (catalogued as Masaccio) was bought by the National Gallery for £108.

Lord Northwick moved into Northwick Park and lived there until his death in 1887. Like his uncle before him, he had no direct heir, and when his widow died in 1912 the entire estate and collection was left to Captain Edward George Spencer-

Churchill, the grandson of the sixth Duke of Marlborough on one side, and great-grandson of Lady Northwick on the other.

Captain George, as he was always known, had been sent to Egypt as a boy for health reasons and had developed a taste for antiquities. While still at Eton, he learnt to translate Egyptian hieroglyphs and he also showed an appreciation and knowledge for pictures as well as huge enthusiasm for the classical world; he was to enlarge and enhance the collection he inherited by a very considerable degree. Before inheriting Northwick, Captain George, a Grenadier, had fought with distinction in the Boer War. In the First World War (1914–18), he was his battalion's intelligence officer. He was severely wounded twice and was awarded the *Croix de guerre* as well as the Military Cross.

Despite the wounds, Captain George's energy, quite extraordinary for one thought so delicate as a child, was inexhaustible and he added tirelessly to his collection at Northwick, not only in the field of Greek and Roman antiquities for which he had a passion, but also old master pictures. Though relatively well-off, he could not regularly buy at important sales as the second Lord Northwick had done. He chose instead, week upon week, to visit Christie's, Sotheby's, Bonham's and Phillips, as well as auctioneers in the country, in order to view their sales of old master pictures. Aided by a large magnifying glass and his considerable acquired knowledge, he added to his collection at Northwick over 200 pictures: the Northwick Rescues, he called them. They were mainly dirty to the point of invisibility and almost always misattributed, enabling him to make some really worthwhile discoveries.

When I knew him first, Captain George was already in his late eighties and, although always defying the odds, he could not live forever. He was unmarried and had made it known that he wished his collection to be sold on his death. He had made clear his preference for Christie's but I am sure he had received blandishments from our rivals. The knowledge that in the foreseeable future this great collection would come up for sale inevitably meant that quite a lot of time and effort was devoted to looking after Captain George when he came to London for the sales, and to visiting him at Northwick. He knew and liked Peter Chance and he had asked Patrick Lindsay to write a description of the collection for Weidenfeld and Nicolson's excellent book, *Great Private Collections*, edited by Douglas Cooper. I had been introduced to George by Peter Chance during my first summer at Christie's. We became friends and, despite the discomfort of the house, I enjoyed my weekends at Northwick, talking to him about pictures and learning something about his amazing antiquities. He liked me, I think, because I had recently been a Coldstreamer and his life had been saved by an officer in my regiment. On top of that, his best friend in the Grenadiers, Charles Britten, had been married to my great-aunt Dorothy. She was one of the few ladies the distinctly misogynistic George really liked.

I had, on several occasions, helped him show visitors round the house and it was with a view to this that I had driven down from London rather late on a Friday evening in the summer of 1964, aiming to be there in time for dinner. Captain George was, as could be expected of someone of his age and background, a stickler for punctuality. I was late. I parked my car, grabbed my bag and darted into the house through the back door, pausing past the kitchen to call to the wonderful cook, Mrs George: 'Has the Captain gone into dinner?' 'No, Mr Allsopp, haven't you heard? The Captain met with an accident in London and you are to call Mr Chance.' This I did, to be told the gruesome news that poor George had fallen into a bath of near boiling water and had probably passed out and, having been unable to get out of the bath, had been horribly scalded. It had been foul weather all week, so the racegoers who had come to London for Ascot did not get up and draw water for their baths as anticipated by the management of the Guards' Club, who had turned the boilers full on. When Captain George, who was not a racing man, got up at his usual time, the water which came out of the taps was close to boiling. By the time Peter Chance talked to me, George was still alive but in hospital, in agony. I stayed on at the house, showed round the visitors as best I could, and on either the Sunday evening or Monday morning, Peter rang me with the inevitable news that Captain George had died.

The will specified that Christie's should sell the entire collection, other than a specific bequest of antiquities and vases that was to go to the British Museum and the Ashmolean. Captain George had also, in a gesture typical of his quirky sense of humour, left one of the least attractive pictures, a *Still Life* by Pieter Hardyme, to the National Gallery, having said to me and I am sure to others before his death, 'They don't have one'. Almost half the staff at Christie's were sent down to Northwick and billeted in the bedrooms of the third floor of the house which were not usually used. As I have mentioned earlier, the house had not been comfortable when Captain George was living there. In his absence, it became even less so. I had recently been given a sponge bag as a present, which had a metal soap-box. After the first night, I never again failed to put the soap in the metal box because the one night I did not, on waking up, I noticed that the soap had teeth and claw marks all over it, which were easily recognisable. The Latin description of the culprit, which Captain George would have used himself, was *rattus rattus*. There was more than one of this particular rodent living in the upper floors at Northwick Park.

The enormous task of cataloguing everything in the house began. Interesting though it was, I will not try and describe anything other than the sale of the paintings as these, along with pictures from the Cook Collection which I will come to shortly, were to fuel Christie's first significant steps towards catching up with their rivals. It is at this point that I should mention another twist of fate, which seemed at the time particularly cruel.

LEFT TO RIGHT

Rembrandt van Rijn. **Portrait of a Boy**, 1655–60

Domenico Beccafumi. **Tanaquil**, c.1519

OPPOSITE

Quentin Massys. **Portrait of a Notary in the character of St Fiacre**, c.1510–20

Despite the fact that George Spencer-Churchill had specified in his will that he wished Christie's to sell his collection, the executors still had the power to overturn this wish if it were not in the interests of the beneficiaries. His estate was subject to the full rate of death duties; at the time this was 80 per cent but, if pictures were accepted in lieu, 25 per cent of the tax due was remitted. This meant that if a work of art was sold to a museum, the beneficiary received almost exactly double what they would get from selling it at auction. The executors decided to surrender the two Roman heroines *Tanaquil* and *Marcia* by Domenico Beccafumi to the National Gallery; Reynolds's sublime *Portrait of Warren Hastings* and an early *Self-Portrait* by Gainsborough to the National Portrait Gallery; the exceptionally fine *Portrait of a Notary in the character of St Fiacre* by Quentin Massys to the National Gallery of Scotland; and a Cosimo Rosselli altarpiece – *The Adoration of the Infant Christ* – to Birmingham. I don't know who the executors' advisers were at the time but they made a fairly astute choice, and not one which coincided with Patrick Lindsay's and Captain George's remarkably similar opinion. The latter were convinced of the merits of Pieter Bruegel the Elder's *Peasant Wedding*, Gerard David's *Adoration of the Magi*, the little Fra Angelico panel entitled *A Miracle of SS Cosmos and Damian*, and Lorenzo Monaco's *The Presentation in the Temple*. Today these pictures are all in some way disputed and in fact were so at the time of the sale. It was sad to see what were undoubtedly the best pictures taken out of the sale; those pictures that were left, Captain George's favourites, were not a great consolation. There is little doubt, however, that it was in favour of the beneficiaries, although it was certainly not what Captain George wanted. He used to say: 'I don't know what these pictures are worth, but my ghosts will.' Sadly, in some cases, they did not, but in other cases, they would have been pleasantly surprised. We will come to that, but before doing so we must turn to the Cook Collection.

By a matter of a few months, George Spencer-Churchill's death preceded Sir Francis Cook's decision to sell the most important pictures remaining in his family collection, known previously as the Doughty House Collection. It had been founded in the nineteenth century by Francis's great-grandfather, Sir Francis Cook, the first Baronet, a successful merchant and haberdasher. He had formed his collection with the help of Sir John Charles Robinson, the superintendent of collections of the newly opened South Kensington Museum, later called the Victoria and Albert Museum. The collection was housed in Doughty House, Richmond, and had never contained as many pictures as the Northwick and Thirlestane collections, amounting at its peak to about 400 – the Northwick Collection in its prime comprised over 2,000 pictures. The Cook Collection had had its share of masterpieces, amongst them Velázquez's *Old Woman Cooking Eggs* (sold in 1955 to the National Gallery of Scotland), Jan and Hubert Van Eyck's *Three Marys at the Tomb* and Filippo Lippi's *The Adoration of the Magi*, which had all gone. However, by 1964 there remained in the collection a substantial number of pictures, including Rembrandt's *Portrait of a Boy ('Titus')*, Velázquez's *Don Juan Calabazas*, Antonello da Messina's *Christ at the Column*, a Fra Bartolomeo, a beautiful Rubens, a Poussin, and a large and rare picture by Michiel Sweerts (*see p.135*).

Just after Christmas 1965, as I remember it, Sir Francis asked us to consider including in the spring sale the Rembrandt and three other pictures. He wanted the best service and the best results, and to make matters more difficult, a couple of years earlier he had already entrusted the Rembrandt to Agnew's for a private sale at a price lower than the one he was asking us now to achieve for him. Although he was also being hotly pursued by Sotheby's and knew their chairman Peter Wilson, his respect for our new employee David Carritt and his fondness for Peter Chance inclined him towards entrusting the collection to Christie's. We were asked to go to Jersey to discuss the final details and, if these could be agreed, take the pictures away with us.

With this visit in view, Peter Chance asked me one morning to go and buy a cosh. I found one in that admirable shop Swaine, Adeney Brigg & Sons Ltd, which still exists in truncated form but no longer sells coshes. I was used to fairly eccentric requests but this was quite unusual and I asked him respectfully why. He said we were going to Jersey to collect a very important picture which was a tremendous secret. We were not permitted to be armed, obviously, and it was difficult to arrange an escort at the last moment, so I was to accompany him with the cosh and help guard the picture on the return from Jersey. We would be travelling in his Bentley and in a Dakota because Patrick Lindsay, who knew about aeroplanes, said they were the safest mode of transport. Safe they may have been but comfortable they were not. Peter and David Carritt had seats. I sat on the floor with several empty crates and with Jim Taylor, a foreman porter, both of us clutching a rope in lieu of seatbelts. Thus we set off from Northolt to St Helier Airport. It was also very cold. We arrived, looked at the pictures which, with the exception of the Dürer, were very impressive, and sat down to an agreeable lunch, interrupted towards the end by Sir Francis's butler whispering to him that there was 'a Mr Wilson on the telephone'. Sir Francis asked to be excused and went into another room to receive Sotheby's final terms. While this conversation was taking place, the pictures were actually being removed from the house and marched past the dining room windows.

Fortunately, the terms offered by Sotheby's were not sufficient to change Sir Francis's mind and we left with an agreement and the four pictures in the Dakota. We returned to Northolt where Rogers, our favourite carrier, met us with their van. We loaded the pictures and drove to Christie's, escorted by the Bentley, the Chairman at the wheel, David Carritt beside him, and me in the back with the cosh. Safely delivered, the pictures were duly catalogued and advertised along with the best pictures from the Northwick Collection. The Cook pictures would be included in the regular old master picture sale which was to take place in March and the Northwick pictures in a special auction in May.

The day before the first sale I was summoned again by Peter Chance to his office and asked a series of slightly strange questions. Did I have a blue suit? Yes, I was wearing one. Did I have a black briefcase? Yes. Blue tie? Yes, I was wearing one. I was to go out and buy a copy of the *Financial Times* and a buttonhole, and to go with Mr Jack, Peter's chauffeur, who would take a Daimler (the Bentley being too ostentatious) and meet a flight from Los Angeles which was meant to get in at 11.45pm, but which was apparently often late. I was to wait until it arrived at whatever time because there would be someone on it who would identify himself and who was to come and look at the pictures before the sale took place. 'Could I ask who I am to meet?' 'Well, it's a secret, but yes, he is an American collector called Norton Simon'. 'OK,' I said. The instructions continued: if the flight arrived before midnight, Peter would see Mr Simon himself; if it arrived later, Peter, who was to take the sale the following day, would go to bed and I was to bring Mr Simon to Christie's where Patrick Lindsay and David Carritt would show him the pictures. The flight was indeed very late and arrived around 3am. I had rung Peter to say he should go to bed, and we arrived at about 4am at Christie's to look at the paintings.

Norton Simon was not interested in any of those from the Northwick Collection – not a great omen – but he did study the Velázquez in considerable detail and gave a cursory glance at the Rembrandt which, he said, he was not particularly interested in because he had already been offered it by Agnew's and thought it too expensive. He then asked, still in my hearing, if Patrick Lindsay might help him in the event of him wanting to bid, which he said he might do, on the Velázquez. He thought he would rather not be identified so Patrick very sensibly suggested that he employ an agent: Dudley Tooth, or failing that, Geoffrey Agnew. Norton Simon said no, he did not want to do that, he wanted to bid himself, but secretly. Patrick made some suggestions: 'Mr Simon, I see you wear spectacles, might you wear them when bidding, and take them off when not bidding? This would be easy to understand and never noticed.' But no, Mr Simon had other ideas. He asked for a legal pad and a room where he could sit and write and concentrate. We gave him Peter Chance's office and Patrick, David and I sat and waited with some trepidation in the room next door. After about fifteen or twenty minutes, he came in with a large sheet of lined paper on which were written his suggestions as to how he would bid. Patrick read this and said it was much too complicated for the auctioneer to understand, particularly in the heat of what might be an exciting sale. Norton Simon made some adjustments and said this was what he wanted to do. Patrick kept the piece of paper and promised to show it to the auctioneer, Peter Chance, in the morning. Even in its simplified form, it was still very complicated. He then asked to be taken to Claridge's, where he was staying.

I should add at this point that Peter Chance was a very good auctioneer, but he did get quite tense before a sale and could be nervous while taking one. He was even more nervous when he read Norton Simon's instructions but he had little alternative but to accept them. Norton Simon said that although they applied to the sale of the Velázquez, Peter could apply the instructions to any of the other pictures in the sale as well if he chose to bid.

The Velázquez, *Portrait of Don Juan Calabazas*, came up just before the Rembrandt and was eventually bought by Dr Sherman Lee from the Cleveland Museum. Norton Simon did not bid on the picture. Next came the Rembrandt and, far from wishing to remain anonymous, when the bidding was opened at around 100,000 guineas, Norton Simon immediately called out '200,000!' and bid several more times before appearing to stop. It was only after the picture had been knocked down to David Somerset of the Marlborough Gallery that Norton Simon rose from his seat and said: 'Mr Chance, read the agreement we had, I am still bidding.' At this point I have a slight disagreement with John Herbert, who states it was Dudley Tooth who was asked to read the agreement. I remember it as Julius Weitzner, the dealer who was seated next to Norton Simon, but that is just a detail.

Interpreting the agreement, in one way you could see that Norton Simon was right, but poor Peter Chance as auctioneer felt that Simon, by bidding openly as he had, had negated his wish to bid anonymously and voided the agreement. This, I have always felt, was part of some scheme in Norton Simon's mind to attract the maximum attention; he certainly succeeded. Otherwise the sale was a triumph: the picture fetched 760,000 guineas (£800,000 or $2,234,000), more than the price Agnew's had offered it for, making it the most expensive picture sold in London and only just short of the $2.3 million which had been achieved in 1961 for the Erickson Rembrandt of *Aristotle Contemplating the Bust of Homer* in New York. Not surprisingly, perhaps, some of the publicity surrounding the sale was quite negative and was not made any better by Geoffrey Agnew, Peter Chance's cousin (and not even the underbidder), writing a spiteful letter to *The Times* about the way the sale had been conducted. To finish the story, when the picture was put up for sale again, the underbidder, David Somerset, was asked if he wanted to go on; he declined (he had already overrun his commission) and left the saleroom in a dignified and uncomplaining way with the less-than-easy task of explaining what had happened to his client.

The collector who had instructed David was someone who appears a number of times in this narrative: Stavros Niarchos. Although there were others in my earlier years at Christie's (Paul Mellon, a charming, courteous, old-fashioned American gentleman and Walter Annenberg, one-time US ambassador to the Court of St James's), the two collectors who towered over the art market in the 1960s, 1970s and 1980s were the two men who had fought it out over Rembrandt's *Titus*: Stavros Niarchos and Norton Simon. In this particular case Norton Simon had outbid his rival. In later years, when I had become lucky enough to count him as a friend, Stavros Niarchos told me that he had sought legal advice as to whether he had a case against Christie's. Without being able to prove loss, there could be no case, and he let the matter drop. In fact, of these two collecting giants – and giants they were – the right man probably won, because Niarchos went on to concentrate on nineteenth and twentieth-century paintings, whereas Simon chose to buy old masters as well.

Before his death, Simon founded the Norton Simon Foundation in Pasadena, where his pictures and sculptures are on permanent exhibition. The Niarchos Collection, as well as being featured in Douglas Cooper's book, *Great Private Collections*, was exhibited at the Tate from May to June 1958. It has grown exponentially in subsequent years and the greatest pictures in the collection are regularly exhibited during the summer months in the Kunsthaus in Zürich, as well as being frequently loaned to various exhibitions. This is not the place to say – and I am not the person to decide – which is the greater of the two collections. They are both worthy guardians of some of the world's greatest masterpieces. What is beyond doubt is that public access to the Norton Simon Foundation makes California a better place and I am a very lucky person to have had access to the Niarchos Collection, both to the original pictures that Stavros bought and later to the remarkable additions of his son, Philip. It should always be remembered that it is not just a small group who are able to enjoy these pictures, but anybody visiting Zürich during the summer. More of this later.

Despite the success of the Cook sale, and nothing to do with Geoffrey Agnew's whinging letter, Peter Chance felt that he had made a mistake over the Rembrandt and this affected his confidence when it came to conducting the first part of the Northwick sale. He realised that it was going to be a difficult assignment before he even got onto the rostrum: the omens had been mixed and to an extent ominous.

Any auctioneer, unless he is taking a sale of his own specialist subject, relies to a large extent on information supplied to him by the department concerned. In this case, this information was woefully inaccurate. The first of the early Italian pictures, Lot 9, catalogued merely as 'Florentine School', made a creditable 4,200 guineas against a reserve of 1,000. The next, attributed to the Master of the Castello Nativity, made 2,600 guineas against a reserve of 2,000 – hardly encouraging. The picture attributed to Lorenzo Monaco, *The Presentation in the Temple*, of which much was expected, was bought by Belle Linsky. It now hangs in the Metropolitan Museum with the rest of her collection, attributed no longer to Lorenzo Monaco but to a Portuguese painter who did work in Italy, Alvaro Pirez, although even now there seems to be some doubt as to the attribution. It sold for 8,500 guineas, only just above its reserve of 8,000, which was a definite disappointment. The next lot, attributed to Niccolò di Tommaso, made 2,800 guineas against a reserve of 3,000. Lot 13, Bicci di Lorenzo's *The Virgin of Mercy*, just sold at 3,800 guineas against a reserve of 5,000, and what was to be the star item, the picture attributed to Fra Angelico, *A Miracle of SS Cosmos and Damian* (and incorrectly measured in the catalogue), made just under 14,000 guineas against a reserve of 10,000. This was a real blow because the picture, despite having been attributed to a number of artists, probably was, in the main, by Fra Angelico himself.

Orazio Gentileschi. **Lot and his Daughters**, 1622

Any real excitement from the Italian pictures did not come until Lot 22, Orazio Gentileschi's *Lot and his Daughters*, which made 38,000 guineas against a reserve of 5,000. This pattern continued with all the baroque pictures, most notably the first of the two Guercinos, *Christ and the Woman of Samaria*, which made 15,000 guineas against a reserve of 5,000; Salvator Rosa's *The Vision of Aeneas*, 17,000 guineas against a reserve of 3,000; and Guido Reni's *Angel Appearing to St Jerome*, 22,000 guineas against a reserve of 1,000. By this time the poor Chairman must have been wondering if his much-vaunted Old Master Picture Department had a clue what they were doing.

Bad times reasserted themselves with Gerard David's *The Adoration of the Magi*, which was almost certainly not by that artist and consequently, beautiful though it is, was bought, again by the Linskys, for 25,000 guineas against a reserve of 20,000. In the catalogue of the Linsky Collection (where the picture, now cleaned, looks beautiful), it is only described as 'Workshop of Gerard David'. The most recent scholarship on the picture generally attributes it to Simon Bening.

Other than the Bruegel (which we will get to later), the star of the Flemish paintings was Jacob Jordaens's *Allegory of the Education of a Young Prince*, again from the seventeenth century, which was fiercely bid for and which made 65,000 guineas against a reserve of 10,000. The beautiful little panel attributed to Dirk Bouts, *The Madonna and Child*, the most exciting of the Northwick Rescues (although the attribution is no longer accepted), made 15,000 guineas against a reserve of 8,000. The last Flemish picture, Pieter Bruegel the Elder's *Peasant Wedding*, despite not being generally considered to be by that artist, made 78,000 guineas, the highest price in the sale.

This would have been very confusing for any auctioneer, the more so given that Peter Chance had had such a torrid experience with the Rembrandt. In Christie's *Review of the Year*, David Carritt publishes something of an explanation (or is it a mea culpa?) when he says, in an article entitled 'Change of Taste', 'the sale on 28 May of 65 paintings from the Northwick Park Collection produced a variety of prices which to the lay observer [and probably to the auctioneer as well] may well have appeared inexplicable to the point of fantasy'. All this is made no better by the fact that in *Sotheby's Annual Review* (1961–2), there is an excellent article entitled

TOP TO BOTTOM

Salvator Rosa. **The Dream of Aeneas**, 1660-5

Workshop of Gerard David. **The Adoration of the Magi**, *c.*1520

Guido Reni. **Angel Appearing to St Jerome**, *c.*1638

'The English Taste for Italian Seventeenth-Century Painting' by Denys Sutton, in which he writes (three years before the Northwick sale), 'one of the most striking and instructive recent developments on the international art market has been the resurgent interest in Italian painting of the seventeenth century'. This had obviously not been widely read at Christie's.

Of the two principal actors in this complicated plot, Peter Chance was far more a victim than a culprit. Yet the part played by Patrick Lindsay deserves an explanation.

Patrick was knowledgeable about early pictures and could talk with real authority about Piero della Francesca (who was incidentally his favourite artist). He had, though, an almost total blank spot about the Italian baroque, in common with many of his generation. He neither liked nor understood artists like Guido Reni or the Carracci family. One cannot expect everyone to like everything. His failing was the greater, however, in his dislike of asking for help from other authorities. He was not one to 'phone a friend'. He also had a view, bordering on the arrogant, that if he did not like something, it was not worth liking. This made him, in some ways, a difficult colleague. He was, however, a wonderful friend, and in that respect his dislike of Guido Reni was made up for by his skill as a helmsman, as a pilot and as a very, very fast driver. He took the same slightly high-handed approach to traffic police as he did to Reni. He did not like them and he expressed this view to the exasperation of his QC who had manoeuvred Patrick, when he was for the umpteenth time up for speeding, into a more favourable position than he deserved. He was probably not going to lose his licence until the judge asked him: 'Mr Lindsay, who did you think the two men in the red sports car were?' 'Me Lud, I took them for sportsmen and not spoilsports.' This was the wrong answer and Patrick lost his driving licence for three years. It was about this time that he took up flying, bought a Fieseler Storch – the plane that Hitler sent to rescue Mussolini and which could almost land like a helicopter – and built himself a runway at his house, Folly Farm, in Berkshire. He pretty much refused to do valuations for clients who did not have fields on which he could land. But then, Patrick would have calculated, if they did not have big enough fields they probably did not have pictures of any consequence!

Christie's season, though, had more excitements and pleasant surprises to come. In a sale in July, Lord Margadale's *Portrait of a Lady* by Bernardino de' Conti (a picture that I knew well and loved) made 29,000 guineas, as did the same owner's Rubens, *Eléonore de Bourbon*. Another picture in that sale, Paris Bordone's *Venetian General Armed by Two Pages*, did not to my mind excite the interest it should have done and I remember at the time thinking of bidding for it myself. It was so beautiful and it too went to the Metropolitan Museum. They had a field day at Christie's that summer. The painting by Bordone mentioned above came from the collection of Lord Harewood, who is also in the first eleven of Christie's supporters. He was forced to sell a large number of works of art for the usual reasons: death duties and to maintain his magnificent Harewood House. He also, in the summer of 1964, sold the celebrated Harewood House desk, a masterpiece designed by Robert Adam and made by Thomas Chippendale, with mounts by Matthew Boulton. The price, 41,000 guineas, was, unsurprisingly, a record for a piece of English furniture. It was a demonstration of technical brilliance, usually found only in the work of the great French *ébénistes*.

Chapter 5

Guy Hannen and my first sale; America with Jo Floyd; a first visit to the Loebs; New Jersey; Mrs Kramarsky; Sarah Russell and Mme Balsan's estate; trouble spelling Tchelitchew

Christie's in 1965 was still a very small firm: only seven Directors, including the Chairman, and a staff of about 150 – a slight increase on the 96 people who made up the firm when I joined in 1962. It was, on the whole, a friendly place and everyone was pretty much on Christian-name terms. Guy Hannen, Lance Hannen's grandson, whose father had acquired James Christie III's shares for him, could be the most severe of the Directors. He had a temper and one always recognised the signs: he became very silent and all the colour drained from his face. But he was also extremely kind and supportive if he thought one was doing a good job. In my case, this was not always so but on the whole we got on well. I became extremely fond of him, but 1965 was still early days.

One morning in June he asked me if I was free to have lunch with him, and what I was doing the following day. 'Going to look at some pictures but I could change it' was my reply. 'There's something else I'd like you to do so if you can change it, do,' he said. 'I'll see you at Wheeler's at one o'clock.' Wheeler's in Duke of York Street was the favourite restaurant of us all; it is sadly now demolished.

We had our usual bottle of Chablis, talked about this and that, and then he told me that there was a Board meeting the following day and that there would be no one to take the morning sale. In those days sales took place every day and they were taken only by Directors. Would I please take the drawings sale? 'You know what to do and if you have any queries, just ask Ray.' Ray Perman was about my age and had just become the Chief Sales Clerk. He later became a very good auctioneer himself. Nowadays Christie's has an expensive training programme for auctioneers, going into every aspect of the process. Whether it is any better than dropping people in at the deep end and seeing if they can swim, I don't know. That night I slept a bit, having asked Ray what on earth I was expected to do.

At the appointed eleven o'clock, clutching a borrowed hammer, the auctioneer's book and a rather leaky fountain pen, I climbed into the rostrum and was just about brave enough to say 'Lot 1. Five guineas I have, six guineas, thank you, seven …'

OPPOSITE

Vincent van Gogh. **Le Pont de Trinquetaille**, 1888

and so on. To be fair to the old system and the old regime, sales like the one I was embarking on had an average price per lot of well under £100. Just to make matters more difficult, we had to sell in guineas but convert the guineas into pounds to write down the price in the book. We also had to be able to work out, instantly, one against another, as bids and reserves could be written in the book in either. But even if you made a mistake, which you were expected to pay for yourself, it was not a catastrophe. Now, with the average price per lot in the smallest sales being several thousands, the stakes are much higher.

I struggled through, making just one serious mistake. I missed a written bid from Brian Sewell, who was quite cross that I, not he, should have been asked to take the sale, and crosser still over my mistake.

John Michael Rysbrack. **Bust of William Shakespeare**, 1760

It was during the frantic summer of 1965 that it was first suggested I should go to New York to manage the office there, our representative, Bob Leyland, having decided to retire. I jumped at the opportunity, seduced by the memory of my National Art-Collections Fund trip to New York. I thought very little about the consequences of going to live in a city where I knew not a soul, and doing a job for which I was completely unprepared. Christie's had not, however, completely taken leave of their collective senses. I was to be joined early the following year by John Richardson, already an established art historian, and we were to share responsibility for running the office. John's appointment was the brainchild of John Herbert, who had the thankless responsibility of managing Christie's relationship with the press. At that time John Richardson had been working for the *Daily Express* and, because of his contract with them, his appointment could not be announced until the following year.

For a time I had to pretend to be in sole charge of Christie's in America. No announcement was made of my appointment, so very few people were interested. Of those who did hear about it, some believed the story, the majority was slightly puzzled, a minority was rather cross and only my mother was really pleased. I had spent the last weekend in England hunting in Warwickshire, staying with my friends, the Wests, at Alscot Park, a dream house on the Warwickshire Stour. My friend's great-great-grandfather, James Alston West, was president of the Royal Society, and a noted bibliophile. He built Alscot as a Gothic pavilion in which to house his library. He commissioned John Michael Rysbrack, who used every known likeness to produce what is generally acknowledged to be the best image of William Shakespeare to stand guard over his folios. Some years later, James West asked me to sell the Rysbrack, which we succeeded in doing, and he very generously gave me a copy of it which has sat on my hall table ever since.

Having finally said goodbye to my mother as if I was off to the trenches, I joined Jo Floyd, recently made Deputy Chairman, who was to help me during the first few weeks. We ensconced ourselves in the back of a BOAC VC10 for the first of many such frugal journeys to New York. Jo Floyd loved to refer to these as 'hard arse'. It was not until the days of CEOs wishing to express their superiority over their fellow workers that anyone in Christie's, with the possible exception of Peter Chance, took to travelling first class and staying in smart hotels.

Jo had booked us a suite in the Blackstone Hotel, near the office, with a sitting room, two small bedrooms and a shared bathroom – *le grand luxe!* Living in such close quarters to this clever and practical man, I picked up one invaluable tip which I recommend to the reader: never go out at night without first putting at least one aspirin on your pillow. This, and the fact that Jo was 6 feet 5 inches tall and had hollow legs, meant that, although fifteen years my senior, he was always ready to go in the morning, and go we did.

He had previously spent a year working in America and had made some very useful friends. The first of these whom he took me to see soon after our arrival were John and Frances (known as Peter) Loeb, who had a magnificent apartment in Park Avenue. Later, in May 1997, we were to sell their collection – more of this later. Any new experience in New York was exciting. By this time, I was quite familiar with English country houses, with the odd great old master painting, family portraits and hunting scenes by John Wootton. However, I had never been in a private house or apartment with a Van Gogh over the mantelpiece, a great 1901 Picasso, a Manet from the legendary Goldschmidt Collection, a large Cézanne portrait, a Monet view of the Boulevard des Capucines, and much else besides … and lived in by real people! I should also mention that Mrs John Loeb was the niece of Governor Herbert Lehman and a cousin of Robert Lehman, whose extraordinary collection I had seen during my first trip to New York. By the time I saw it, though, the Lehman Collection had assumed the character and feel of a museum; the Park Avenue apartment was still very much a family home.

The first weekend, Jo and I boarded a train for New Jersey to stay with Harry and Marian Frelinghuysen. They lived in a modest, comfortable house in Far Hills which typified the very best of American hospitality. They had in their drawing room three beautiful Monets from the 1870s, which were there by descent from Harry's grandparents, Mr and Mrs H.O. Havemeyer. The Havemeyers were friends of the painter Mary Cassatt, with whom they had spent much time in Paris putting together a spectacular collection. The majority of this collection is now in the Metropolitan Museum and is particularly strong in paintings by Mary Cassatt herself, Manet, Degas and Monet. The Havemeyers also owned that particular favourite of mine, Manet's *The Railway*. Mrs Havemeyer was almost certainly the first owner of a painting by Manet in America and did much to introduce impressionism to the American public. We never sold any of the Frelinghuysens' pictures – they were not sellers – but spending time with them and seeing these paintings was reward in itself.

Although I knew no one in New York, I had one much older friend who lived close to the Frelinghuysens in New Jersey. She was called Edith Gambrill and she and her husband, who was master of the local Somerset hunt, had been friends of my grandfather through their shared passion for breeding foxhounds. Edith's son-in-law, James Casey, a lawyer, had become a friend of Jo's and would in time become Christie's attorney. I adored visits to New Jersey. In my homesick moments, and there were quite a few of these, it reminded me of home.

The following week, back in New York, Jo took me to a house in Central Park which belonged to a very dignified lady, Mrs Siegfried Kramarsky. I have never forgotten the large white-and-grey-painted rooms in her Central Park West apartment, across the street from the Dakota Building. They contained very good old master drawings, early Chinese porcelain and a picture by Van Gogh, *Le Pont de Trinquetaille*, which I eventually sold in June 1987. It is one of only two pictures I sold of which I have kept a reproduction. In the adjoining room was Van Gogh's *Portrait du Dr Gachet* which my colleague, Christopher Burge, was to sell for yet another world record, $82,500,000, the last 'hurrah' of the 1990s. Another painting I remember was a very beautiful Toulouse-Lautrec portrait of a girl. This visit to Mrs Kramarsky is the one that sticks most firmly in my memory from my days in New York.

Jo Floyd was at his absolute best with a certain type of American collector. These were the people, particularly collectors of impressionist pictures, that he and his contemporaries at the auction house had realised needed to be won over if Christie's were to survive, let alone one day gain parity with their rivals. The firm could no longer just rely on their traditional English clients, loyal as they were. It is a genuine tribute to Jo that the firm succeeded, albeit with some bumpy patches. He was wonderful with those American ladies and the fact that he bore a striking resemblance to President Reagan did him no harm either. Gone forever were the days when Christie's could afford to tear up envelopes franked with foreign stamps. I am not making this up! In the 1930s, the then Senior Partner at Christie's, Lance Hannen, would retire to his Scottish estate. Once a week, the Chief Sales Clerk would look through the mail in London and bring up on the night train those letters that looked to be of interest, having, it is said, thrown away any with foreign stamps.

We covered a lot of ground, Jo and I and the aspirins, from the Blackstone Hotel, and it was at this time that Jo introduced me to Sarah Russell. I had met Sarah before, briefly. Her brother, Charles Spencer-Churchill, had been my exact contemporary at prep school and I knew their parents, the Duke and Duchess of Marlborough, because Mary Marlborough used to appear in a convoy of cars laden down with plants to coincide with the annual gardening competition at Summer Fields. Spencer-Churchill always won. No one could compete with the gardens at Blenheim! Sarah and I became really close friends and she had just inherited the estate of her grandmother, Consuelo Vanderbilt.

Miss Vanderbilt was a famous beauty and a considerable heiress. Her portrait by Giovanni Boldini hangs in the Metropolitan Museum. She married the ninth Duke of Marlborough but it was not a happy marriage and resulted in a colourful divorce, all the details of which came to the attention of Christie's in a very peculiar manner, which I will describe in a later chapter. After her divorce she married Jacques Balsan, a charming Frenchman and amateur painter who was a friend of André Dunoyer de Segonzac, Paul Maze, Lord John Churchill and his cousin Winston. While they were married, Consuelo and Balsan put together a considerable collection of works of art which were grandly housed in Palm Beach and Southampton, Long Island. Mme Balsan died in 1964, almost exactly coinciding with my arrival in New York.

Despite both Jo's and my friendship with Sarah, Christie's were never formally asked to handle the estate. What happened was that Sarah would ask one or two leading dealers what they would offer for something and then get me up for a weekend in Southampton and ask me what I thought Christie's might get for it. If I guessed right, I would get the goods. It was not a perfect arrangement but it did not work out too badly.

Bill Acquavella, who was just starting out in what was to be a mercurial career, probably got the best pictures, but the Pissarro I was given did well in June 1969 and I also got a Tiepolo gold-and-grey ground grisaille. There was also very good eighteenth-century French and German mounted porcelain, and I managed to salvage some of the French furniture from raids by the American trade. A dealer called Freddy Victoria, I remember, did extraordinarily well out of this. Business and friendship can successfully combine, and Sarah became an integral part of my life in New York. She died, too early, in the year 2000 and I was asked by her brother, Sunny Marlborough, to give the farewell speech at her final resting place in Bladon where all the Churchills, including Sir Winston, are laid to rest.

After about a month, Jo returned to London, leaving me as the only representative of Christie's in a vast country in an even vaster continent. I had only my brief experience at the firm in London, a scant knowledge of old master paintings and the even scanter help of a rather bad-tempered, late middle-aged secretary to fall back on.

The day after Jo left, someone rang the office to ask if an expert could come and look at some drawings. 'Yes,' I replied, noted the address and went round the following day. The first thing I was shown was a drawing by Auguste Rodin. Somebody had warned me that a great many Rodin drawings are not in fact by Rodin. I did not think this one was but it was so faded it was difficult to tell. At least I knew a little about the artist and bluffed my way through. The next was a drawing by Jules Pascin. This artist, little known in Britain, Bulgarian by birth, settled in Paris where he made a slight impression, and then took up residence in New York where he eventually gained citizenship and every New Yorker aspiring to be a Frick or a Mellon from Newark to Yonkers bought pictures and drawings by him. The

one I was shown was definitely from the lower end and I said regretfully that it would not reward the expense of sending it to London for sale – almost certainly true.

The third thing on the list was a picture by Pavel Tchelitchew. This was a problem. I had not heard of Tchelitchew and I could not spell his name. What is more, the client was looking over my shoulder as I was attempting to write it down. Not good. I muttered something about putting the 't's in later. I said I wanted to do some research on the drawing. I should have kept the client's name and address, because I could have sent him, in 1986, the catalogue which I helped to prepare for the Edward James Collection which contained no less than ninety-two drawings by this artist. Things could only get better from here on, and eventually they did.

Camille Pissarro. **Vue de Pontoise**, 1873

OPPOSITE

Giovanni Boldini. **Consuelo Vanderbilt (1876-1964), Duchess of Marlborough, and her son, Lord Ivor Spencer-Churchill (1898-1956)**, 1906

David Carritt and the Pontormo; John Richardson's arrival; Le Nain and Whistler's mother; Miss Brayton, Lizzy Borden's school friend from Fall River; Warhol and Rauschenberg; visit to the Ganzes; sale of the Watney Collection; sale of Monet's *Terrasse à Sainte-Adresse*; I marry Fiona and secure Van Gogh's portrait of his mother

I had a welcome visit around Christmas (I did not return to London until the following summer) when David Carritt came to New York. Sadly, I think it was the only time he came to America while I was there, but sitting in our little office on 57th Street, he told me that he wanted to take me to see the best old master painting in private hands in America. He made a telephone call and the following day we set off on a visit to a rather old-fashioned apartment in a building on Fifth Avenue: not one of those with a crew of fancy doormen, but with just one elderly supervisor, and an even older elevator. We took this elevator to the penthouse and emerged in a dark and dated apartment where on the wall was Pontormo's *Portrait of a Halberdier* (then thought to be Cosimo de' Medici). A more stunning image could not be found anywhere, and it was so completely unexpected.

Chauncey Stillman, the owner, was a very nice man with a charming daughter who had dinner with us. I was to see him several times, but can claim no credit for the eventual sale which was engineered in 1989 by Christopher Burge. The picture made a world record price for an old master painting and was bought by the Getty Museum. It is certainly one of the best half-dozen old master pictures which Christie's sold during my working life and it did fetch the highest price of any old master: $35,200,000. History proved David Carritt right.

Shortly after David's visit, John Richardson arrived in New York. Whatever success Christie's and I may have had in America in the five years I was there would never

OPPOSITE

Pontormo (Jacopo Carucci).
Portrait of a Halberdier, 1528-30

have been possible without John. I had not met him before and he came with a fearsome reputation, both as an art historian and as a character. In many respects it was brave of Christie's to have employed such a frankly controversial figure. However, from the first day we met, John and I struck up a friendship which lasts to this day and he is, among other things, godfather to my son, Henry.

When John came to Christie's he had really no experience of the commercial art trade, although he had bought and sold things himself, but he had an extraordinarily wide knowledge of nineteenth-century works of art derived partly from his own God-given eye and partly from his training at the Slade. There he encountered two of his closest friends, Lucian Freud and David Hockney, but more important even than this was his friendship with that most difficult, irascible but brilliant of art historians, Douglas Cooper. John had become a close friend of Cooper in 1952 and they had lived together at the Château de Castille, near Avignon, as neighbours of Picasso, where Cooper had amassed a remarkable collection of cubist pictures and drawings by Braque, Picasso, Gris and Léger.

Picasso, like everyone else who met John, became his friend and for ten years they went together to bullfights, exhibitions, restaurants and bars. This friendship gave John a unique insight into the artist's life and work. It contributed to the success of the three volumes on Pablo Picasso which John has already published; Waldemar Januszczak, writing in the *Sunday Times*, described Volume III as 'the latest instalment of the finest artistic biography ever written [...] Picasso had a blessed life, and was blessed after his death in having John Richardson as a biographer.'

John had already done much of the work on these remarkable volumes when I met him for the first time at the beginning of 1966. Not only had he become immersed in Picasso, he had published an excellent book on Manet in 1959, recorded a series of conversations with Braque for the BBC in the late 1950s, and curated a major retrospective of that artist in 1964. He worked on a catalogue of Juan Gris for the museum in Dortmund and had written on Monet, Léger and de Staël as well as claiming friendship with the majority of those artists.

Maxfield Parrish. **Old King Cole Mural**, 1906

John was also – and this was my particular good fortune – someone who loved to share his knowledge, and though never seeking to educate, he did so without trying and made everything such fun at the same time. He was a tireless perfectionist. The only problem I ever had with John was that it was almost impossible to get him to finish a letter. He would write, rewrite, rewrite and rewrite … Sometimes I had to point out to him that the client did not require perfection, just an answer.

John probably acquired his extraordinary work ethic from his father, General Sir Wodehouse Richardson, KCB, DSO, who had been quartermaster general in the Boer War and once he retired from the army, founded the Army & Navy Stores. He had married late, when he was seventy, and John was born in 1924. Sir Wodehouse's father, Guildford Richardson, a colonial servant, had also married late and was born back in the eighteenth century. The three generations spanned four centuries, from the eighteenth to the twenty-first: this must be unique.

John had already lived in New York. He had a wonderful apartment, the bottom two floors of a brownstone on 68th Street, which contained what by any standards was already a pretty impressive collection of works of art, mainly gifts from Picasso and Braque, but also things that John had bought, including a remarkable picture by Maxfield Parrish.

Maxfield Parrish was the American painter whose huge 'Old King Cole' Mural decorates the wall of the King Cole Bar at the St Regis Hotel on East 55th Street where the first ever Bloody Mary was mixed in 1934. Before 1950 the King Cole Bar was off limits for the fairer sex because the picture was thought indecent: Old King Cole has clearly broken wind and his attendants have their hands to their noses with expressions of distaste on their faces.

This was just one of the many fascinating things John taught me about paintings and the city. On a more serious note, I would like to record something which John was to show me in 1975 when we met up again in New York, after I had gone back to England and John had sadly left Christie's. He was then working at Knoedler & Co., where he helped to organise a loan exhibition of works of art from the Hermitage and State Russian Museum in Leningrad, the first loan exhibition of the emerging era of glasnost. It included, amongst other masterpieces, Louis Le Nain's *A Visit to Grandmother* and I was looking at this picture when John suddenly said, 'Oh my God … do you see what I see?' I passed. He said, 'Look, there is Whistler's mother!' He was right. This is, as far as I can find, a piece of unpublished information not even mentioned by Sarah Walden in her excellent book, *Whistler and His Mother*. John appears to have been the only person to have spotted the origins of this great American icon, and to have realised that Whistler would have seen the Le Nain painting while living with his parents in St Petersburg, where his father worked on the railways. I would like John to have the credit for this discovery as a small thank-you for the years I spent with him in America.

Louis Le Nain. **A Visit to Grandmother**, *c.*1645-8

John introduced me to a great variety of his friends and acquaintances, to Bob Silvers, editor of the *New York Review of Books*, and to perhaps his closest friend, Bowden Broadwater, sometime husband of the novelist Mary McCarthy. She wrote, amongst other things, one of the funniest short stories about the commercial art world in her book *The Company She Keeps*. The chapter entitled 'Rogue's Gallery' bears a strong similarity to the House of Wildenstein.

John also introduced me to his friend Jim Parker, who ran the Metropolitan Museum's Furniture Department, with whom we spent happy weekends in Newport, Rhode Island, and who in turn introduced me to a legendary Newport lady, Miss Alice Brayton, whose topiary gardens were the pride of Old Newport. More fascinating still was the fact that she had been at school with Lizzie Borden. Lovers of light music will recall from Michael Brown's song 'Fall River Hoedown (Lizzie Borden)', composed for Leonard Sillman's *New Faces of 1952* on Broadway, that she 'chopped her papa and her mama up in Massachusetts' and got off with a caution. Here are the first two verses of the song:

Yesterday in old Fall River, Mr Andrew Borden died
And they got his daughter Lizzie on a charge of homicide
Some folks say she didn't do it, and others say of course she did
But they all agree Miss Lizzie B. was a problem kind of kid

James Abbott McNeill Whistler.
Portrait of the Artist's Mother, 1871

> 'Cause you can't chop your papa up in Massachusetts
> Not even if it's planned as a surprise
> No, you can't chop your papa up in Massachusetts
> You know how neighbors love to criticize

It was through John that I also met Andy Warhol, whose paintings I have always hugely admired, and Robert Rauschenberg, who became for a short time a friend of mine. With Andy Warhol there were often mysterious substances I did not feel completely at ease with, but Bob Rauschenberg's dinners were much more simple: a bottle or two – I cannot remember any more – of bourbon. This friendship resulted in Christie's first sale in New York, sadly not recorded anywhere. It was a single lot, a massive model aeroplane, auctioned by me in Bob's huge studio loft for charity.

Rauschenberg, Jasper Johns (whom I sadly never got to know) and Picasso were the favourite painters of Victor and Sally Ganz. John knew the Ganzes well and he took me to see them very soon after he arrived. I was overwhelmed by what they had. I wish I had spent slightly more time with John before I went to see them and I might have better appreciated the extraordinary collection they had put together. As many reading this will know, it eventually formed, in November 1997, the largest sale that Christie's had undertaken up to that time.

John and I often travelled together, but sometimes we would go our separate ways and on one such occasion, in March of our first year together, I set off to the bitter cold of Montreal, where we had just opened an office, and John went south to Palm Beach, Florida. When, after two weeks, we met up again in New York I asked John how he had got on, saying he was lucky to have gone to Palm Beach. He said he did not think he was at all lucky: he had spent a terrible time watching, as he said, ghastly middle-aged women walking past the swimming pool of his hotel, 'skeletons covered in chicken skin all held together with diamond clips'. John always had a very keen eye and a way with words.

By the autumn of 1966, I had been working with John for over six months and had already realised how lucky I was to have such an amusing and intelligent comrade-in-arms. We had moved our offices from the tiny brownstone on 57th Street to two floors with a street-level entrance at 867 Madison Avenue, then known by its old New York name, the Rhinelander Building (now rebranded the Ralph Lauren Building). Despite the fact that we had been allowed a telex machine, which somebody in the office knew how to operate, it was still a slightly lonely existence and we both felt cut off from and sometimes ignored by our colleagues in London. This sense of isolation was often exacerbated by our almost total ignorance of what was going on back at King Street.

A splendid example of this was when we received an envelope from John Herbert, the Press Director, containing about twenty photographs of what was clearly a very important collection of old master paintings. They had belonged to the late O.V. Watney of Cornbury Park, Oxford. John and I could only hope that some of the directors of the main American museums had been forewarned of this impending sale which, had it taken place today, would have made headlines the world over.

The importance given to it by our Press Office has got to be judged, without wishing to be beastly, by the fact that it is completely omitted from John Herbert's book *Inside Christie's*. It included a rare *Portrait of a Man* by Andrea del Sarto; an

LEFT TO RIGHT

Juan de Flandes. **The Marriage Feast at Cana**, *c.*1500-04

Sandro Botticelli. **Marriage of Nastagio degli Onesti and the Daughter of Paolo Traversaro**, *c.*1483

Claude Monet. **La Terrasse à Sainte-Adresse**, 1867

excellent Frans Hals, *Portrait of Pieter Jacobsz Olycan*; and a good Corneille de Lyon, *Portrait of the Chancellor Henart*. Most notable was a beautiful panel, *The Virgin and Child with Saints*, by that rare Renaissance master Nicola di Maestro Antonio d'Ancona (who was associated with Fra Carnevale, the Master of the Barberini Panels), whose panel in the Metropolitan Museum I had fallen in love with on my first visit and constantly revisited. Two even rarer pictures, examples of the work of Juan de Flandes, stayed in the United States: *The Temptation of Christ* went to Washington and the other, *The Marriage Feast at Cana*, was bequeathed to the Metropolitan by Belle Linsky (she and her husband Jack were becoming serious and independently minded collectors). The remaining twenty-five panels from this series are in the Prado.

There was also a ravishing panel, mainly by Botticelli, depicting *The Marriage of Nastagio degli Onesti and the Daughter of Paolo Traversaro*. This last picture was bought for 100,000 guineas by the Pucci family, and returned to their palace in Florence, its original home, where it happily remains to this day and where I was lucky enough to see it. I thought at the time of the sale that it was one of the most beautiful works of art I had witnessed pass through the salerooms and seeing it in Florence reinforced this view.

The Watney Collection was amassed in the nineteenth century by Vernon Watney, head of the brewing family who, in the 1960s, ended up acquiring my old family firm, Allsopp's, and forming it into Allied Breweries. The Watneys never gained a peerage, but they certainly held on to their money and were far better at collecting works of art than any Allsopp was.

Cornbury was a beautiful estate. It now belongs to Lord Rotherwick of the Cayzer shipping dynasty. The Watney Collection also contained (although there are question marks about some of the lesser figures in the picture) an *Altarpiece* by Giovanni Bellini, another masterpiece, which was kept back to settle tax and finally negotiated to the nation by Christie's in 1977. It can now be enjoyed in the Birmingham Museum and Art Gallery.

It has to be admitted that John and I had not made huge contributions to Christie's during our first year, but we were hard at work on various projects which did bear spectacular fruit the following year. Success has many fathers, while failure is an orphan. This the *Oxford Dictionary of Quotations* gives to Mussolini's son-in-law, Count Ciano, although I suspect it has more than one father itself. It certainly applied to what was to be the sale of the most important impressionist picture up to that moment: Monet's *La Terrasse à Sainte-Adresse*.

My old friend, David Bathurst, who had joined Christie's in the spring of 1963, the year after I did, was the first accredited impressionist and modern specialist in the firm. As soon as he arrived, he assiduously pursued those paintings illustrated in colour in John Rewald's book *The History of Impressionism*. The Monet appears in all its glory on page 153, giving the owner as the Reverend Theodore Pitcairn of Bryn Athyn, Pennsylvania. David contacted him and they got on extremely well. His efforts were rewarded, to begin with, not by gaining the first prize, the Monet, but a substantial one nonetheless: Van Gogh's *Portrait of Mademoiselle Ravoux*, the daughter of the innkeeper in Auvers-sur-Oise where Van Gogh spent his last days. In addition there was a strange, haunting drawing, reminiscent of Burne-Jones, also by Van Gogh and entitled *Sorrow*. These appeared in a sale on 6 June 1966. *Mademoiselle Ravoux* fetched a then record price for Van Gogh, 150,000 guineas ($441,000).

Even after this success, and despite his obvious liking for David, the Reverend Pitcairn held back and it was left to Jo Floyd, chauffeured by me, to sign up the Monet the following spring. I remember sitting with Jo at the Reverend's large desk before he came into the room, desperately trying to read the letter from Sotheby's, upside down. We could not, but we came away with the contract and I was told to organise the transport of the picture from Bryn Athyn to London.

John and I went to collect the picture on a very hot day in June 1967. The Reverend had specifically asked us to be at the house between 10 and 11am as his wife would be out shopping and he admitted to us when we arrived that he had not told her he was selling the picture, which had been bought for her as a present. It was vitally important that the van arrived and we got the picture out of the house before she returned from the local grocery store.

As luck would have it – and in those days so very often did not – the van sent by the very reliable firm of packers, Hudsons, who were used by Christie's, had a puncture and the driver had a problem changing the wheel. He had forgotten the jack. By 10.45am there was no sign of the van. The Reverend was getting increasingly anxious that his wife would return and we were getting still more anxious that, after all our colleagues' hard work, he would change his mind about selling the picture. So we took it down from the wall and carried it out to a barn where we sat clutching it firmly until finally the van arrived and we were able to sneak it out unobserved by Mrs Pitcairn, who by this time had indeed returned from shopping. Its journey to London was uneventful and it came up for sale in December 1967 when it made 410,000 guineas (just over $1 million), another record.

It was my happy task to ring the Reverend Pitcairn's attorney, Fred Drews, to tell him the

Vincent van Gogh. **Portrait of the Artist's Mother**, October 1888

news from London. His response was initial silence, followed by an expression I had never heard before: 'Holy Dog!' The Reverend had told Peter Chance, who had conducted the sale, that in 1926, when he bought the picture, he and his wife had been walking down 57th Street and had seen the Monet in a dealer's window. They bought it in ten minutes for $11,500. They were 'not thinking of investment', he said, but they 'were struck by its cheerful quality and thought that it was the type of picture which would always give [them] a lift. At the time some people had thought [them] rather odd. In those days Monet wasn't too well known there.'

The Pitcairn family had one more happy piece of business for us – particularly so for me. I had stopped off in New York on 19 April the following year, the day after my wedding to Fiona, on the way to our honeymoon in Jamaica, and received a message from Fred Drews telling me that the Reverend had decided to sell Van Gogh's *Portrait of the Artist's Mother*, which we managed to get into a sale on 28 June and which made 110,000 guineas, this time only $277,000. The rate of exchange fluctuated almost daily. However it was a good price for a small picture which Van Gogh had done from a photograph and was never entirely happy with.

Chapter 7

Jack R. Dick; the first telephone bid; guarantees; Patrick Lindsay visits; the Parker Estate; Michael Tree and the business with Stavros Niarchos; Mrs Tippett

During the summer of 1968, which was a happy one, I made two visits to clients with my colleague Patrick Lindsay, who was by then firmly installed as the Head of the Old Master Picture Department. The first was a trip up the New England coast to Greenwich, Connecticut, to see a man who had almost single-handedly reinvigorated the market for British sporting pictures. Jack R. Dick had discovered that it was possible to obtain huge tax advantages from breeding pedigree beef cattle. He spent the proceeds on British sporting pictures. He had the field pretty much to himself, except for competition from that truest of gentlemen collectors, Paul Mellon. Dick paid very high prices for pictures by Stubbs and his contemporaries with the same enthusiasm as he broke records for the prices paid for Aberdeen Angus bulls. Both his bulls and his collection of pictures were housed at Black Watch Farm, Greenwich, which had gained legendary status. Patrick wanted to see it and I had arranged the visit. Jack Dick was no stranger to Christie's; he had bought, amongst other things, two beautiful Stubbs paintings: *Goldfinder* and *Two Mares and a Foal* sold by the executors of General Sir Allan Adair, the distinguished commander of the Guards Armoured Division in the Second World War.

The sale of the Stubbs had introduced something new to Christie's. Dick had insisted on bidding for the pictures on the telephone, the first time this practice – common today – had been used. The bids were taken and relayed to the rather reluctant auctioneer, Peter Chance, by that stalwart servant of Christie's, Roy Davidge. It was hardly cutting-edge e-commerce but it was the first halting step towards online bidding and online sales. It seemed to the younger Directors rather a good idea and it had considerable advantages, both to the bidders and the auction house. However, it led to something not so appealing. At a recent sale organised by Christie's in a marquee in the country, the sale was not a failure but the tent was almost completely empty. All the bidding was between members of the auction house's staff on banks of telephones relaying bids to the auctioneer. There was none of the excitement of a normal live auction and the expertise of the auctioneer, such as he had, became completely redundant.

OPPOSITE

George Stubbs. **Goldfinder**, 1774

was uncovered and awaiting an occupant, since Mrs Parker was still alive, cared for in a twilight home in the city. Beside these two sarcophagi was another much smaller one, which informed us that the Parkers had lost a child in infancy.

This was a fitting end to a frightful visit and we emerged into the sunlight, passing a farewell message again written on a large boulder by the door: 'Get out and stay out.' We had every intention of obeying but before leaving I was asked my views on the pictures and recommendations for their sale. I passed the buck to Patrick who, never at a loss, with a completely straight face said how much we had enjoyed the visit, 'one of the most extraordinary of my career to date'.

'I have two suggestions,' he continued. 'The first would be, if possible, to hire the house and its contents to a film company. I would suggest an English firm, Hammer Films (otherwise known as the 'Hammer House of Horrors'), or failing that' – and Patrick said this was his personal choice – to 'acquire a large quantity of dynamite and blow up the house with its contents.' 'Oh my God,' exclaimed the attorney, 'thank you Mr Lindsay, I was just hoping someone would say that!' We struggled down the drive and returned to the station and so ended the most bizarre visit any of us had ever made or ever would make.

Sir Joshua Reynolds. **Warren Hastings**, 1766-8

I would like to say this account is the absolute truth as far as my memory allows me to record, but a kind friend found some interesting facts after I had written it which I now include as a postscript. The house I described still stands on a hill on 70 acres of woodland just outside the Baltimore Beltway. I had forgotten that it is called The Cloisters and was built in 1932. It is recorded as having been built of 'large random size blocks of grey and gold Butler stone quarried on the estate or other Maryland quarries, and the roof, consisting of heavy Butler's stone flagstone, secured by iron pins, is the only one of its kind in the United States'. This comes as no surprise. It also comes as no surprise that the house has been used as a venue for television and films, not entirely as Patrick Lindsay suggested, but with some titles in the same genre, including *Homicide* and *The Wire*, and several movies, such as John Waters's *Cry-Baby*, starring Johnny Depp, about the lives of delinquent adolescents, which seems very appropriate. The Cloisters did indeed belong to the Parker family. Sumner A. Parker was born in 1882 and ran a successful iron business. His wife,

Dudrea, was six years younger. The poor child referred to in the vault, Sumner A. Parker Jr., is recorded as having died in infancy. Sumner Parker died in 1945 and Dudrea finally in 1972, having narrowly escaped death shortly before when she threw an aerosol can into the fire she was sitting in front of and was blasted across the room by the explosion. Another example of truth winning out against fiction. The Cloisters, though, has been given a facelift and is currently used as a wedding venue; small wonder that marriage as an institution is now on the decline!

I returned to London that Christmas with Fiona, and there was one incident I remember with particular pleasure. I had been introduced to Michael Tree, who had just been made a Director of Christie's. In the fullness of time, Michael became what can only be described as a close friend. He was a gifted amateur painter and,

The Cloisters, Falls Road, Baltimore County

amongst his other subjects, he painted Fiona. The management of Christie's at this time was very anxious to be on better terms with Stavros Niarchos and Michael's appointment was largely due to the fact that he and Niarchos were already friends. A discussion took place between Peter Chance, Patrick Lindsay and Jo Floyd on the one hand, and Michael on the other, when it was made clear that Michael's principal task would be to cement a relationship between that legendary collector and the firm. His reply somewhat disconcerted his colleagues. Puffing on his pipe, he said he was awfully sorry but 'Boys, you see, Stavros is such a close friend of mine that I really cannot discuss business with him'. Michael remained on the Board of Christie's until the firm went public, when he retired. He was much missed for the warmth of his friendship and the smell of his pipe at early morning Board meetings.

Mary Elizabeth Altemus, later Mrs Tippett

Jim Casey, who I mentioned earlier, had become Christie's attorney in 1968. He put me in touch with a client of his who wanted a valuation of English sporting pictures. The client was the wonderfully eccentric Liz Tippett, born Mary Elizabeth Altemus. She grew up to be a great beauty and a beautiful rider. Her first husband was the rich, elegant and eligible John Hay (Jock) Whitney, who later became the popular US ambassador to the Court of St James's (by then married to his second wife, Betsey).

Liz Tippett's fourth husband, Colonel Joe Tippett, also flew her helicopter and had been an old footballing friend of Jim Casey. Liz Tippett was still living on the estate that Jock Whitney had bought at the time of their marriage and generously left her on their divorce: Llangollen, Upperville, Virginia. The list of pictures I had to value included a good Stubbs and a group of other good sporting pictures by Herring, Ferneley and the like. I arrived at the house at about 11am to be greeted in a very friendly way by a large lady armed with a pair of shotguns, mounted on a mule and accompanied by several big dogs. 'You're Jim Casey's friend?', she asked. 'Yes.' 'Good,' she replied, 'you know what you've got to look at?' 'Thank you, yes.' 'It will take you a while, help yourself to a drink, and if I am not back by 1pm – there are a lot of quail come in – there is a freezer in the kitchen with some cold lobster. Help yourself.' With this, she gave the mule a kick, whistled up the dogs and rode away. It was difficult, and with the benefit of hindsight no easier, to describe Liz Tippett's legendary beauty. Beauty was not the thing which immediately came to mind looking at her very old jodhpurs, even older woolly coat and large battered straw hat, but the remains of great good looks struggled through. Mrs T. could certainly ride and, I am sure, shoot, and any doubt about this was dispelled when she arrived back, the panniers of the mule groaning under the weight of dead quail.

I looked at all the pictures. The Ferneleys and J.F. Herrings were excellent and the Stubbs, if not the greatest, was not a bad picture. There were about twenty in all. I noted them down and measured them and finished sometime before one o'clock. I did help myself to a drink but I waited until after one to investigate the freezer.

Eventually hunger got the better of me. I found the freezer and lifted the lid. The lobsters were not immediately evident. What was evident was a very dead black Labrador. I closed the freezer, hunger fled and I poured myself another drink. Eventually, at about 1.45, Mrs Tippett returned with, as I said, a lot of quail and asked me if had I enjoyed the lobster. 'No,' I said. Memory dawned on her once beautiful features: 'Oh my God, I am so sorry, it died in the night and I didn't have time to bury it, so I just chucked it in the freezer.' There may have been stranger valuations than this, but not many.

Chapter 8

Sale of Heywood-Lonsdale Rembrandt; Tiepolo's ceiling; Henry McIlhenny's Seurat; first appearance of *Yo, Picasso*; Bassano's *Flight into Egypt* sold to Norton Simon; the Van Alen Bruguière sale contrasted to Adenauer; return to London

The 1968–9 season lacked the excitements of the year before, with its Monet and two Van Goghs from the Reverend Pitcairn, and certainly lacked the excitements of the year to follow. It was getting towards the time when old master pictures no longer dominated the marketplace. Dominate, however, they did in 1968–9 when the top price was 460,000 guineas ($1,159,000) for Colonel Heywood-Lonsdale's *Self-Portrait* by Rembrandt, another of Christie's most faithful clients coming up trumps with his sensitive, contemplative picture which was bought again by Norton Simon, albeit with less brio than in earlier years.

The picture which stole the headlines was David Carritt's discovery from the Egyptian Embassy, the Tiepolo ceiling painting, *Allegory of Venus Entrusting Eros to Chronos*. There is some confusion here regarding the classical Greek/Roman iconography. Venus didn't give birth to Eros, Aphrodite did and I hope she was giving Eros (or was it Cupid?) to Chronos not Cronus. If to the latter, also known as Saturn, the child would not stand a chance. Cronus has some very nasty habits, among them castrating his father and eating his children; nonetheless it makes a lovely picture. David had taken me with him on his first trip to the Embassy when he had unravelled the mystery of where the picture was. It had disappeared sometime after the death of Henry Bischoffsheim and David had found a reference to it in a Tiepolo catalogue in 1962 as 'formerly in the Bischoffsheim collection'. He very cleverly discovered that the Bischoffsheims had lived at 75 South Audley Street and felt that this could be where pictures might still be. They were. Plans for a sale, however, had to be put on hold due to the Arab–Israeli War of 1967. After diplomatic relations had been restored, the sale again became a possibility and the picture was sold for 390,000 guineas ($982,000) to the National Gallery in London where it filled a significant gap in the national collection. It was at the time a record for any eighteenth-century picture.

OPPOSITE

Pablo Picasso. **Yo, Picasso**, 1901

BELOW

Giovanni Battista Tiepolo. **Allegory of Venus entrusting Eros to Chronos**, *c.*1754–8

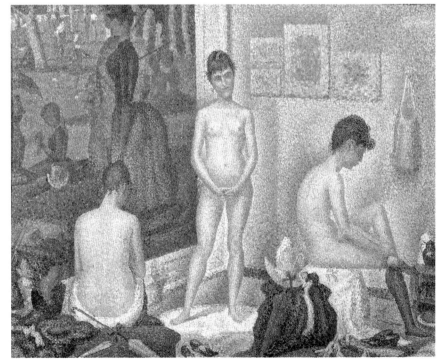

Jacopo Bassano (Jacopo da Ponte). **The Flight into Egypt**, c.1544–5

LEFT

Georges Seurat. **Les Poseuses (petite version)**, 1888

Claude Monet. **Les Bords de la Seine**, Argenteuil, 1872

After these two exceptional old masters, the next best pictures Christie's sold that year were Madame Balsan's *Vue de Pontoise* by Pissarro, entrusted to me by her granddaughter, which made 85,000 guineas and at 75,000 guineas, Van Gogh's *Le Semeur*. There was another picture which intrigued me, Sir E.J. Poynter PRA's *Cave of the Storm Nymphs*, which sold for 3,500 guineas. The painting came up for sale twice at Christie's and twice at Sotheby's, ending in 1994 when it achieved £551,500.

The year 1969–70 was not dominated by old masters but by three exceptional impressionist, post-impressionist and modern pictures. Post-impressionism won the race with Seurat's *Les Poseuses (petite version)* making 410,000 guineas, just over $1 million. This exquisite painting came from Henry McIlhenny's collection entirely *grâce à* John Richardson. It was rightly praised by critics and favourably compared with the larger version in the Barnes Foundation, a collection not often bettered. It was, in the words of John Russell, writing in that year's *Review*, 'one of the three or four most beautiful works of art to have come on the international art market since the war'.

John was also responsible for the first appearance at auction of another seminal work, Picasso's *Yo*. This time round, *Yo* was knocked down for 140,000 guineas ($353,000) which was frankly rather a disappointment, certainly for John. The purchase came from his friends Mr and Mrs Michael Zimmer. Mrs Zimmer was the granddaughter of Hugo von Hofmannsthal, who had bought the picture in 1911 with the proceeds of his libretto for Strauss's opera *Der Rosenkavalier*. Too much has been written about this fascinating picture for me to add anything here. It came in and out of my life for the next fifty years and I would only say that if anybody were looking for a bridge from classical to modern painting, this would be a good one. It

was sold again by Christie's in 1975 and after that by Sotheby's in 1981, before making its final appearance in 1989 – again at Sotheby's – where it made $47.9 million.

Aelbert Cuyp. **Extensive Landscape**, c.1641-44

Drawn into the sale by these two wonderful pictures was another beauty, this time from an old friend of Peter Chance's, Hanning Phillips. Monet's *Les Bords de la Seine, Argenteuil* was painted in 1872 and took second place on the day at 240,000 guineas ($605,000). If the race were rerun today, it is without peradventure that the order would be first Picasso, second Seurat and third Monet, but what does it matter? They were three masterpieces and Christie's were lucky to have them. There was also a good supporting cast: two Sisleys, *Printemps à Bougival* and *Une route en Seine-et-Marne*, and a Monet, *La Seine à Chatou, près d'Argenteuil*, all from the Blackwell family. John was also responsible for bringing in another good post-impressionist picture, *Bonjour Monsieur Gauguin*, which, for reasons I never quite understood, was sent to a one-off sale at Le Richemond in Geneva where it made £131,707 – strangely at that time, a record for Gauguin. It belonged to a Mrs Mary Ermolaev and her son Vladimir Pogdoursky, whom we had got to know in New York.

To return to the old masters, there were two stars, including one as luminous as any of the aforementioned later works, Jacopo Bassano's *The Flight into Egypt*. This picture was something of a parting gift from David Carritt, who left Christie's the following year to join a new art combine, Artemis, which incidentally bought *Les Poseuses (petite version)*. He had found the picture in a convent, Prinknash Abbey, near Stroud, to whom it had been left by Lord Rendel of Hatchlands. It had made its last appearance as the property of Lord Harrington at Christie's in April 1812 where it was bought in! My sometime colleague and friend Simon Dickinson, who has, many would agree, an eye as good if not quite so well tutored as Messrs Richardson and Carritt, always rates it as the favourite old master picture of his career. So incidentally did my wife, who did not have a bad eye either and neither presumably did Norton Simon who bought the picture.

Andrea Appiani. **Napoleon as First Consul**, *c.*1798

The supporting cast was made up largely from a collection of the late Margaret Louise Van Alen Bruguière of Wakehurst, Bellevue Avenue Newport, Rhode Island. In a rare nod to modesty, all the grand Newport houses were known as a cottages. Wakehurst, a replica of the house in Sussex, now the property of the National Trust, was not as grand as some, but still a substantial mansion and housed a very good collection of old master pictures. Mrs Bruguière had first been married to Mr Van Alen, whose son James I had met on previous trips to Newport. He was an ebullient character who was responsible for the foundation of the Tennis Hall of Fame and the introduction of the tiebreak. He had been, in his time, a leading amateur player. I took Jo Floyd with me to Newport to see the collection and we won it against Sotheby's. The sale in December of that year went extremely well. There was an excellent Salomon Van Ruysdael, *River Scene with a Ferryboat*, at 50,000 guineas; an early Cuyp, *Extensive Landscape*, at the same price, which was then a record for the artist; a Willem Van de Velde the Younger, *Fishing Boats and Other Vessels in a Calm*, which went for 26,000 guineas – another record for the artist; and a Jan Van Goyen, *An Estuary Landscape* at 37,000 guineas, also another record. In addition there was an excellent Aert van der Neer, *River Scene by Night*; a Jan Steen; a dashing portrait by Andrea Appiani of Napoleon Bonaparte at 24,000 guineas (the artist painted several versions of this subject and this was the best) and, in another sale, Gainsborough's *Portrait of Dr Richard Warren*, King George III's doctor, strangely reminiscent of his portrait of James Christie. The input of the Picture Department that summer had been the disastrous sale of the Adenauer Collection which Frank Davis, in his foreword to the *Review*, wrote, 'not unnaturally failed to interest the international market'. In fact it sold only five out of the twenty-five pictures for less than 2 per cent of the total as opposed to the 96 per-cent success rate of the Van Alen Collection.

The goings-on of 1969–70, while gratifying at the time, were soured by the fact that neither John nor I was given the one thing we wanted: a Directorship of Christie's. John would leave a couple of years later because of Christie's refusal to grant his wish, which was a grievous loss to the firm. I returned to London and was allowed to join the Board, but I was not granted what I wanted at the time (although latterly I have often wondered why), the place in Christie's Old Master Picture Department that I had vacated to go to New York.

Velázquez's *Juan de Pareja*; trip to Sydney; the Dodge Sale and sales of pictures from Lord Harewood; Lord Derby and the Tournon-Charpentier family

Sometime later I discovered from reading John Herbert's book that my success with the Van Alen pictures was the deciding factor in Christie's getting one of the best collections of all to sell in London from America: the works of art left by the late Mrs Horace Dodge, Anna Thomson Dodge. Before I describe the Dodge Collection, I should mention a picture sold at Christie's in November 1970 which made an impression on the market and on people's perception of the firm, rivalled only by the sale of Van Gogh's *Sunflowers*. I refer of course to the Earl of Radnor's *Portrait of Juan de Pareja* by Velázquez.

The picture, which had always been regarded as one of the great masterpieces in private hands in Britain, was painted in Rome in 1650 as an exercise for the artist prior to painting his portrait of Pope Innocent X. Juan de Pareja was Velázquez's servant, friend and an accomplished painter. Sometimes described as the artist's slave, there is nothing subservient in his intelligent, handsome face. The picture was an instant success and, just under 150 years later, had found its way to Naples where it was acquired by Sir William Hamilton. It reached London, with some help from Nelson on his ship the *Foudroyant*, and was sold at Christie's for 39 guineas. Ten years later it was acquired by the second Earl of Radnor for £152 and remained at Longford Castle until the sale. It has been variously published and exhibited. I first saw it in Christie's bicentennial exhibition, where it occupied pride of place in the great rooms to which it would return for its last appearance before leaving home for the Metropolitan Museum, efforts to retain it in this country having failed. For this sale, Peter Chance stepped aside at the last moment in favour of Patrick Lindsay, who clearly did a magnificent job. The picture made £2,310,000 or just over $5,500,000, way above expectations and over twice the previous record for a painting.

Unfortunately I was not in the room when the picture was sold because, due to the manoeuvrings over who was to sell the Velázquez, I was sent to Australia to fill in for Patrick, who was to have taken our sale in Sydney the same day. I was sad that I was going to miss at first hand what was clearly going to be a dramatic day. I was,

'Marc' (Mark Boxer) on the controversial departure of Juan de Pareja to New York

OPPOSITE

Diego Velázquez. **Portrait of Juan de Pareja**, 1650

however, excited to be going to Sydney, a city of which I had heard so much, although it was a long flight. For once, I was given a first-class ticket, which made the prospect of twenty-four hours on the old Boeing 707 slightly better. The plane was supposed to stop in Bahrain, Delhi and Singapore but it didn't because there was a typhoon over the Singapore peninsula, so we headed back to Kuala Lumpur and landed there to wait for the typhoon to blow itself out before returning to Singapore. This diversion added twelve hours to an already long flight. We set off again to Perth. Perth! I thought we were nearly there. Not quite. Australia from its western tip to its eastern is 2,553 miles, and when I finally arrived in Sydney, just over five hours on from Perth, I was exhausted, not sure what day it was, and was met by a friend of a friend who was putting me up in Paddington. It might have been King's Cross or Euston for all I knew. My friend's friend asked me if I liked sailing. 'Yes,' I replied. 'Good,' he said, 'we will wake you up at seven, we're going on the Sydney Harbour race and we need an extra crew.' 'Sounds fine,' I said as I went to sleep.

Seven came in what felt about ten minutes. I dragged myself out of bed, put on some wholly inadequate clothes and set off for the boat. The rest of the crew were suitably clad, clearly fit, rested and raring to go. My enduring good memory is of the beauty of Sydney Harbour. No one had told me that Sydney was so beautiful! My enduring bad memory is of a mixture of lingering exhaustion and a desperate, unrequited desire to answer a serious call of nature brought on by thirty-six hours sitting in a 707. Every tack up the harbour was buttock-clenching agony and the bladder situation wasn't good either. I can't remember whether we came first, second or last; I can only remember the relief when we finally made it back to the Club House.

The sale was that evening. I had a bit of a rest in the afternoon and was then greeted in the rented hall by the redoubtable Sue Hewitt, and our other representative, the charming John Henshaw, who was actually a New Zealander, but, aged fifteen, had fled the South Island where he was born because the rainfall was 365 inches per year. He never returned but he became a leading authority on Australian painting and a very entertaining colleague. The sale itself was not so entertaining. In fact, the high point for the audience and low point for me was when I stepped into the rostrum to discover that those in charge of the mechanics of the sale had failed to put in the floor. I stepped boldly into the abyss and a second later the enraptured audience could only see eight white knuckles gripping the rim of the rostrum and a pair of well-shod feet flailing around in the space below. It was a great evening once the sale was over and I awoke the next morning to discover the amazing news about the Velázquez. The danger with a successful sale is always the anticlimax afterwards. This, with the Velázquez, would not be the case. The following spring and summer, Christie's would sell the Dodge Collection and much else besides.

This famous collection included highly important French furniture. The star was Tsarina Marie-Feodorovna's Louis XVI Carlin bureau plat, mounted with Sèvres

plaques, as delicate and beautiful a table as ever there was. It was bought by an Iranian collector, Habib Sabet, for a record price, 165,000 guineas. It also gave rise to a superbly surreal photograph of foreman porter Jim Taylor and an assistant carrying the bureau plat off the aeroplane at London airport which appears to defy the laws of physics. Jim Taylor was the same wonderful character who had accompanied me to Jersey in the back of the Dakota.

There was also a pair of exceptional Louis XV marquetry commodes by BVRB and another bureau plat said to have belonged to Catherine the Great. There was not just furniture. There was a beautiful Van Dyck, *Portrait of Mountjoy Blount, Earl of Newport* (this went for 85,000 guineas but could have fetched more) and a pair of paintings by François Boucher, *La Fontaine d'amour* and *La Pipée aux oiseaux*, traditionally thought to have been painted for Madame de Pompadour (these measured 3 by 4 metres and made just over $1 million). There was much more besides and in this instance, the collection did not come over in a Dakota but in a specially chartered 707 direct from Detroit to London (although the Bouchers were actually too big and came by sea). Credit where credit is due, getting this collection mainly went again to Jo Floyd. Put together as it was, with Lord Harewood's *The Death of Actaeon* by Titian and Lord Derby's beautiful *Four Studies of a Negro's Head* (then attributed to Van Dyck), it gave Christie's the follow-up sale for the Radnor Velázquez. It should be noted that the Impressionist and Modern Picture Department was now playing its full part and their star of the year was undoubtedly the absolutely beautiful Renoir, *Le Pêcheur à la ligne*, which came direct from the family for whom it was painted, the Tournon-Charpentiers. The Renoir made fractionally more than the Bouchers and was bought for $1,104,000 by Nigel

LEFT TO RIGHT

Jim Taylor (left) carrying the bureau plat

François Boucher. **La Fontaine d'amour**, 1748

Titian. **The Death of Actaeon**, *c.*1559-75

Broackes, one of a new generation of English collectors. The Titian, which many expected to exceed the price of the Velázquez, eventually sold for $4,065,600. The season's total was just over £25 million or $60 million. For the first time since the Second World War, Sotheby's must have felt us breathing down their necks.

In 1973, Christie's became a public company which involved much discussion both with the firm's bankers Hambro's and with the newly formed business advisory arm of our accountants, Peat Marwick Mitchell.

Peats came up with a new world order, advocating originally an outsider as Managing Director. Fortunately, this was played down to the boundary at long leg. Guy Hannen was confirmed in his post as MD and a compromise was reached whereby an outside operations manager, or some such nomenclature, was appointed. Someone asked Patrick what he did: 'He orders the paperclips, I think,' was the reply but Guy set up a Management Committee. He was the Chairman and I was the Secretary and responsible for the minutes and I soon realised that the man who writes the minutes has considerable power since, after a week, few people can remember what they themselves – let alone anyone else – have said. I enjoyed this and it was better than helping Geoffrey Corbett weigh the silver. I also had to assist

the Operations Manager and by a small miracle, I remember what he was called: Denis Mann. I am almost sure he went mad and left. I am absolutely sure of something else: it is impossible to survive, let alone thrive, in an auction house – which is a sort of madhouse – unless sustained by a love and knowledge of works of art. To my mind, and based on a lifetime's experience, the asylum functions best when the lunatics are in charge

My three-year stint on the management team was in addition to my work in the Silver Department and I sometimes accompanied Arthur Grimwade on valuation trips and visits to clients. As I have said, I was very grateful to Arthur. He was a dear man. He had come to Christie's from an ecclesiastical family, at the same time as Peter Chance, via St Paul's School and the Boy Scout movement and he served in the Royal Navy Volunteer Reserve (RNVR) in the Second World War on the Arctic convoys. He had been given a place in the Silver Department in 1931 under the titular command of Charles Brocklehurst. Arthur, according to his own memoirs *Silver for Sale*, did not rate him. He turned himself into one of the world's leading experts on English silver but he was, in fact, more interested and knowledgeable in English watercolours and in the flint churches of Suffolk. Arthur was sometimes impatient of the world as he found it in the 1970s and travel with the L.O.E. (Lovable Old Eccentric), as Patrick called him, could be a bit of a challenge but always fun, except at breakfast when he would make the most appalling fuss about coffee. The most unforgettable of these adventures came that year when we were working in Ireland.

Associate of Peter Paul Rubens. **Four Studies of a Negro's Head**, *c.*1617-20

Rogier van der Weyden's *St Ivo*; Lady Baird and Lord Dunalley; Desmond Dunalley's silver client in Ireland, a wasted journey with Arthur Grimwade; the porcelain vase and the refuse tip; my godfather George Burns and the wonderful Bellotto; Sir Victor Crutchley VC, his Bellotto versus Canaletto; the Czernin Guariento di Arpo and Norton Simon once more; Reynolds's *Mrs Abington*; Peter Chance's last sale

In that annus mirabilis 1970–1 there was a picture not sold at auction but negotiated to the National Gallery: Rogier van der Weyden's *St Ivo*. This picture, hailed as a great discovery, was much praised by the Gallery's then director, Sir Martin Davies. Two or three years after its acquisition, doubts were raised about its authenticity, which were then quashed, but the doubts have reawakened and it is now labelled as 'Workshop of van der Weyden'. Personally, I have always felt that the picture was strange insofar as the hands are not well drawn, the background is strangely confused, and St Ivo's back is out of all proportion to the rest of his body. But its authenticity is not at the heart of this story.

Martin Davies's article in Christie's *Review* credited this discovery to David Carritt. The picture certainly came from the late Joan, Lady Baird, from her home in Bray, near Dublin, but it was really discovered by a charming man, Lord Dunalley. Desmond Dunalley subsequently became Christie's representative in Ireland, entirely on the strength of finding Lady Baird and her picture. He told me that he had a client with possibly some very good silver, but he did not know anything about silver so he could not be sure. He thought we should go and see her. Arthur Grimwade and I had been in Ireland doing valuations in the north, but agreed it was worth while making a detour down to Dublin. Desmond met us at our hotel and we set off in his Volvo to somewhere west of the capital. Arthur complained a bit about the state of the back of the car: it had quite a lot of corn growing in it, but Desmond was a working farmer. Arthur sat, slightly querulously, in the back seat, and I sat in

OPPOSITE

Workshop of Rogier van der Weyden. **A Man Reading (St Ivo?)**, *c.*1450 the front with Desmond because he said he wanted me to help him map-read. We drove for about an hour, Arthur, like children young and old the world over, continually asking 'Are we nearly there?' Desmond replied, with a slight lack of confidence in his voice, 'Yes, pretty nearly', and I said quite quietly, 'Where is the house actually?' He said he had forgotten but thought it was 'Off this road somewhere'.

We drove on for another half-hour, time and the rather flat, monotonous interior of Ireland passing, when Desmond suddenly took a lightning turn to the right. Thank goodness nothing was coming either towards us or fast from behind. 'I think it's up here,' he said. We drove on for about another ten minutes until we reached the driveway of a nice but unpretentious house. I asked Desmond, 'What is your client called?' 'I've forgotten,' he replied. We pulled up, got out, and Arthur asked, 'What is her name?' Desmond replied, 'I will introduce you,' and then rang the bell and walked in, pushing past a slightly surprised lady. Fortunately, there was a bill on the hall table. 'Ah,' he said, and addressed her by the name on the bill. 'Lord Dunalley, I wasn't expecting you,' she said. 'These are my colleagues from Christie's. We have come to see the silver,' said Desmond. 'Oh,' she replied, 'you should have warned me … It's in the bank in Dublin.' It was after two o'clock, long after Arthur would normally be lunching at his club, the Garrick. Mrs Name-on-the-Bill rang the bank and asked to speak to the manager, who said yes, it would be fine for us to come and look at the silver. Were we in Dublin, because the bank closed at three o'clock? Desmond turned, hardly saying goodbye, and bolted from the house, followed by Arthur and me.

We sped back to Dublin. We must have done it in record time because we got to the bank, absolutely next door to the Shelbourne Hotel where Arthur and I had been staying the night before, to see the clerk pulling up the metal grille of the windows. The door was firmly locked. We had just failed to make it. I cannot remember whether Arthur subsequently ever got to see the silver but Desmond soon afterwards stopped being Christie's representative in Ireland.

Arthur and I returned to London and he soon regained his equanimity. I was extremely grateful to him for giving me a berth. He did not really need another pair of hands in the Silver Department. He already had as his principal assistant Tom Milnes Gaskell, and Anthony Phillips, who continued to work in the Department for the next forty years. They were both first-class experts and I still see Anthony. Also confined to the Silver strongroom was a remarkable character, Geoffrey Corbett, whose sole task, although he was intelligent and knew an enormous amount about silver, was to measure and weigh it.

Arthur was very tolerant of my wanderlust. I was always darting off on expeditions, either on my own initiative or to help out someone else in almost any field other than silver. There was even a consolation for being forced to work in the Silver Department: the absolutely exquisite Paul de Lamerie

George II coffee pot by Paul de Lamerie, 1738

Bernardo Bellotto. **View of Verona with the Ponte delle Navi, looking downstream**, *c.*1745

coffee pot, sold in 1971, from the Dodge Collection. It made £24,000, which was a remarkable price given that in 1968 the silver market had completely collapsed.

The porcelain market, on the other hand, had not collapsed. One particularly beautiful piece, a Southern Song dynasty Kuan Yao octagonal bottle of the palest celadon, perfectly modelled and glazed, had a very lucky escape. It eventually made a world record price of 90,000 guineas. But the fact that it made its way to the saleroom at all was something of a miracle because although it was originally delivered to Christie's, it was never removed from its box and was then consigned to a council refuse tip. It was rescued in the nick of time before it would most certainly have been crushed and buried. There were anxious faces that day.

The 1972 season saw a continuation in Christie's revival and successful rivalry with Sotheby's. There were masterpieces from every discipline. The season's prize has to go to Bernardo Bellotto's *Ponte delle Navi, Verona*, which was sold by my godfather, Major General Sir George Burns, from his house in North Mymms Park on 26 November 1971. It made 300,000 guineas which was more than any other picture by a Venetian view painter, including, obviously, the artist's uncle Canaletto. No one doubted the importance of that picture. The only point with which I would take issue was William Mostyn-Owen's contention in Christie's *Review* of that year that with no other work did Bellotto ever surpass his uncle Canaletto. I think this neglects the brilliance of Bellotto's views of Dresden and Warsaw, and even some closer to both artists' home town, Venice. The present picture, the *Ponte delle Navi*, already had a distinguished history with Christie's, having first been sold by James Christie himself on 9 March 1771, when it was described as 'Canaletti [*sic*] a large and most capital picture being a remarkably fine view of the city of Verona. Its light and shadow, fine, and uncommonly highly finished.' It was sold for 255 guineas to Lord Dover and again on 25 May 1895 for 2,000 guineas – a substantial price in those days – and bought by Agnew's on behalf of George Burns's grandfather, Walter H. Burns. As good a painter as Canaletto undoubtedly was, and a brilliant draughtsman (as anybody who has had the privilege of seeing the Royal Collection at Windsor will know), who is the better painter?

Sometime after the sale of the Mymms picture, I was asked to go and look at a painting in Somerset belonging to a formidable character, Admiral Sir Victor Crutchley, who had won the Victoria Cross as a young lieutenant on board HMS *Vindictive* during the First World War. He was the owner of a beautiful small picture of *The Tower of Marghera*, another early work painted by Bellotto in the Veneto and, as this illustration shows, a view which was also painted, slightly later, by his uncle, Canaletto. The way the buildings and the landscape are painted shows skilful execution in both pictures but with the Bellotto, the light in the sky and the way that it picks out the details in the buildings is sharper and more dramatic. The overall effect in the work of the young artist, still an apprentice, is every bit as good as that of the elder master. This same light is evident in the Mymms picture and in all his views of Dresden and Warsaw and, to me, this places Bellotto, in the end, ahead of his better-known uncle. The Mymms picture is certainly a masterpiece, as anyone who visits the National Gallery of Scotland, where it is still on loan, can attest.

TOP TO BOTTOM

Bernardo Bellotto. **The Tower of Marghera**, *c*.1741

Giovanni Antonio Canal (Canaletto). **The Tower of Marghera**, *c*.1755

The other fascinating old master that year was an entire altarpiece by Guariento di Arpo, the able and colourful pupil of Giotto. Although not in its original framing, which was replaced in 1847, in every other respect the altarpiece, of palatial proportions (over 2 by 2.5 metres), was complete and in a remarkable state of conservation. It came from the home of the Czernin family in Vienna, not from their amazing palace in Prague which is so large it had to be built outside the walls of the city. The picture made 245,000 guineas and was bought again by Mr Norton Simon. It is without doubt the finest early painting in his remarkable collection.

That year again saw very good English pictures come under the hammer, pride of place going to Sir Joshua Reynolds's *Portrait of Mrs Abington*, which made 100,000 guineas, the sort of price it would have made had it come up for sale in 1930, when it would have been a world record for a painting. Romney's *The Gower Family*, in the same sale, made slightly more at 140,000 guineas.

That summer, Peter Chance took his last major sale, the Leo Rogers Collection, which he did with all his old charm and brio, selling every lot and for some excellent prices. The collection made just under $2 million and contained a first-class Modigliani, *Portrait du peintre Moïse Kisling*. Whether it was a good picture or not, the Modigliani was certainly much better than anything Kisling could ever have painted. Another record was achieved later for Beckmann's *Bildnis Quappi mit weissem Pelz*: 24,000 guineas. Whether or not it was a record really does not matter. What does matter is that Beckmann was, at his best, a very good painter.

Two people whose taste I admired bought beautiful Beckmanns. One, Baron Thyssen, suffered on a number of counts: he married several very beautiful women, which makes people jealous; his firm had some questions to answer about the war; and he suffered as a collector from having a father who was in the really great category, with which it was difficult to compete. However, Thyssen himself bought some very good things, including pictures by Beckmann and Hopper. The other Beckmann collector, who is still with us, is the dealer Richard Feigen. Dick has been a very successful dealer because he has a really good eye, as witnessed by his love of Beckmann.

That year also saw some noteworthy furniture from the Hillingdon Collection. Charles Hedworth Mills was a successful banker. He was ennobled in 1886 along with my great-great-grandfather, Lord Hindlip, to the distress of some commentators who objected to men in trade being made peers. Of the two of them, Lord Hindlip made more money, but Lord Hillingdon won out hand over fist by putting together a collection of French furniture and pictures. The furniture, in particular, was rivalled as a collection only by that of the Rothschilds. Most of it by the second half of the twentieth century was in the Metropolitan Museum in New York, but there were still treasures with the family. One of these was Martin Carlin's Louis XVI black lacquer *secrétaire à abattant*, which made 120,000 guineas on 29 June 1972.

In a sale earlier that month, topping the price of even the Carlin, was a Chinese red, blue and white porcelain Southern Song wine jar, which was leading a double life as an umbrella stand. It had been discovered by Anthony Derham, the leading light in Christie's Oriental Porcelain Department, who secured the vase for sale and managed to get it to the rooms – this time without a trip to the refuse tip. The result was a record, not just for a piece of porcelain, but for any work of art other than a picture: 210,000 guineas. At the time it was sold, the wine jar was still the most collectable, most treasured type of Chinese porcelain. However, as in the West, Chinese taste can go through rapid changes and a short time earlier, a Yung Cheng famille rose pilgrim flask from the Summer Palace – the property of Lord Margadale – sold for a modest 3,600 guineas. Were it to come up now, it would make a price which would far outstrip that of the wine jar.

TOP TO BOTTOM

Sir Joshua Reynolds. **Portrait of Mrs Abington**, 1771

Louis XVI black lacquer secrétaire à abattant by Martin Carlin

Ten years at Christie's; disappointment over Sebastiano del Piombo head; Cuyp and Sir Harry Oakes; Verspronck goes west and Christie's shares south; Guy Hannen and Patrick Lindsay at odds; a Gilman portrait; Lady Sefton and Ansdell's *Waterloo Cup* at Croxteth; Degas and Barbra Streisand; *Patience Escalier*, my favourite Van Gogh

The year 1972 had been my tenth anniversary at Christie's. On 8 December that year, a picture came up for sale, originally part of the Panshanger Collection: Sebastiano del Piombo's *Head of the Madonna*, at one time attributed to Leonardo. When I saw it, I thought it was one of the most beautiful things I had ever seen. I asked Fiona, my wife, to come and look at it. She agreed. It had an estimate of

OPPOSITE

Vincent van Gogh. **Portrait of Patience Escalier**, 1888

BELOW LEFT

Aelbert Cuyp. **Wooded River Landscape**, *c.*1650

BELOW

Sebastiano del Piombo. **Head of the Madonna**, *c.*1530

4,000–6,000 guineas and I was fairly convinced that it would make more than this. I went to see my bank manager and arranged a facility which would allow me to bid up to 10,000 guineas. Come the sale, I don't think I even got my hand up. The bidding rose inexorably from 5,000 to 10,000 to 15,000 to 20,000 … and eventually to 55,000 guineas. The picture was bought by David Carritt who had, by that time, left Christie's and who died shortly afterwards. A couple of years later, I saw the Sebastiano again, carefully restored but, although brighter and cleaner, not the same as the vision in the 8 December sale. Some of the old magic had disappeared in the restoration. It was, in a strange way, some sort of consolation that Fiona and I had not been able to acquire a thing we had fallen in love with. The price by this time was over £100,000, but it was also an object lesson in what can be lost when you clean a picture. I reproduce it here as it was in the catalogue.

We were yet to equal the achievements of our friends in Bond Street but we were closing the gap and continued to do so. Our turnover in 1973 increased

by £14 million to nearly £34 million. The best picture was undoubtedly the Aelbert Cuyp, *Wooded River Landscape*, from the family of Sir Harry Oakes, the Canadian-born mining millionaire who had become the largest landowner and almost certainly the richest resident of the Bahamas. He was murdered in 1943 when the Bahamas were under the governorship of the late Duke of Windsor. His son-in-law was tried for his murder and acquitted; no one else was ever charged and the murder remained unsolved, although it was the subject of considerable speculation and inspired several books and four films. Whatever the unfortunate circumstances surrounding its ownership, the picture was one of the best works by this much-loved painter and somewhat unsurprisingly made a record 580,000 guineas.

Le Rixe des musiciens (*The Beggars' Brawl*), a painting by the great French Caravaggesque painter Georges de la Tour, was another rare and exciting picture: it made 380,000 guineas. If minor painters can paint masterpieces, Johannes Corneliszoon Verspronck's *Portrait of a Lady* was one such picture. It came from the Clarke Collection of Borde Hill through a client of Guy Hannen, now sadly missed. It was bought, I need hardly add, by Norton Simon. Turning to things more modern, it seems extraordinary today that Juan Gris's *L'Intransigeant*, from the collection of L.A. Basmadjieff, could have been bought for 65,000 guineas the season before.

TOP TO BOTTOM

Johannes Corneliszoon Verspronck. **Portrait of a Lady**, 1641

Harold Gilman. **Girl with a Teacup**, 1915

The year 1974 saw the introduction of the three-day week, imposed because of the miners' strike. The value of Christie's recently issued shares plunged from 100p to 20p in the blink of an eye. However, Christie's increased their turnover by £10 million from the previous year to £44 million and, all things considered, it was a very successful year. Although we had special dispensation to hold sales five days a week since we had already published the catalogues, there were difficulties as we were not allowed to use electric light. Unfortunately, it was before the days when bidders were issued with paddles. In the unlit rooms on winter afternoons, it was difficult to see and some auctioneers struggled. Patrick Lindsay rather unkindly suggested that if one particular colleague was to take sales in the afternoon, the potential bidders should be supplied with flags to wave.

In this general air of austerity, Guy Hannen, by now named Managing Director, tried to instil some sense of financial responsibility among his colleagues, particularly with regard to the use of cars or taxis to go between King Street and the newly acquired Christie's South Kensington. Patrick, half-heartedly taking up the theme, addressed a meeting of the Old Master Picture Department thus: 'I am led to believe that the underground railway runs from Green Park Station to South Kensington, quite close to our office, and I would suggest that you use it.' He himself continued to travel either in his Ferrari or, on high days and holidays, in what had been the Maharajah of Jaipur's Phantom III Rolls Royce.

Richard Ansdell. **The Waterloo Cup Coursing Meeting**, 1840

Despite all this, there were some good things sold in 1974. These included more pictures from the collection of Edward Le Bas, such as Harold Gilman's *Girl with a Teacup*, which fetched 18,000 guineas. Harold Gilman is not a name to conjure with but, some day in the future, our descendants will appreciate that he was a far better painter than any single artist in the Sensation exhibition, a subject which we will come to. Richard Ansdell's *The Waterloo Cup Coursing Meeting* is illustrated on the front cover of the *Review* of the year. I sold it at the house sale at Croxteth from the estate of Lord Sefton and it was the first really expensive picture I ever sold, though not the most expensive picture Christie's sold that year, good though it was. It gets a mention in one of the funniest poems I have ever read, 'Magna Carta' by Marriott Edgar, found in John Julius Norwich's wonderful *A Christmas Cracker:*

> So they set about making a Charter,
> When at finish they'd got it drawn up,
> It looked like a paper on cattle disease,
> Or the entries for t' Waterloo Cup.

From Croxteth, the best of the pictures were settled in lieu of tax and included a Gainsborough, *Isabella, Viscountess Molyneux, later Countess of Sefton*, which went to the Walker Art Gallery. Croxteth Hall was a very large house in the centre of a very large park, some 3,000 acres, within the city limits of Liverpool. The Molyneux family had held nearby Sefton since about 1100 and when the house there was demolished in 1720, the family moved to Croxteth. The family also owned the famous Abbeystead estate, some 30 miles to the north, and the grouse moors of Abbeystead had produced record bags on any number of occasions. The sixth Earl, Hugh, had died in 1962, leaving his American wife, 'Foxy', sadly childless. There was, as far as could reasonably be established, no heir to inherit either the large and valuable estates or the large and valuable collection of works of art.

Hugh and Foxy Sefton were close friends of my parents-in-law, although sadly I did not really know the legendary Lord Sefton myself. I wish I had. Tales of his wit and repartee are legendary. My favourite was the story of Sefton popping into his club, White's, for a quick lunch. On seeing him looking quite out of sorts at the bar afterwards, a friend asked the reason for his distress. He replied that he had just had lunch upstairs and a younger member whom he had not known and who clearly did not know him had asked what he did. 'What I do?', stammered Sefton; 'It's like asking a Hottentot who his tailor is.' Michael Tree, painter, pipe-smoker and confidant of Stavros Niarchos, was in the Blues with Lord Sefton during the war and knew all the stories off by heart. I tried to get him to write some down for posterity, but Michael was not a scribbler and so they are lost, along with so much else, scattered to the wind.

Lord Sefton's lawyer, another charming man whose instructions were a pleasure to take, was the executor of the estate. He told me that some years before the Earl's death he had been on a trip to Canada on the family's business and he thought that he might have found an heir. On his return to Liverpool, he contacted Lord Sefton, asking, 'Shall I get him to come over so you could have a look at him?' 'No, I don't think so,' said Lord Sefton, 'I might not like the feller.' It was the end of the conversation and, in turn, the end of the Molyneuxs of Croxteth.

Foxy, Lady Sefton, was left well endowed for life, certainly well enough endowed to buy a huge corsage of orchids which she wore on her bosom as she stood on the steps of Croxteth for the last time to welcome friends and local dignitaries to a private view, or bunfight, the evening prior to the sale. One of the more intriguing sections of this was devoted to various sporting accoutrements. Croxteth was a well-known and respected home of hare-coursing and was also known for a slightly less-respected sport, cockfighting. The collars and spurs attracted a colourful crowd of sportsmen, who came to the view with red-and-white spotted handkerchiefs, stubble, scars, earrings and whippets. I suppose they were 'Travellers'. Lord Sefton would probably have known and welcomed them. The spurs were all included as one lot and made 100 guineas. The total for the sale was £519,393.

Tureen from the Sèvres œil-de-perdrix service, 1788

All the best pictures from Abbeystead also went in lieu to the Walker Art Gallery, including Richard Ansdell's *The Molyneux Family Picnicking on the Moors at Abbeystead* and several other charming views with the family and their ponies. The house, minus most of its works of art, was left to the Liverpool Corporation, along with the park, for the enjoyment of Liverpudlians in posterity. Abbeystead sold for a *prix d'amitié* to the Duke of Westminster: 'unto he that hath shall it be given'. This gift extended to the contents of the cellar, including a very large quantity of wine. If my memory serves me right, there were many dozen bottles of non-vintage Bollinger which, if laid down and left undisturbed for ten years, drinks better than any other champagne and drink it they did, I am told, in jugs.

Among the good crop of modern pictures that year, I would have taken home Degas's *Femme mettant ses gants*, which fetched £152,250. This slightly odd amount takes into account the introduction of the firm's premium that year and also the fact that we had by then abandoned guineas. Dare I say it, the subject of the picture looks just like Barbra Streisand!

Edgar Degas. **Femme mettant ses gants**, 1890

The introduction of the buyer's premium has given rise, like Sir Harry Oakes's murder, to several books, which I am in no position to discuss. However, I was asked – somebody had to be the fall guy – to take the first premium-added sale in London (a buyer's premium had, incidentally, always been charged on sales in Geneva). It was a book sale and a representative of the book trade read out a statement deploring the introduction of the premium and then left the sale, followed by a number of his colleagues. I thought it was going to be a disaster, but it was not. They had clearly all left their bids with one person who bought almost everything. I will not speculate on what happened after this. Suffice it to say that pots often call kettles black.

The best things that year really fell outside the picture field, with the collection of Sydney J. Lamon of New York, which was exceptional. It had everything: good seventeenth-century Dutch pictures; some beautiful German silver birds and animals; a silver-gilt model of a chamois from Nuremberg *c.*1627 (this was the prize), and even better porcelain and fabulous French furniture. His ormolu and porcelain-mounted *table à café* by Bernard II van Risenburgh made £115,500: it was a small masterpiece and appeared again later. Coming only three years before Christie's opened in New York and the first sale took place there in 1977, the Lamon Collection was the last to be shipped in its entirety from America to London. It was sold over several sales and the first made £1,621,128, with every lot selling.

Inevitably, when you have worked in the auction world for so long, people imagine you must have discovered a lot of things. In fact I didn't. But in 1974 I did discover a rather remarkable Chelsea botanical circular soup-tureen and cover which had been used for growing bulbs in a potting shed at a house in Surrey. It belonged to a charming man called Stephen Cave, who also owned the oldest house on Barbados, St Nicholas Abbey. I think the £10,500 he got for the tureen was all eaten up in Barbados.

I did also once discover a missing picture by Zuccarelli from a set of ten pictures, most of which are at Windsor. I had gone to see an old friend of Peter Chance, called, I think, Commander Benskins, whose house was one of the last lived in by a single family in Belgrave Square. Peter cautioned me before I went: 'Make sure you look at everything.' It was during Ascot week, so the family were all off at the races and had left before I made my great discovery. The front of the house had a large collection of pictures of sheep by an artist called Joseph Farquharson, who was to painting what William McGonagall was to poetry. I counted the sheep and, before leaving, asked the butler if there was anything I had not looked at. 'Well, sir,' he said, 'there is the back stairs.' 'Is there anything on the back stairs?' I asked. 'Well I think there might be but there is no electric

Table à café by Bernard II van Risenburgh, 1761

BELOW

Soup tureen, Chelsea. Raised red anchor mark, 1753-7

light.' I had taken a torch and halfway up the stairs I saw the shape of a picture covered in dust. I asked the butler for his help and we got it down. Underneath the dust even I, hardly off the Front Counter, recognised the Zuccarelli. I got very excited and came back the next day with David Carritt who confirmed my attribution and told me about the pictures at Windsor. The family, who initially had also been excited about the price they could achieve and counted the number of racehorses they could acquire with the proceeds, suddenly changed their minds and said they had never had any good pictures before. Now I had found it, they said they wanted to hold on to it. I am sure if I thought really hard I could come up with a few more discoveries, but I have got a book to finish …

The market reacted rather negatively to the arrival of the new Labour government at the end of 1974. This was hardly surprising, but things did pick up in 1975 and although the turnover was down about £10 million, there were some interesting sales. Edmund de Rothschild, one of Christie's most faithful clients, consigned two extremely good lots for sale. One was a Sèvres ornithological and œil-de-perdrix service, so large that Edmund – the banker – never managed to count the number of dinner plates. In the end, we gave up and gave him a receipt for approximately 150. Edmund de Rothschild was an extremely nice man, but I do not think he could have fixed the LIBOR even if he had tried – certainly not on the evidence of his plate-counting abilities. He also consigned to us the Louis XVI black lacquer ebony commode by J. Baumhauer (called Joseph), which I have always felt was as good a piece of French furniture as is possible to buy. It fetched £115,500. Carlin's Louis XVI black lacquer and ebony bureau plat and *cartonnier* at £157,750 was perhaps even better and was bought by Stavros Niarchos.

Mr Niarchos also bought the best picture that Christie's should have sold but did not that year: Vincent van Gogh's majestic *Portrait of Patience Escalier. Patience* had belonged to Sir Alfred Chester Beatty, whose son had consigned it for sale at Christie's after long negotiations with the then Chairman, Jo Floyd (who had succeeded Peter Chance in 1974). He had reached an agreement with Chester Beatty's lawyer but matters went horribly wrong over the press release. This strange, sad story is described in John Herbert's book, *Inside Christie's*. John tells of his own part in the extraordinarily sloppy way that the publicity of this incomparable picture was dealt with.

Briefly, the press announcement of the sale went out before the client was expecting it to, before he had had an opportunity to tell his wife that he was selling the picture and before he had signed a contract with Christie's. The result was that a consortium of dealers discovered the estimate. Martin Summers, then with Lefevre, had simply rung up the Press Office and been told. He, in turn, called David Somerset, who then rang Chester Beatty and offered him double Christie's estimate. That was the end of any public sale. There is no doubt in my mind that we had hugely underestimated the picture and that the dealers' offer was much more realistic, although this too was on the conservative side. It was sold to Stavros Niarchos for an undisclosed price. If it had

been sold at auction it would without any doubt have made a world record price and would have had the same effect on the market as the *Sunflowers* did over eleven years later. However, this pales into insignificance when compared with its value today and, more importantly, with the impact that the picture makes.

In 1990, Mr Niarchos wanted to talk to me about a project and asked me to meet him at the great Van Gogh Centennial Exhibition at the Rijksmuseum. We agreed to meet underneath *Patience*, which he had generously lent. I arrived slightly early for our assignation and for about a quarter of an hour watched the reactions of the hundreds of people who visited the exhibition. Without exception they stopped in front of *Patience*, astonished by the picture's beauty and size. One can argue endlessly about the merits of one Van Gogh portrait against another, but it is very difficult to find anything which holds its head up when set against *Patience*. Losing it was a galling day for Christie's, but the story does have a slightly happier ending because I suspect Beatty felt guilty about his treatment of the firm and this influenced the decision of his family in 1987 to give us the *Sunflowers*. We will talk about that later.

I must continue with the theme of loyalty and, my word, Christie's owed a lot to the loyalty of its old clients: Fiona, Countess of Normanton, was one of our most faithful and consigned us her Parmigianino, *The Mystic Marriage of St Catherine*, for private sale to the National Gallery. It is an exquisite picture. Harking back a few years to 1969, I had always been puzzled as to why the early pictures by Jacopo Bassano, like *The Flight into Egypt*, which Norton Simon bought that year, were so much better than the later pictures. I was discussing this with my sometime colleague Francis Russell and I am sure he is correct that Bassano, early in his career, came under the influence of Parmigianino. If you compare these two pictures, it shows.

Late in 1975 was a sale that included, for the second time at Christie's, Picasso's self-portrait, *Yo, Picasso*. This time it had edged its way up to £283,500. It made one further appearance at auction and has joined *Patience* with whom I am sure it will stay forever. The bravado of *Yo* was captured in Gainsborough's portrait of the dancer Giovanna Baccelli who died in 1801, exactly one hundred years before Picasso painted his self-portrait. Baccelli was the leading ballerina of her day, and Gainsborough exhibited the picture at the Royal Academy in 1782 to great applause. It came, along with other pictures, following the death of Mary, Countess of Swinton, and can now be seen in the Tate Gallery. The highest price paid that year for a picture at auction was for Mary, Countess of Crawford's Duccio *Crucifixion*, sold by her son Patrick Lindsay on 11 July for £1 million. This did not seem, even then, a vast price for a work by an artist as rare and important as Duccio, and the explanation lies in the fact that it was never wholly accepted as being by that master. Other attributions have been made, notably to Ugolino, and not even the efforts of Patrick Lindsay, an undoubtedly brilliant auctioneer, could lift the picture to what it would have made if accepted by all.

Two weeks before, Patrick had sold Turner's *The Bridgewater Sea Piece*, which was bought by Harry Hyams, the property tycoon, who died at the time of writing this book. The picture used to be on loan to the National Gallery. The property of another of Christie's faithful clients, the trustees of the Ellesmere Settlement, was Reynolds's *Portrait of George Clive, His Wife Sidney and Daughter Louisa with an Ayah*. I always find the little girl Louisa's head strangely unattached to her body. That year also saw the sale of Hans Hoffmann's *Squirrel*. It is not Dürer, but it is the next best thing and it is one of those 'once seen never forgotten' drawings. In the modern field, there was the dispersal of a large part of the Zumsteg Collection, which used to hang in the delicious Kronenhalle Restaurant in Zürich.

Sebastiano del Piombo. **A Prophet Addressed by an Angel**, 1516-17

No account of the 1976 season would be complete without a mention of the best old master drawing, certainly in my time, to be brought into the Front Counter. Fortunately, it was shown to Noël Annesley who, after thinking about it for a week or so, was able to identify it as the work of Sebastiano del Piombo and relate it with absolute certainty to the frescoed altarpiece of the *Transfiguration* at the Borgherini Chapel, San Pietro in Montorio, Rome. As a result, *A Prophet Addressed by an Angel* made £104,000. The owner must have been thrilled.

Chapter 12

Founding of the House Sale Department with Anthony Coleridge and his confused introduction to Christie's; Cullen tent and table linen; the Swythamley Trophies; two sales in Ireland; Prince Littler sale; Sotheby's sale at Mentmore; back again to Ireland for Charleville; Knight of Glin finds a label; Andy Warhol's *Purple Jumping Man* sold in London; the Kingston tureens

The 1977 season, setting aside the state of the economy, was an exciting one. The year before, my old friend Anthony Coleridge and I had been given joint responsibility for House Sales. The description 'House Sales' or, as they were sometimes called, 'Sales on the Premises', was a double misnomer. At that time, houses were the one thing that we did not sell and the sales were not held on our premises but off them, at the houses or estates so named. What we did sell were their contents. It was the job I had wanted most for a long time, since being denied a place in the Picture Department, and in Tony I had another wonderful partner in crime.

Tony Coleridge is a direct descendant of the poet Samuel Taylor Coleridge. He is an honest person and claimed that while at Eton he had learnt off by heart those two great poems of his ancestor, 'Kubla Khan' and 'The Rime of the Ancient Mariner'. I can, just about, believe him over 'Kubla Khan'. I can almost see myself committing that great drug-induced tale to memory. 'The Rime of the Ancient Mariner', though, is another story. I usually get to the bit where 'he stoppeth one of three', and then I have to wake up the prompter.

Tony Coleridge had arrived at Christie's very shortly after me, probably a couple of months later, and in distinctly humoresque circumstances. He came as something of a fully fledged expert, having worked in the Chattels Department at

OPPOSITE

Thomas Gainsborough.
Giovanna Baccelli, Exhibited 1782

his father's firm, Knight, Frank & Rutley, and he had already published some serious work on Chippendale. His arrival coincided with, and was rather overshadowed by, another new recruit to the firm, David Carritt, who had been preceded by a fanfare of publicity from the Press Office and some rather barbed comments from Brian Sewell.

In those days everyone joining the firm did time on the Front Counter under the watchful eye of Ridley Leadbeater. All of us thus employed – Mr Leadbeater, Verity Raymond, John Bowes-Lyon and I – were fascinated to see what this controversial gay art historian would be like. But David had bypassed the Front Counter and gone straight to a smart office in the Picture Department. We knew that he would be arriving that day so we were baffled when a very smartly dressed figure wearing a well-cut Prince of Wales check suit, a regimental tie with the green-and-black broad stripes on it (I think with the colours of the Devon and Dorset Regiment), and bearing a furled umbrella and a bowler hat, presented himself to a puzzled Mr Leadbeater. None of us could see in this military figure the much-heralded pal of Bernard Berenson. The confusion was eventually sorted out. Tony stayed on the Counter for a couple of weeks before taking root in the Furniture Department, to which he was to make a considerable contribution over the next dozen years.

Our House Sale Department was further strengthened by Elizabeth Lane, Connal Mcfarlane and James Alabaster. The first sale of the new Department was at Malahide Castle, Co. Dublin. Tony was in sole charge on this occasion and the sale made £529,790, with every one of the 1,462 lots selling. Quite a number of the lots were paid for with IOUs as the Irish banks were on strike for over two months that summer. All the IOUs were honoured. That would not happen everywhere. One commentator wrote: 'The strike provided economists with a unique opportunity to study the functioning of a modern economy without access to bank deposits.' I don't think I would ever have been any good at economics.

Tony's and my collaboration in fact started the previous September, when we had jointly organised the sale at Cullen House for the Earl of Seafield, a very old friend of mine. It was sad to see him moving out from what had been the family's home since the seventeenth century. Cullen is situated on the coast, in Banffshire; there are more difficult places to get to in the British Isles, but not very many, so it was not as well attended as it might have been. Tony became extremely anxious about the lack of cars in the car park and every half-hour he went out in the pouring rain to see if more people had arrived. The trickle never turned into a flood of clients and the weather forecast worsened during the view, as did the weather itself. The night before the sale, the forecast actually predicted a major storm. Tony and I slept fitfully in a nearby hotel and arrived early the next morning to see the catering tent impaled on the turrets of Cullen House. This was without any doubt the low moment of Christie's newly fledged House Sale Department, but we managed to get the tent down and had it re-erected just in time. Quite a substantial number of people, whom Tony had counted drifting in and out of the car park over the last four days, did come to the sale. It made just under £300,000 and contained one or two very good pictures. But probably of more interest than anything else, was the extraordinary number, 398 large and 60 small, of damask tablecloths which had been accumulating over the centuries, some of them barely used. Ian Seafield was, I think, pleased with the results of the sale, and we were relieved.

Relieved we may have been, but we still had to hand over 458 tablecloths, some whiter than others. To our porters, cultured men though they were, one half-dozen damask tablecloths looks pretty much like another. Not so to the sometimes excitable lady buyers (few men in Banffshire buy table linen), and I remember being called up to quieten down a very cross client who felt cheated on the whiteness front. 'I am really sorry,' I said; 'this is Christie's and we are not trying to sell you anything you haven't had a chance to examine before the sale.' 'Don't you put on that high and mighty tone with me, young man,' she said; 'you may be Christie's but I am Thistle Antiques!' This time I did not have Patrick Lindsay to pass the buck to.

That May, Tony and Christie's South Kensington were in charge of a remarkable sale in Cheshire, Swythamley Hall, near Macclesfield, on behalf of the executors of the late Lt Col Sir Philip Brocklehurst, whose cousin, Charles, had been a partner in Christie's during the war. It was notable mainly for the Brocklehurst Collection of Hunting Trophies. The Brocklehursts, on Sir Philip's death, had become an extinct species, but not before Sir Philip and his brother Courtney, who had

The Swythamley Hall Hunting Trophies

been the senior game warden in the Sudan in the 1920s, had done their best to help a number of other species towards extinction. Sir Philip had been on Shackleton's Antarctic expedition to the South Pole in 1907–9 and came back with a couple of penguins. In 1912, he bagged a large walrus in the Arctic and the year prior to that he had taken his toll of India. In the Punjab he got a very good urial (a type of Himalayan sheep and nothing to do with Marcel Duchamp). The three caribou that perished the following year in Newfoundland probably didn't affect sustainability of the species.

However, his most prodigious year was 1910, in Africa, where he accounted for two black and two white rhinoceroses, buffalo, wildebeest, elands, bongo, topi, Grant's and Thompson's gazelles, waterbuck, bushbuck, reedbuck, gerenuk and dik-dik, duiker, roan and sable antelopes, greater and lesser kudu, zebras, giraffes, impala, crocodile, warthogs, wild dogs, spotted hyena, a wolf and a fox. He also brought back a python and a puff adder and these, with lion skins, cheetah skins and leopard skins, all decorated the house. The trophies made somewhat over £7,000, but the rest of the sale was not very interesting.

In September 1976, we were back in Ireland for a good sale at Newtown Park House, Blackrock, for Senator Ned McGuire in conjunction with the Dublin firm of Hamilton and Hamilton. It featured two very handsome mirrors by the Booker Brothers of Dublin, which were written about in the 1976 *Review* by our new representative in Ireland, Desmond FitzGerald, the Knight of Glin. In the same sale was an absolutely charming picture by Walter Osborne, RHA, entitled *In St Stephen's Green*, which made a record price of £16,000 for this appealing Irish artist. In all the sales we conducted in Ireland we received tremendous support from the Gardaí: they could not have been nicer and on this occasion they sorted out the small problem of one of the local worthies turning up disguised as a bishop of the Roman Catholic Church and trying to make off with quite a number of pieces of Senator McGuire's silver under his scarlet cassock.

That November, Tony and I moved to Clonbrock, Ahascragh, Ballinasloe, Co. Galway where we sold an extraordinary collection of pictures, furniture and porcelain which had been left untouched since the last male member of the Dillon-Mahon family to have lived at Clonbrock had died around the turn of the century. Almost all of the furniture was made in England by Gillow and in those days, before the demise of brown furniture, it caused considerable interest. The pictures were nothing special but the porcelain, which looked wonderful in the catalogue, must have cost a lot of money when it was purchased since much of it could be dated to the Chelsea gold anchor period. Unfortunately it had obviously been kept warm in the oven and had developed a distinctive and disturbing craquelure. It had also not been washed since it was last used eighty years before. However, the house was a 'good survival' and the sale was a success, helped by the catering, just what one wanted on a cold November day in Co. Galway: oysters and Irish stew. If you did not like oysters or Irish stew you could always have a piece of soda bread and a Guinness.

Back in the United Kingdom, there was a sale at Chestham Park, Henfield, for Mrs Norah Prince Littler, widow of the famous theatrical entrepreneur who was responsible for Ivor Novello and who had some good works of art, including a Canaletto that was later sold in London, and a masterpiece of German cabinetmaking in very rare blue lacquer. This secretaire made a respectable £65,000. I should think it changed hands for a good deal more later.

Christian Reinow. **Writing cabinet (bureau)**, *c.*1745-9

In May 1977, Sotheby's held an extraordinary sale at Mentmore Towers for the Earl of Rosebery, lasting over a week, which made £6.4 million. No one could pretend that it was not beautifully organised and conducted for the most part by the still suave Peter Wilson. After this, one would have thought that all, or certainly the higher proportion, of country house sales, would follow it to Sotheby's. Fortunately for Tony and me, this was not the case. Almost immediately after the Mentmore sale, we received a series of requests to organise similar, if lesser, events. It would be some time before we surpassed Sotheby's total, but in 1978 alone, as Jo Floyd generously points out in the foreword of that year's *Review*, 'Sales on the premises had been a particularly successful feature of the season […] with a combined total of £4,462,000.' These included Bois Doré in Newport, Rhode Island; Charleville in Ireland; Childwick Bury near St Alban's for Mr Jim Joel and Wateringbury Place near Maidstone for Mr David Style.

Joseph Wright of Derby. **The Boy Archers (Francis and Charles Mundy)**, 1780-5

In January 1978, again in collaboration with Hamilton and Hamilton, we had a sale at Charleville, Enniskerry, a beautiful house which survives in an even better state today. The house belonged for three hundred years to the Monck family and was built by an architect called Whitmore Davis, and a very good architect he was too. The very fine proportions of the fenestration at the front of the house were emphasised by the use of copper glazing bars, which gave a much finer and more delicate look than the usual wooden ones.

By the time the contents of the house were consigned to us for sale, little of the original was left, but what had been collected by the then owners, the Davies family, included another good Booker mirror, some good furniture and one notable picture, *Francis and Charles Mundy* by Joseph Wright of Derby. Tony and I, not for the first or the last time, had a tussle with the Picture Department to keep it in the house sale. But our stubbornness paid off and the picture fetched £68,000, a record at the time for a Wright of Derby.

Tony reminds me in the article about the sale he wrote in the *Review*, that it was the only house sale we ever conducted without a marquee. His experience of the catering tent at Cullen had obviously left its mark and we arranged closed-circuit television to operate between the hall and the drawing room so that the large crowd, which was expected and which materialised, could all bid. I knew the sale would be a success because on the way to the house from Desmond FitzGerald's apartment in Dublin, I was uplifted by the sound of Terry Wogan singing the Cornish 'Floral Dance'. I was then one of the millions who tuned in to BBC Radio 2 wherever I could pick it up and much miss the great man today.

While we were in Dublin, either Tony or I – or it might have been Desmond himself – received a request from a lady some considerable distance away, asking if we could come and value the contents of her house which included what she thought were two rather important mirrors. The Knight of Glin, who had become Christie's representative after the charming Desmond Dunalley had driven his Volvo off into the sunset, had built up a considerable reputation for his extensive knowledge of Irish paintings and he collaborated with Anne Crookshank in producing the definitive catalogue of Irish Painters. He was also an authority on furniture and, in particular, Irish mirrors by the Booker Brothers of Dublin. No house in Ireland is complete without one of the brothers' pier glasses above a mantelpiece somewhere.

We agreed to go, possibly slightly unwisely the day after a reception was being held in Desmond's Dublin residence, where a good time was had by all, not least by Desmond himself. The following morning Desmond, Tony, Fiona and I set off to give this house the once-over. On this occasion we had no trouble finding it. I drove since Tony, a cautious driver, did not really like taking the wheel. Desmond did have a licence but, had anybody wearing any sort of uniform stopped us on this particular morning, he would not have had one for very much longer. Desmond slept, though not exactly the peaceful sleep of the blessed.

We arrived at our destination, got out of the car and rang the bell. Our client opened the door and asked if, before starting the valuation, we would like a cup of coffee. Desmond, by this time quite awake, said he did not want a cup of coffee but would like to avail himself of the facilities. He was directed to a door to the right of the hall. Desmond did not need a second invitation to dash in, quickly shutting the door behind him. After the briefest of pauses there emerged a series of sounds which I suppose could have been mistaken for somebody finding the right key on a tuba, but were pretty obviously emanating from the backside rather than the front of the human frame. But this was not all, because before the end of the tuning-up process there was another unmistakable noise, followed by a pause, followed by a flush, then another flush, and then Desmond emerged, having regained quite a lot of his colour and looking much more like a man ready to opine on the Booker Brothers.

While this was going on, and slightly to distract our hostess's attention, we had asked for a ladder so that we could better inspect the mirrors. Desmond scaled the ladder and achieved – not always an easy feat while standing on the top step – an examination of the back of one of them. He said that there was something on a label but he could not quite see it, and he asked me if I would like to replace him on the top rung and see what I could make of it. I did. I said, 'I can see the label, Desmond, you are absolutely right, but I am not sure it is quite the one we are looking for.' It distinctly said 'John Lewis'. We thanked the lady for the coffee, looked at one or two other things, gave some probably rather flattering estimates to make up for the disappointment of the mirrors, and then took our departure. We did stop a couple more times on the way back to Dublin, not to look at any more mirrors, but to try and lessen our own disappointment and the length of the journey. But it just goes to show, even with Irish mirrors, you cannot get it right every time.

I now turn to Childwick Bury Manor in Hertfordshire, which contained a really fine collection of English furniture, most of which had been acquired by Mr H.J. Joel (always known as Jim) from Frank Partridge, and which we were to sell on 15 May 1978. Jim Joel was the heir through his father to one of the great diamond mining fortunes. A very keen and discerning owner of racehorses, he was a popular figure on the turf. He never married and his considerable wealth and the proceeds of the various sales conducted after his death all went to a charitable foundation which, to this day, makes generous contributions mainly in the field of medicine. For a time, though, his great-nephew, Andrew Brudenell-Bruce, a close friend of my brother (and others who may read this book), had been led to believe that he would inherit a substantial part of his great-uncle's estate. When the will was read, Andrew, or 'BB' as he was known to his many friends, discovered that his share was to be considerably less than he expected. Disappointed but not daunted by the news, BB asked a number of his friends to a party, where he provided food and drink but set aside the remainder of the legacy to buy one huge firework, which was ignited at the party. In other words, the entire fortune went up with a bang, a stylish way to meet with disappointment. The sale of the collection was in itself a firework display and there were extraordinary prices paid for English furniture. A pair of George III mahogany commodes attributed to William Vile fetched £95,000, and another commode, also by Vile, made £38,000. There was a great deal else besides, and almost nothing failed to sell.

An ormolu-mounted bust of Vitellius, Roman, c.1600

The sale at Wateringbury two weeks later was a sharp contrast but no less successful in its results, making over £1 million in its first two days. It was an extraordinary, eclectic collection of furniture and works of art. I really enjoyed it. After a call from David Style's companion, Jonathan Vickers, I took Tony Coleridge down the old A20 to Wateringbury, which is outside Maidstone, and from the moment we arrived in the front hall of the very pretty red brick house in the manner of Roger Pratt, we knew it was something special.

Like so many late Carolean and early Georgian houses it consisted of a series of rectangular reception rooms on the ground floor, each filled to bursting with very attractive furniture, some of serious quality. David Style had inherited the house, which had been in his family since it was built, and had reassembled most of the family pictures. But it was his extraordinary ability to find, buy, sometimes even make furniture and put it together in the house which made it so special.

The distinguished architectural historian John Harris wrote a rather touching foreword to the catalogue. He began by saying,

> the emptying of a country house, whose collection and furnishings are refulgent of the taste of an idiosyncratic owner, is more than just one of those sadnesses that come and go with each country house auction […] Wateringbury is more precious than many of our great houses furnished with stock 'grand tour' effects.

He compares David Style not unfairly with Nancy Lancaster.

It is difficult to pick out a favourite or even a few favourite lots from this extraordinary house, but these illustrate its unique character: a pair of fine early George II white-painted and parcel-gilt console tables attributed to William Kent, probably from Raynham Hall; the ormolu, ebony and pietra dura side cabinet from Hamilton Palace; and the ormolu and marble bust of Vitellius. The pictures so lovingly put together by David Style did not sell so well but one, dated 1636, by an unknown English hand, made £20,000 and is now in the Tate Britain where a wider audience can enjoy it.

David Style was as lucky as he was innovative. If ever a house should have that great warning 'caveat emptor' over the door, it was Wateringbury. I remember so well looking at one of the Kent console tables with John Partridge and him saying: 'I don't know; I suppose it's right.' Whether it was or not, the charm of the place and everything in it was enough to persuade cataloguers and buyers alike to give everything the benefit of the doubt. The result was a sale totalling £1,556,876. It was no Mentmore, but a huge success and huge fun.

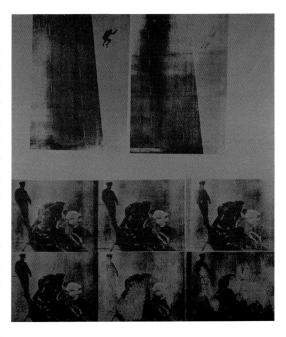

Andy Warhol. **Suicide (Purple Jumping Man)**, 1963

One of our most interesting and innovative colleagues, Jorg Bertz, working out of our office in Düsseldorf, put on a sale on 7 December 1977. Then head of Christie's fledgling Contemporary Department, he had arranged to sell an important group of pictures in London – the first major contemporary sale in King Street – which included Andy Warhol's *Suicide (Purple Jumping Man)*. It sold for £40,000, less than David Style's Louis XIV Boulle *bureau mazarin*. It was bought by Ernst Beyeler, who sold it on to the Shah of Persia. The picture remains in Iran to this day, the property of the government, and is worth upwards of $150 million. Only a Francis Bacon, which I will discuss later, has increased in value in percentage terms more than this Warhol and either of these two pictures would almost certainly today be worth more than the entire contents of Mentmore Towers.

But for all the toing and froing from Kent to Hertfordshire to Wicklow and Westport, Rhode Island, life and a series of successful sales went on in King Street. The sale of one old master painting in particular struck me as quite exceptional the following summer: Annibale Carracci's *Butcher's Shop*, which sold for £2.6 million.

The most remarkable sale of the season, however, did not take place in London or New York, but in Geneva, with Meissonnier's Kingston tureens making 2.45 million Swiss francs, the equivalent of £2 million today, making them fifty times more expensive than *Purple Suicide*. Whatever the vicissitudes of currency, the value of

silver and indeed the value of a picture by Andy Warhol, the Kingston tureens leave three lasting memories.

Firstly, they are notable for their beauty and wonderfully eccentric design – they really are close to the ultimate expression of the rococo. Secondly, they belonged to a woman, the Duchess of Kingston. Here she is, illustrated in the role of Iphigenia, a slightly troubling character who was sacrificed by her father Agamemnon because he had offended Artemis. I very much hope that this does not happen to either me or any of my three daughters, because I am sure that there are one or two things in this book which might offend Artémis, the present owners of Christie's. But, back from the brink, to the Duchess of Kingston. When not playing Iphigenia, she was the daughter of a quite respectable Devon squire, yet had a series of love affairs: first with William Pulteney, the first Earl of Bath, who was famous for his bridge in Bath; secondly with the Duke of Hamilton; and thirdly, on the rebound, with Lieutenant Augustus Hervey, later Earl of Bristol. There's a family for you! After that, she was the mistress of George II until, finally, she hoped to settle down to a quiet and comfortable home life with the Duke of Kingston. She succeeded in convincing the ecclesiastical court that she had never been married to Hervey and married Kingston, who did what everybody in his position should do: he died, leaving her his entire estate. Things then went slightly pear-shaped because there was a witness to her marriage to Hervey, but, because she was either the Countess of Bristol or the Duchess of Kingston, when put on trial for bigamy, she was entitled to be heard by her peers who let her off with a caution, telling her that if she ever did it again, she would be beheaded. There may be clients at Christie's with a more colourful past than this but I cannot honestly think of any; Madame du Barry was beheaded after consigning her jewels to Christie's, but that's another story. Back again to the tureens, because the third point about them is they represent, in real terms, a price unequalled, even today. I suppose one has to believe that art is certainly a good investment but it has to be taken in the round.

LEFT TO RIGHT

Kingston soup tureens by Juste-Aurèle Meissonnier, 1734-6

The Duchess of Kingston as Iphigenia

Parmigianino's *Portrait of a Collector*; Thomas Brudenell saves the day; Patrick Lindsay – model sales and the British Engineerium; Gladys, Duchess of Marlborough and the Master in Lunacy; collection of Baron Paul Hatvany; the Mettler Collection; the House Sale Department organises twelve sales in the year

Christie's finally launched their New York sales on Park Avenue in 1977. The opening sale did not go too badly, although the most important lot was bought by someone who could not pay for it. What happens in these circumstances could fill half a book in itself, but it is actually quite a rare occurrence. In this case, the buyer of Renoir's *Baigneuse couchée* was clever and had arranged his antics very carefully so there was no way we could have checked. He appeared to have an excellent credit rating and was indeed the son of a very rich man. However, he had no money whatsoever and the sale had to be cancelled. This cast a pall over the opening sale, but it had happened and there was no going back.

There was a lot going on elsewhere that season, including some good sales in London. A particularly beautiful painting executed by Léger in 1920, entitled *Les Femmes à la toilette*, made £130,000. A record-breaking David Hockney, *Man Taking Shower*, fetched £26,000, and one of the most interesting pieces of silver Christie's had ever sold, a silver-gilt ewer by Adam van Vianen (the most celebrated Dutch goldsmith of his time and the leading practitioner of the Auricular style), made a serious sum of money – £164,686, a very high price for a piece of silver, which only goes to further underline the extraordinary price achieved for the Kingston tureens.

It was also a season which saw the sale of two remarkable lots, not bought by Iranians but both created in Persia. One, by far the most significant, consisted of seven folios

OPPOSITE

Parmigianino. **Portrait of a Collector**, c.1523

from the Houghton Shahnameh, the most important miniatures to come on the market for many years, which made a price commensurate with their rarity: £785,000. Completely different but ravishingly beautiful and again from the Morrisons of Fonthill, was the *jambiya* or dagger which sold for £48,000.

The best old master by far to sell in London was Parmigianino's *Portrait of a Collector*, which came from another faithful client of Christie's, Julian Byng of Wrotham Park. I shall never forget this sale. Patrick Lindsay was the principal auctioneer in the main room and I was the backup in the West Room, linked by telephone. I had been told by the clerk that a representative of the National Gallery would be bidding in the main room, but that I should watch out for someone in my room who had come over to bid, up to a serious level, for the Louvre. When we got to the Parmigianino, the

Giovanni Bellini. **The Madonna and Child with a Donor**, 1505

bidding rose, as predicted, between Geoffrey Agnew on behalf of the National Gallery and my lady from the Louvre. Suddenly, the telephone link went dead and I heard Patrick Lindsay saying from the main room, 'It is against you in the side room.' A young man called Thomas Brudenell had recently joined Christie's Front Counter and was standing in the packed anteroom. He was also, I knew, visible to Patrick Lindsay in the main room. I shouted at him, 'Bid Thomas, bid!' He had never bid in a sale before but realised what he was to do and raised his hand. Patrick, who I think was related to him (some people are related to everybody), said 'Are you bidding, Thomas?' He replied, 'I think so.' Patrick took his bid but the National Gallery went on. My lady bid once more, which I relayed to Thomas, but that was the end for the Louvre and the picture went to the National Gallery for £650,000. Severe embarrassment was avoided and Christie's will forever be indebted to Thomas Brudenell. The picture is one of those works which gets better every time one looks at it and although the National Gallery is well represented in works by the artist, this picture always shines.

In the same sale was a beautiful panel, *The Madonna and Child with a Donor*, signed by Giovanni Bellini but probably executed in part in his studio by another hand. I

Edgar Degas. **Femme se peignant**, c.1887-90

mention it mainly because it is lovely, but also because it belonged to Lady Mairi Bury, whose husband, Derek Bury, heir to the earldom of Albemarle, had first introduced me to Christie's. I am forever in his debt, I think.

The 1978 season was improved by an initiative of Patrick Lindsay. This man of extraordinary abilities – most of the time – had a hugely wide compass of things he liked and quite a wide compass of things he did not, as discussed earlier, but among the things he liked were models and engineering. He taught himself to be a first-rate woodturner. He knew about epicycloidal chucks and was the proud possessor of a

Holtzapffel lathe. He was a stalwart supporter of Christie's model sales, most of which he took himself but which were organised by a charming eccentric called Jonathan Minns. He got involved with, and got Christie's involved with as well, a splendid project to save the Brighton and Hove pumping station known as the British Engineerium and to turn it into an engineering museum based around the great beam engines. He drew into this project such diverse talents as those of HRH Prince Philip, Patrick, myself and most of the Board of Christie's, the Department of the Environment, the Southern Water Authority and several councils. The museum still flourishes and here is a photograph of the magnificent engine installed in 1875 to pump water to the citizens of Brighton and Hove.

The British Engineerium, Hove

Sometime in the 1970s, my friend and colleague David Bathurst had received a letter from the Office of the Master in Lunacy. (They must have been using old writing paper as the Office of the Master in Lunacy became the Court of Protection in 1947.) This strange title referred to a member of the Solicitor General's Department who was in charge of the affairs of those unfortunates who had been 'committed' (what is now known as 'sectioned'). One such was Gladys, Duchess of Marlborough, the second wife of the ninth Duke. The Master in Lunacy no longer exists in this politically correct age; he is referred to as 'Social Services'.

In her day Gladys was a famous beauty, a friend of Bernard Berenson and a number of other artists, including Rodin, who also fell for her, but she had set her sights on the Duke while he was still married to Consuelo Vanderbilt. After the Duke had left Consuelo, Gladys and he married but by this time she was over forty and had started to lose her legendary good looks. One of the reasons for this decline and eventual lapse into insanity was that, aged only twenty-two, she had allowed herself to be injected with an early form of Botox – paraffin wax. The injections went wrong. Marriage to the ninth Duke probably didn't help; fond as I was of his grandchildren, he never sounds the most sympathetic of men. In 1962, Gladys was confined to St Andrews, where my grandfather was governor and where David Bathurst visited her when she still had a very good collection of impressionist pictures.

One was a beautiful Degas, a charcoal and red chalk drawing entitled *Femme se peignant*, sold by Christie's after her death. Could it have reminded the Duchess of her youth? Hugo Vickers, who helped me with the sale of Cecil Beaton drawings, has written a biography of Gladys, which is well worth reading, sad though it is.

The year 1978 was marked by the dispersal in London of a large part of the collection of Baron Paul Hatvany, a friend of Peter Chance and Noël Annesley. Paul Hatvany was of Hungarian descent and had lived in London in exile during the war. Endowed with a more than adequate family fortune and considerable knowledge, he was able to take advantage of the strange wartime art market where notable works of art came up for sale with very few serious collectors to buy them.

By a strange coincidence, the same year as Hatvany decided to sell part of his collection, another even better-off and more avid collector, Count Antoine Seilern, died in July. The majority of his collection, housed in a large house in Prince's Gate, was gifted to the Courtauld Institute and represented one of the most significant bequests of the second half of the twentieth century. We were asked to value the collection for probate which was both fascinating and instructive and we later sold his collection of Dürer engravings and the Chinese porcelain which he had left to his nephew, Peter. The Hatvany Collection included, among some fine drawings, *Madonna and Child with Saint Julian, Saint Francis and Two Angels* by Francesco Pesellino, now attributed to Filippo Lippi, which fetched £70,000.

In 1979, a number of other good old master pictures were sold, the most expensive of which was a painting in the collection of the late Lord Hillingdon, Jan van de Cappelle's *Estuary in a Calm*, which fetched £510,000 (just over $1 million). However, this was almost certainly the first year (and by no means the last) when Christie's New York salerooms, so recently opened, achieved more than the sales in London. Monet's *Argenteuil, fin d'après-midi*, which had made £39,900 ($111,720) in London in 1964, was sold in New York for $350,000 (£171,568) in May 1979. It had succeeded in a threefold increase in value in dollar terms, but a fourfold increase in sterling terms. More interesting than the price for this picture, for me anyway, is the fact that this classic early painting, which would have enthused the market in 1964 when it first appeared, still looks just as beautiful today. I think it survives unaffected

LEFT TO RIGHT

Henri de Toulouse-Lautrec. **Study for La Grande Loge**, *c.*1896

Pietro da Cortona. **Study of the Head of an Angel**, *c.*1630 by any change of taste. Not all early impressionist pictures do.

In London, we sold the collection of the Swiss textile merchant Hans Mettler, organised again by John Lumley. Mettler was related to Mrs Hedy Hahnloser-Bühler and had put together an excellent collection, including this rare Toulouse-Lautrec, *La Grande Loge*, which made £370,000.

However, the picture which aroused the most interest, and would indeed arouse the most interest were it to come on the market today, was Henri Matisse's *Le Jeune Marin I*, which made £720,000 – one could add a few noughts today! Another picture that sold in New York was a Mondrian from 1928, *Large Composition with Red, Blue and Yellow*, which made a record price of $800,000, while a Brancusi in the same sale fetched $400,000 – a good price but not a record. One has to be careful with records for Brancusi because, not long before this beautiful object appeared, a well-known collector had instructed two members of the same family to bid on his behalf for a work by Brancusi, forgetting that he had done so, and the two brothers vigorously bid against each other, slightly distorting the market!

But I think from such rich pickings I would want most – and could actually have afforded the £7,000 then paid – this Pietro da Cortona drawing of the truly angelic *Study of the Head of an Angel*. By far the most beautiful picture was the Giovanni Bellini from Cornbury, *Madonna and Child*, which was finally negotiated in lieu of tax.

There was a piece of furniture sold in New York, a Louis XV black lacquer commode, which I think was one of the most beautiful pieces of French furniture I have ever seen. I would very much like to have joined the members of the club that had owned it, all of whom in some way or another figure on other pages in this book: Lord Cowper, the one-time owner of the Sebastiano del Piombo *Head of the Madonna* I admired so much in its uncleaned state, Baron Alphonse de Rothschild, Sir Philip Sassoon and Stavros Niarchos. The only problem is that I would not be able to afford the membership fees of the club.

Louis XV Black Lacquer commode by François-Antoine Mondon.

The London old master sales were not terribly exciting. I am not a huge lover of Victorian painting, but we sold that year for £27,000 Burne-Jones's *The Challenge in the Wilderness* which really appealed to me as, we are led to believe, it appealed to Picasso.

Our House Sale Department held no less than twelve sales that year, the most important of which, North Mymms Park, belonged to my godfather, Major General Sir George Burns, who was the owner of the Bellotto mentioned earlier. Mymms was one of the largest house sales we ever conducted. It took place in September 1979 and totalled £2,400,000, second only to Mentmore in value for a country house sale. There is so much to say about this sale one hardly knows where to begin. I should possibly start with George Burns himself.

Burns had been an inspirational soldier, rising to the rank of major general and commanding the London District, but in the war he took the 3rd Battalion Coldstream Guards up through the tortuous battles of the Italian campaign, being awarded the DSO and MC. Possibly more important than being a brave and resourceful commander was the fact that he was beloved by everyone throughout his long career and when commanding the London District with thousands of troops, he knew the names and personal circumstances of every soldier above the rank of corporal. His only problem commanding this large body of men was when, once a year at the Birthday Parade, he had to mount a horse. Although quite a successful racehorse owner, he hated riding. In later life, while he was colonel-in-chief of the Coldstream Guards, the Queen realised his dislike of riding and allowed him a place in the carriage procession.

He maintained North Mymms Park, a large house, sometimes known as Little Hatfield but not so little, 21 miles from Hyde Park Corner. He never married and continued to live in the house with his mother, who was used to a standard of living which made considerable inroads into godfather George's inheritance. Old Mrs Burns, whose mother-in-law was Pierpont Morgan's sister, had only one concession to economy, and that was to use a Greenline bus to take her from the end of the drive at Mymms, where she was dropped by her chauffeur in the Rolls-Royce. When the bus reached Victoria Coach Station she was picked up by the same taxi driver every time she made the journey and taken to Claridge's. There she would have lunch and gamble. If she won, she would spend the money. If she lost, she would take one of her large collection of gold boxes to S.J. Phillips and sell it for cash. When she died, that firm was good enough to inform godfather George that they had a number of boxes that had been left by his mother for a rainy day. The rain, however, fell mainly on godfather George who by this time had to foot the bill for these excursions.

Mymms, as it was, could not go on forever and the sad decision was taken to sell while assets still outweighed the overdraft. Fortunately, the sale was an almost unqualified success. It consisted of exceptional sculpture of which the undoubted star, and certainly the best example of baroque sculpture to be sold at either auction house during my working life, was Alessandro Algardi's white marble *Bust of Monsignor Antonio Cerri*, which made £150,000 – at the time a record price for a piece of classical sculpture. Of almost equal appeal was the bronze *Bust of a Gentleman*, attributed to Johan Gregor van der Schardt, which sold for £45,000.

There was excellent furniture. A rare set of early eighteenth-century Piedmontese chairs made £17,000 and an extraordinary group of tapestries, the best of which was a set of three of the early history of Venus, made £46,000. But this was not all. There was porcelain, quantities of it, including a 205-piece early Meissen service, and the best piece of French furniture, a *bureau à cylindre* by Jean-François Oeben, which made £34,000. There was also an extensive library, bound entirely in scarlet morocco, which was an interior decorator's dream. The sale was sad for me because I knew the house so well.

There is an interesting postscript to the Mymms sale which relates to a conversation I had at the time with Dick Kingzett, a partner in Agnew's and by popular consent the nicest man in the art world. He told me that the mezzotints at Mymms – there were twenty lots of them, one of which fetched over £1,000 – had been part of a group put together by Agnew's in around 1912 for one of their last ever major exhibitions of these once very expensive prints. The exhibition had not been a success but, on the last day, J.P. Morgan appeared. He always spoke to one of the porters who took him round to do his bidding, watched from behind a curtain by the anxious partners of the firm. On this occasion, Morgan made very few marks in the catalogue and the watching partners were pretty depressed, but it did seem that they might get at least some revenue from the collection which otherwise had been untouched by the public. The financial situation was as bad in 1912 as it was in 1980.

On leaving the gallery Morgan handed the catalogue to his favourite porter, saying 'Would you tell Mr Agnew that I have marked the prints that I do not wish to acquire?' He bought virtually the whole exhibition and obviously gave some to his sister.

This marked the end of the 1970s, which were something of the calm before the storm. As I hope I have shown, there were some exciting sales and exciting prices, none more so than Velázquez's *Juan de Pareja*, and Christie's sales turnover rose over that decade from £20 million to £100 million, giving an average annual turnover of £55 million. The steady rise in the value of works of art and the performance of the art market was, not for the first or the last time, in sharp contrast to the ups and downs of the financial world in general and the stock market in particular. It all seemed exciting at the time but it was nothing compared with the firework display which was the art market in the 1980s. The £100 million became £1,000 million and relatively modest pictures by the end of the 1980s were fetching over £1 million. With this in prospect we move into 1980, where the firm's turnover reached £150 million and Peter Wilson finally retired from Sotheby's. For reasons I know not why, Sotheby's did not disclose its turnover that year. We had not yet caught up but we were getting very close.

OPPOSITE

Alessandro Algardi. **Monsignor Antonio Cerri**, c.1630-40

Lord Northampton's vases; Ford Collection of impressionists in New York; more pictures from Baron Paul Hatvany; Rubens's *Samson and Delilah* sold in London and Brian Sewell's review in the *Evening Standard*; the Cecil Beaton sale; Oswald Birley's studio; the *Codex Leicester*; the Cristallina collection; Havemeyer sale at Sotheby's

The Northampton Vase, probably Etruria. c.530–540BC

OPPOSITE

Peter Paul Rubens. **Samson and Delilah**, c.1609

Sotheby's must have been worried when Lord Northampton, whose family had a long association with Christie's and who was a good friend of mine, asked me to sell his unique collection of Greek vases. The sale, which took place on 2 July 1980, totalled £1,340,180 and the Northampton vase was bought by Stavros Niarchos for £190,000 to join his great collection of Greek, Roman and Etruscan art.

But everything that was happening in London, eye-catching though it sometimes was, paled into insignificance compared with the sale on 13 May of the Henry Ford II Collection of Impressionist and Modern Paintings which had been secured by David Bathurst and Christopher Burge. The sale was a triumph, totalling just under $18.5 million – beyond all conceivable expectations. Van Gogh's *Le jardin du poète à Arles*, was bought for $5,200,000, a record for any nineteenth- or twentieth-century work of art. Cézanne's *Paysan en blouse bleue* made $3,900,000, a record for the artist, and went to the Kimbell Art Museum, Fort Worth. Degas's *Etude du nu pour 'la petite danseuse de quatorze ans'* sold for $900,000, another record. Modigliani's *Nudo seduto* made $600,000, yet another record. Finally, Paul Gauguin's *La Plage au Pouldu*, a particularly beautiful picture, looking forward to those in Tahiti, made $2,900,000, again a record.

Modern pictures in England suffered by comparison, but old masters did not. From the late Baron Paul Hatvany came *The Madonna and Child* by Gherardo Starnina (Master of the Bambino Vispo), which made £95,000, and the same price was paid for a ravishing *Madonna Adoring the Child* by Neroccio di Bartolomeo de' Landi. An excellent

Bellotto of the Piazzetta in Venice made £260,000, less than the Burns picture nearly ten years earlier but still a good price for a good picture. A rare picture by Hans Muelich, *Portrait of a Bearded Gentleman*, from Lord Margadale made £75,000. But the most important work by far – just a pip in price ahead of the Van Gogh and, to be honest, a picture which was expected at £2.3 million ($5.5 million) to fetch more – was Rubens's *Samson and Delilah*. There had been hopes that it would overtake Sotheby's Turner *Juliet and Her Nurse*, sold in New York two months before for $7.04 million.

Both sales received considerable coverage in the press but no account quite matched Brian Sewell's report of Christie's sale which I have borrowed from John Julius Norwich's *Christmas Cracker* for 2009:

> With the auctioneer's premium the Nation has paid more than two and a half million pounds for a painting that, when all is said and done, is a picture of post-coital *tristesse*. Samson's is an unedifying story of harlots, arson, cruelty to animals, and random vengeance […] For the full squalor of the tale look up Judges XIV and read on.

Why should Brian Sewell, who liked and appreciated baroque paintings in general and Rubens in particular, have written this vituperative review? He was trying, rather unsuccessfully, to settle an old score.

In writing this book, I have drawn extensively on Christie's *Reviews* and the author of the *Review of 1966–1967*, when Christie's sold the modello for the picture discussed above, credits its discovery to David Carritt. This never tallied with my memories and, on checking with old friend Noël Annesley, he confirmed that it was not David but Brian who identified the picture. At the time the powers that be were anxious to promote David Carritt's career in Christie's and less so Brian's, hence this causal attitude towards the truth. He was upset, with some reason, and had delayed his moment of revenge until this sale.

As I write this, I am being entertained by accounts both in the newspapers and on the wireless of the life of my old friend Brian Sewell, who died the week before. His career in Christie's came to an end shortly after the sale of the Rubens. I cannot help finding it funny that, although he never managed to achieve a seat on the Board of Christie's, he received on his death far greater acknowledgement than anyone else connected in my lifetime with the firm – not, I suspect, because of his association with that awful old spy Anthony Blunt, but because he made people laugh.

Back in London, the sale of the Hatvany Collection continued with the best of his old master drawings. The highlight was, without doubt, Mantegna's *Saint Andrew and Two Saints with Books*, which made £165,000 – a record for a Mantegna drawing. The whole collection totalled almost £2.5 million. The best old master picture in 1980 came from the Proby family and was sold by private treaty to the National Gallery: Frans Hals's *Young Man Holding a Skull*.

Lot 14 - 'The Bidding Lady'. Reddish House Sale, 9th June 1980.

In June 1980 we held a sale which attracted almost more publicity than Mymms, for a small percentage of the value. This was the sale of the late Sir Cecil Beaton's effects at Reddish House. We had to construct a road to enable the traffic to flow in and out of the grounds and this we were allowed to do with the cooperation of the amazingly supportive Wiltshire County Council. Working on the sale was made immensely pleasurable by the presence of Eileen Hose, Beaton's most indispensable friend and secretary for over a quarter of a century. The sale contained a few good works of art. Augustus John's *Dorelia in the Garden* was one of that artist's better pictures and made £20,000. A set of four early eighteenth-century marble medallions of the Four Seasons made £10,000, and on the second day the rose given to Beaton by Greta Garbo in 1932 sold for £750, to great applause.

The afternoon session of the first day, though, was very long and contained 242 lots and the tent was rather dark at the back. Tony Coleridge, whose eyesight was never perfect, took several bids from – not for – Lot 14, a partially draped female figure with her arm raised, who was positioned at the back of the tent. When he discovered this, ever the gentleman, he offered to refund the buyer part of the price but the buyer was so pleased by the gesture and so amused by the story that he refused Tony's generous offer or proffered refund. Fun though it was, the sale had one unfortunate incident, which resulted in a row with my wife of epic proportions due entirely to a misunderstanding (isn't it always?).

The first day of the view had been extremely hot and I had taken my son directly from his ghastly prep school near Newbury to the sale. Around lunchtime I had bought for myself a pint of ginger beer shandy from the bar. I had allowed my son Henry to drink a bit from my glass. I thought no more of it until about an hour later when my wife arrived, caught up with Henry, then with me. I have never seen her so cross. She said she knew I was an idiot but she did not know I was so irresponsible as to give our nine-year-old son very strong alcohol. I asked what she was talking about. Henry had said I had given him half a pint of brandy. 'No, no, no, not brandy,' I explained, 'but sips of shandy.' My wife was a very sparing drinker. Had this not been the case she might have realised that it was unlikely that a nine-year-old, even a son of mine, would have been able to remain standing, let alone lucid, after half a pint of brandy; oh well.

If you can tell a gentleman from his shoes, Mark Birley was the quintessential English gentleman. This, despite the fact that his father, the painter Sir Oswald Birley, was a New Zealander, and his mother Irish. He was educated at Eton and married Annabel Vane-Tempest-Stewart, second daughter of the eighth Marquess of Londonderry after whom he named the nightclub. Annabel's was not just a nightclub; it was quite simply THE nightclub. There had not been, nor ever will be, another nightclub like it. Mark was a perfectionist and ran it to perfection. I am sure he could have done anything he put his hand to, but he chose to run Annabel's where an entire generation dined, danced and found romance. It was there that I asked Fiona to marry me and it was there that countless other couples popped the question on the red plush banquettes that lined the walls, which were hung with wonderful drawings, paintings and cartoons. Mark was a passionate collector and a passionate dog lover and he combined these two passions by collecting amazing pictures of dogs. He was also an accomplished draughtsman but kept his talents very much to himself. For all his style, he was a shy man, almost certainly because he had had an unhappy childhood with very selfish parents. His father, the painter, had some considerable, if sometimes wasted, talent, but he was selfish and self-absorbed. However, he flourished as a society portrait painter and died in 1952.

In early 1980, Mark had asked me to arrange a sale of the contents of his father's studio. I was very fond of Mark and I liked many of his father's pictures. They were not great works of art, but many had charm and some were really accomplished. This, and Mark's popularity as a man – and by this time legendary host – could have almost guaranteed the success of the sales. But, as indicated elsewhere, 1980 was a pretty poor time to sell works of art. The sale, 'Charleston Manor, The Remaining Contents of Sir Oswald Birley's Studio', was very hard work. The best picture was without doubt *The Opera Box*, bought by my very close friend Charlie Shelburne, now the Marquis of Lansdowne. Another friend, Nicholas Villiers, bought the best of the Indian pictures; Birley had produced some of his best work in Rajasthan and I ended

Oswald Birley. **Female Nude Reclining on a Sofa**, 1911

up picking up the pieces of a refusenik bidder, a reclining nude, which had quite clearly been Birley's last model before he married Mark's unloving mother.

During the run-up to the sale I was inveigled by Mark into buying a book of the most expensive raffle tickets I had ever seen. But my luck was in and I won the first prize: a Cadillac. I took delivery of the great green, greedy monster just in time to collect Fiona and my third child, Sofie, from the Princess Margaret Hospital in Swindon, where Fiona had just given birth. I hope the luck that brought the Cadillac will always favour Sofie. The Cadillac had to be sold prematurely as the MD of Christie's refused to fund the petrol. I don't blame him. At 9 mpg, it was difficult to justify! The man then in charge of the paperclips was someone I remain fond of, Paul Whitfield, who was before his management role an expert on bronzes and furniture and, unlike those who subsequently filled his post and never dared to show their faces in the rostrum, he was one of the best auctioneers.

By comparison, 1981 was quite a quiet season. The turnover increased, which was in itself remarkable. Again, the financial climate was terrible. We did have important lots to sell, the best probably being what was then known as the *Codex Leicester*, which had been acquired by the Coke family for their library at Holkham in Norfolk. Although it sold for £2.2 million, it was expected to achieve more. Indeed, Christie's knew that a substantial bid had been received for it but cancelled due to the terrible earthquake which occurred just before the sale in the hills above Naples.

There were a number of good old masters on the market that year. The most expensive was a beautiful Poussin, *The Holy Family* from Chatsworth, which fetched £1,650,000 (also below expectations), and it was bought, I think for the first time,

123

Alfred Sisley. **La Seine à Argenteuil**, 1872

by Norton Simon and the Getty Museum in concert. They share the picture and this may have depressed the price. Stubbs's portrait of *Tristram Shandy* (you can't get away from shandy!), which I discovered on a trip to South Africa, sold well for £280,000, and this time the slight shortage of works of art in London was not made up for by sales in New York. There was, however, a flash of light: a group of pictures from the Edward James Collection at West Dean. Dalí's *Le Sommeil* fetched £360,000 and the same artist's *Banlieue* sold for £170,000, *Solitude* for £145,000 and – made much of by the press – the *Téléphone-Homard* achieved £19,000.

What was supposed to have been the highlight of the year for modern picture sales, the Cristallina Collection, contributed little to the annual total. One picture, Degas's *Portrait of Edouard Manet*, did sell for just over £1 million ($2,200,000). Almost all the remaining lots failed. The main reason for David Bathurst's rash decision to take on the Cristallina Collection was that he already knew that Sotheby's had received a number of very good consignments and that his huge success with the Ford pictures would very soon be eclipsed. In fact, the actual year that the Cristallina things came up for sale was not the year when Sotheby's sold the collection that David feared most – that was to be eighteen months later. But even so, Sotheby's made considerable strides in 1981.

The real triumph for Sotheby's, and the corresponding problem for Christie's, was the sale in May 1983 of sixteen pictures collected by Mr and Mrs H.O. Havemeyer, which made $16,835,000. The star lot was Degas's ravishing *L'Attente*. There were also pictures by Manet, Cézanne and Mary Cassatt, each exceeding $1 million. The extraordinary prices for this sale were unexpected, but David had known for two years that Sotheby's had the collection and this must surely have been on his mind both when he accepted the Cristallina sale and when he gave his rather panicked response to the press afterwards about the number of paintings actually sold.

Sotheby's made a leap forward when they sold our old friend *Yo, Picasso* for £5.3 million in May 1981, a good price this time for this masterpiece. They also sold an important picture by Sisley. Alfred Sisley is a painter who, at his best, is as good as his two great contemporaries, Claude Monet and Camille Pissarro. The reason why there is no other illustration of Sisley's work in this book is that so much of what he painted did not

Edgar Degas. **L'Attente**, *c.*1882

match up to his own very high standards. However, this view of *La Seine à Argenteuil* shows just how lyrical his painting could be and in the saleroom it fetched £320,000. From Mr and Mrs Sydney Barlow, who had returned to Sotheby's from Christie's, Renoir's *Jeunes filles lisant* made $2 million, and went to the same home as *Yo*. They also sold two contemporary pictures, Franz Kline's *West Brand*, for $350,000 and Robert Motherwell's *Summertime in Italy, No. 10*, for $150,000.

The year 1982 was very difficult financially. Sales had not done too badly. The old masters were thin but English pictures did well. A very handsome early Turner, *The Temple of Jupiter* from Lord Wraxall (a member of the Gibbs family, whose house, Tyntesfield, was recently accepted by the National Trust), made £648,000. Thomas Lawrence's *Portrait of Miss Julia Beatrice Peel*, daughter of the prime minister, sold for £216,000. (Peel is unique among British prime ministers for having acted as a pall-bearer for the then president of the Royal Academy, Sir Thomas Lawrence.) Raeburn's *Mrs Margaret Stewart* achieved £162,000 and the same price was paid for Hoppner's *Princess Royal of Prussia*.

John Lumley repeated his successes with Salvador Dalí's *L'Enigme du désir*, which he sold for £453,600. More interesting than the price was the fact that the picture belonged to a distinguished psychoanalyst, Mr Oskar Schlag. Lumley refers to the fact that in the thirty-five years that Schlag owned the picture he never completely understood its meaning (but he said it did help him in his work). I have often looked at the photograph reproduced here and wondered whether I ever understood its meaning; at moments I thought I had (which is even more disturbing) and I can appreciate that it is an accomplished painting, but I never find myself able to like the works of Salvador Dalí.

Salvador Dalí. **L'Enigme du désir**, 1929

The Mostyn and Grafton Tompions;
Rothschild box sale; Lord Astor sells Hever
through Sotheby's to Jo Floyd's chagrin;
Lansdowne Leleu bureau plat; Stoneleigh
Abbey; Godmersham Park; Degas in New
York; sale at Luttrellstown for Guinness heiress
Aileen Plunket; Chatsworth drawings; Belton;
more pictures from the Cook Collection;
another beautiful Pissarro – *La Route de
Sydenham*; Sir John Lavery's *Weighing Rooms*

Lord Mostyn's Thomas Tompion was the greatest British clock ever made, with a year-going quarter-repeater movement, ebony, silver and silver-gilt case, designed in part by Daniel Marot. I brought it back from Mostyn in the back of my car (very safe, Volvos). It was decided in the end not to auction it but to sell it privately to the British Museum. While I am happy that it has remained in England, I think it would have fetched more at auction and would probably have been bought by an English buyer. It was a wonderful thing and we settled on a price with a private treaty sale of £500,000.

As to whether or not it was unique depends on how you interpret the facts surrounding the other externally identical clock made by Tompion, not this time for William III, but for Charles II's illegitimate son Henry Fitzroy, the first Duke of Grafton. In the Fitzroy family home at Euston, there is still what looks like, and was once the pair to, the Mostyn clock, but it lacks Tompion's amazing movement. The reason was that in around 1810 the clock stopped and the then Duke enlisted the help of the leading clockmaker of the day, Justin Vulliamy. Vulliamy, with a great deal more ingenuity than honesty, informed the Duke that the clock, though the best in the world when it was made, was now old-fashioned and it was not surprising it

The Mostyn Tompion Clock, 1689

OPPOSITE

Piet Mondrian. **Composition No.II / Composition I // Composition en Rouge, Bleu et Jaune**, 1930 had gone wrong. He suggested, rather than repairing it (it needed, incidentally, nothing other than a good clean), that he should make his own movement for the Tompion case. The poor old Duke of Grafton considered this to be a good idea and paid Vulliamy quite a lot of money to have him install something far less good than the original which Vulliamy kept to his dying day, doubtless studying it almost every day left to him and bequeathing it on his death to the Worshipful Company of Clockmakers. According to the late Duke, the Vulliamy movement never ran particularly well and the clock, beautiful though it is, is worth a fraction of the Mostyn one.

I had the most difficult job that year as an auctioneer, having to sell Lord Rothschild's collection of gold boxes. There was not a single bid on any of the first six lots although there were plenty of flashing camera lights. In the end, the sale did not do too badly and a beautiful box in gold and lapis lazuli by Jean Ducrollay made £48,600. After it was over I asked Jo Floyd how we were going to get the bought-in lots back to Lord Rothschild. 'You are going to take them,' he said, which was slightly unfair as I did not know

Hever Castle

Arms & Armour

Baron Astor of Hever informing his old friend Mr. J.A. Floyd, Chairman of Christie's, of his decision to entrust the sale of his collection to Sotheby's.

Lord Rothschild and the fact that I was the friend of his son Jacob did not help. Any slight feeling I might have had about being ill-used by Jo, I was able to settle when it was announced that Lord Astor had decided to sell the entire contents of Hever through Sotheby's. Gavin Astor had been a very close friend of Jo's and almost everybody in Christie's, myself included, had done quite a lot of work at Hever. I used the occasion to make the cartoon which, I am happy to say, still resides in the gents' of the Floyd family house Ecchinswell.

Very little porcelain so far has been mentioned in this story, but this stunning Vincennes green, gold and white basket made just over £30,000. The autumn before saw the sale of the Marquis of Lansdowne's Louis XVI amaranth bureau plat by Jean-François Leleu. It was bought in this sale by Mrs Barbara Johnson and later by Giovanni Agnelli, who thought it was the most exciting piece of furniture he had ever seen. The very high price of £330,000 may have been explained by the fact that the table once belonged to Talleyrand.

The best house sale that year was again in Ireland, Adare Manor, Co. Limerick, home of another old friend, Lord Dunraven. It was a sad affair but it fetched just under £1 million. A more interesting sale took place the year before at Stoneleigh Park, Francis Smith of Warwick's masterpiece, now a shadow of its former glory and sometime host to the Royal Show. Tony Coleridge and I tried hard to publicise these house sales and market their contents. Generally we succeeded, but from time to time we did not and, sadly, Stoneleigh was one of these occasions. The collection included some really good and interesting things but the sale was poorly attended and, not for the first time, the cleverest of dealers, Christopher Gibbs, took full advantage of the lack of opposition. Christopher was a stalwart of all our house sales and himself consigned the contents of his own family home, the Manor House at Clifton Hampden, in the autumn of 2000. The sale was a catalogue of forty years' worth of country house sales both at Christie's and Sotheby's and included, from Stoneleigh, a set of particularly fine mahogany dining chairs and two linen presses which had cost Lord Leigh £4. 11s. and were sold by Christopher for £18,800.

In those days, and this was certainly to the advantage of the sellers, members of staff were allowed to bid in sales and one like Stoneleigh, where there really were not many people, enabled us sometimes to make some surprisingly good acquisitions. My sitting room at home would not be what it is were it not for Stoneleigh. And I shall never understand why so few people bothered to come to this splendid house just outside Coventry.

The year 1983 was much more interesting and successful, despite Sotheby's getting the Havemeyer Collection. It was dominated not by sales of impressionist pictures or old masters (although there were some good ones that we will come to) but by our house sale at Godmersham Park, Kent, which, unlike Stoneleigh, captured everyone's imagination, partly because it was by repute the setting for Jane Austen's *Mansfield Park*. There is no reason to doubt this. The house once belonged to Edward Austen Knight, the author's brother. In the 1930s it had passed to Robert and Elsie Tritton. Elsie benefited hugely from her first marriage to Louis Baron of the Black Cat cigarette fortune. Her second husband was Robert Tritton, one of the first Old Etonian interior decorators, who had very good taste. The sale attracted the attention of a great many New York ladies over for the summer, including Judy Taubman whose husband, Alfred, was putting the final touches to his acquisition of Sotheby's.

OPPOSITE, TOP TO BOTTOM

Charles Hindlip. **Hever Cartoon**

Louis XV snuff box in lapis lazuli by Jean Ducrollay

Sèvres Basket (panier, deuxième grandeur), 1756

Louis XVI amaranth bureau plat by Jean-François Leleu

Taubman's ownership of Sotheby's was a huge success. He died in April 2015. Although he was a serious and sometimes ruthless rival, I liked him very much. He was a genuine collector of works of art with a particular knowledge of Chinese porcelain and contemporary paintings, and he was a great philanthropist, particularly in the cause of dyslexia, from which he suffered, as do I.

George I cushion covers embroidered in petit point

Although no Mentmore, Godmersham Park was full of really 'wantable' things. The highest price for the sale was £140,400 for a late fifteenth-century Flemish tapestry. An English chair, upholstered in needlework, made £81,000 – the most expensive single English chair ever sold. However, the real excitement of the sale was the cushions. A pair of George I petit point cushions made over £15,000 – a record for cushions. In 1932 they had cost 300 guineas – a substantial amount even then. It has been remarked that Godmersham was beautiful but not pet-friendly!

The Bartos Collection, another triumph for John Lumley's London Impressionist Department, contained some very good material, including an excellent Piet Mondrian *Composition en Rouge, Bleu et Jaune*, the yellow being a tiny flash in the bottom right-hand corner. The picture was a record for the artist, selling at just over £1.5 million. The most engaging pictures in New York were again by Degas: two wonderful pastels of ballet dancers, *Danseuses à la barre* and *Danseuses au repos,* which belonged to the late Mrs Dunbar W. Bostwick, and which made $1,045,000 and $1,320,000 respectively.

Back in London, a record price was paid for Pierre Bonnard's *Femme assoupie sur un lit ou L'Indolente* which has just formed part of the amazing 2015 Bonnard Exhibition at the Musée d'Orsay. It is one of those pictures which is more beautiful than any reproduction will ever show. It fetched £302,400.

Nestling among all these high-priced impressionists was the most beautiful drawing by Peter Lely of *Elizabeth Seymour, Countess of Ailesbury*, executed in black, red and white chalk, on coloured paper. This revealed what a wonderful artist Lely could be when on top form and it made £39,960, apparently a record price for an English drawing. It had belonged to Sir Joshua Reynolds who, as well as being the first president of the Royal Academy and the leading portrait painter of his day, was also one of the greatest of all collectors of old master drawings.

Included in the 1984 *Review* is another house sale which actually took place in 1983 and was a precursor to Elveden. Of the many Guinness houses in Ireland, Luttrellstown was the most exotic. Ernest Guinness bought the estate for his daughter, Aileen Plunket, in 1927 and, with the help (and sometimes I expect the hindrance) of Mrs Plunket's decorating friend Felix Harbord, set about doing it over in the grandest fashion. Grand it certainly was. The hall was slightly smaller than that at Elveden and had been done up in the Gothic style, boasting a pair of very good George II white-painted side tables in the manner of Matthias Lock. The whole house carried on in the same grandeur and included some good furniture and rather beautiful pictures.

My favourite lot was a north Italian giltwood carved panel depicting the story of Pyrrha and Deucalion. Pyrrha and Deucalion were to the ancient Greeks what Noah and his wife Naamah are to Christians and Jews. I wish I had bought the panel. It would be very appropriate in my Dorset mill which is prone to bouts of rising water. The most expensive lot in the sale was Lot 511, George Elgar Hicks's *Portrait of the Countess of Iveagh*. You will also see this portrait at Elveden, where it was again the most expensive lot. Lady Iveagh clearly liked to see herself in all her homes.

The year 1984 was 53 per cent better than the preceding one – according to the figures anyway – with a turnover of just over £350 million. There were good works

George Elgar Hicks. **Portrait of the Countess of Iveagh**, 1894

Raphael. **Study of a Man's Head and Hand**, *c.*1500

Belton House

of art in every field, but there is no doubt whatsoever that pride of place has to go to the sale of the Chatsworth drawings, totalling £21,179,880, which was a personal triumph for Noël Annesley, Christie's long-time Old Master Drawings Director.

He had worked in secret on this project for a number of years, in cahoots with the Duke, his Trustees and his curator, Peter Day. On behalf of the Duke, Noël Annesley had made vigorous efforts to sell the collection to the nation for sums of money considerably less than the eventual price, but to no avail. The drawing which outstripped all the others was Raphael's *Study of a Man's Head and Hand*, which fetched £3,564,000, followed closely by a page from Vasari's *Libro de' disegni*, with studies by Filippino Lippi and Rafaellino del Garbo, which sold for just over £3.2 million. A Mantegna, not dissimilar to the Hatvany drawing mentioned earlier, made £1,188,000. The beautiful Holbein, *Portrait of a Scholar*, reached £1,566,000 and perhaps the surprise of the sale was Barrocci's *The Entombment* which made a huge price for this particular artist – £388,800 – but seemingly quite inexpensive after some of the others. Finally the Rembrandt, *View on the Amstel*, fetched £648,000. It was quite an evening.

The next excitement that year was the series of negotiated sales. A rare and beautiful Lotto, *Virgin and Child with Four Saints*, went to the National Gallery in Scotland and a Bassano, *Christ on the Way to Calvary*, almost as good as the Prinknash picture, albeit not a complete composition, went on behalf of the trustees of Lord Bradford to the National Gallery.

Florentine Lapis Lazuli Chest on a Charles II Stand, 17th century

The National Trust acquired Belton House and the majority of its contents, leaving us to sell the remainder at this most beautiful Carolean home. The best picture left behind was undoubtedly the Van Dyck sketch of *A Grey Horse*. It is a study for the equestrian portrait for the Marchese Anton Giulio Brignole Sale. This book is about works of art and the house at Belton comes very high among them. Here it is as it looked when the National Trust took it over. Edward Brownlow had decided that he could no longer afford to live in his family's magnificent house. He was, incidentally, a charming, well-intentioned, public-spirited man. We had undertaken the probate and valued the house and two offers had been received: one from the National Trust which would have meant that the majority of the contents would have been retained with the house and passed to the nation, but with a guarantee that parts of the house could be used by Edward Brownlow and his family; the second from a member of the public who wished to buy the house, the estate and the contents. This would have been a great sale for Christie's, surpassing anything that we had had, for example, at Mymms. While the trustees and one of the agents favoured accepting the commercial offer, another of the trustees and one of the agents preferred the public sale. The trustees and their advisers were locked fifty-fifty. They asked Lord Brownlow what he would like to do, and he said, 'I would like Charlie to make up his mind on my behalf.' I had not one moment's hesitation in deciding what was the right thing to do, but this meant some considerable sacrifice by Christie's. I felt then and I remain quite sure that, whatever he might have thought at the time, Edward Brownlow was the sort of man who was happier doing the right thing and letting the nation effectively take the house. This they did and we had a relatively small but successful sale on the premises. Not only did the Van Dyck make a good price, but so did the late seventeenth-century lapis lazuli chest, which we had to tussle with the National Trust to retain in the sale. In the end, the chest made £102,600 and was bought back by the National Trust for the house.

Belton House is extremely interesting. The architect was William Winde who was born in Holland of English parents. He became a soldier and is sometimes still referred to as Captain Winde. He would have been familiar with the works of Daniel Marot and there is even a suggestion that, for a time, he worked with him. On returning to England, he is known to have worked with both Christopher Wren and Roger Pratt. As well as Belton, his most enduring works are the gate piers set in the walls of the once-imposing Hampstead Marshall House. The house is now demolished but the walls survive. In the previous chapter I suggested that the

Mostyn Tompion could have been sold at auction. I was, however, never in any doubt that Belton should go to the nation, with as many of its contents as the National Trust wished for. The afternoon after making the decision about the fate of the house, I drove back to London and, being slightly earlier than I had anticipated, stopped at the Wallace Collection to enjoy what had been another act of great generosity. The museum was almost empty so I could not help thinking how unappreciative the public is for much of the time.

Brenda, Lady Cook and the Cook trustees, in their turn, had decided to sell two pictures. The first was Michiel Sweerts's *The Plague at Athens*, which made £972,000. This remarkably fine Poussinesque picture records an event which is of huge topical interest. Some recent research has indicated that the plague which decimated Athens in 430BC was caused by the same Ebola virus which has been responsible for so much suffering in West Africa. There was also an early Poussin, *Venus and Adonis*, which fetched £280,800. This had always been regarded as a copy or a work by one of Poussin's many pupils prior to its being re-established. It is a beautiful thing.

There was, however, no shortage of contemporary and modern pictures. Pride of place went to Pissarro's *La Route de Sydenham*, which made £561,600. Strangely, at that time it was a record price. It was bought by the National Gallery. The previous autumn, Henry McIlhenny's beautiful Cézanne still life, *Sucrier, poires et tapis*, was sold in New York for $3,960,000. Richard Diebenkorn's *Yellow Porch* made a healthy $440,000 and a picture I remember particularly well was sold at Christie's South Kensington: Sir John Lavery's *The Weighing Room*. I cannot include this without mentioning the subject, a group of jockeys, prominent among them one wearing Lord Derby's colours. The late Earl of Derby, uncle of the present Earl, was a stalwart friend of Christie's. During the war, he came forward and lent them Derby House the day after the King Street rooms had been destroyed by incendiary bombs so that they would have somewhere to continue their business. Twenty years or so after that, he sold Rembrandt's *Belshazzar's Feast* privately to the nation, and then a number of things,

THE TOMPIONS; STONELEIGH ABBEY; DEGAS IN NEW YORK; CHATSWORTH DRAWINGS; BELTON; PISSARRO

principally the picture attributed to Van Dyck of *Four Negro Heads*. I do not know a great deal about racing, but I always remember Lord Derby's colours because of a story I was once told, and particularly like. John Derby's stable jockey was an Australian and, after winning a prestigious race in Paris (not the Arc de Triomphe, but something of that sort), he was promised a night out. In contemporary parlance, he liked to party, and after the race he was taken to a well-known watering hole for dinner and afterwards given the pick of the available talent. After one or two false starts, he teamed up with a dark-skinned brunette, scantily clad in white. Asked why he wished to spend the evening with this particular young lady, he replied 'That's easy, Lord Derby's colours, black with a white cap.' To the victor belong the spoils!

That same month, in a sale in New York, an Archaic grey pottery amphora from the Han dynasty was sold for $28,600 (£20,000). The amphora, of which one other example had appeared in a sale sometime before, was thought to be a huge rarity, which is reflected in the price and its inclusion in that year's *Review*. In 1994 I was visiting Hong Kong and I was taken on a shopping spree by our then representative there, Anthony Lin. I bought (for $500, I think, but it could have been less) an identical Han amphora in marginally better condition than the one from the collection of Mr Mottahedeh. Why would something in 1984 be so much more valuable than the same thing in 1994? The reason is perfectly simple: in the intervening ten years, the Chinese, in a huge building programme, had opened up endless sites in the north and discovered any number of Han tombs, and what was thought to be rare is now no longer, but it is still beautiful.

Amphora. Han Dynasty

Michiel Sweerts. **The Plague at Athens**, *c.*1652-54

Sale of Lord Iveagh's house at Elveden; St Osyth's; Mrs Dodge's Carlin table reappears; Mrs Gould's executors sell her jewellery; Lord Northampton sells his Mantegna; death and funeral of Peter Chance; sale for Geoffrey Bennison in London; *Marquesa de Santa Cruz* not sold in London; works by Géricault organised by Noël Annesley

The next house sale after Belton was Elveden, for the trustees of the Earl of Iveagh. I initially took rather a dim view of Elveden because when going to see it, by way of a reconnaissance, with Tony Coleridge, I was quite badly bitten by the caretaker's border collie and had to go to the doctor's surgery in Thetford for a tetanus injection. But the house was amazing and had just about everything in it.

This most extraordinary sale took place over four days in late June that year. Eighteen thousand people attended the view. The house had been built mainly in the nineteenth century by Maharajah Julep Singh, the deposed son of the ruler of Punjab, beloved of Queen Victoria. He remodelled the old eighteenth-century house, both inside and out, like a maharajah's palace and filled it *coûte que coûte*. It had just about everything in it: pictures, furniture, porcelain, silver – in all 2,184 lots which made a total of £6,162,719. But the most remarkable of the contents, fetching by far the most money, were the carpets. I do not think our carpet people quite got it right. I took the sale myself and the estimates bore no relation whatsoever to the prices realised. But I learnt something that day. If you ever see a carpet with a Harvey Nichols label on it, buy it! That remarkable Knightsbridge shop, famed now mainly for its striking window displays, used to be the most important importer of Oriental rugs in England. The other firm represented in the collection was, of course, Liberty. I could not really complain about the disparity between the estimates and the prices because it is our job as auctioneers to get the highest prices we can. However, under any normal circumstances, an auctioneer has to open the

OPPOSITE

Patrick Lindsay selling the Mantegna, 13 April 1985

137

bidding at below the reserve price which in turn has to be below the low estimate. Had I started below these estimates and adhered to the usual increments, I would probably still be selling the carpets at Elveden today. I will not list all the carpets with their estimates and the prices they ultimately fetched, but to take the twelve most notable examples, the total was £315,000 against a low estimate of £9,200. These carpets were all the Harvey Nichols carpets. It is impossible to illustrate any of them here because none was thought worthy of illustration in the catalogue.

St Osyth's Priory is a very beautiful medieval building close to the Essex coast. It belonged to my dear old friend Somerset de Chair who was married to Juliet Fitzwilliam, the most faithful client and kindest friend I had throughout my time at Christie's and who figures elsewhere in this book. The priory's annex, at one time in the 1970s, stabled *Whistlejacket*. The house was the personal property of Somerset and, after his death, his children had some difficulty selling it due to the fact that he had sold the mining rights to the house, which meant that strong men in hard hats could pop up under the drawing room floor at any moment.

I could not end this sketch of 1984 without mentioning the reappearance on the market of Mrs Dodge's Carlin table, sent in by Habib Sabet. It did rather well. The price went up in the ten years he had owned it from £173,250 to £918,000. My favourite piece of furniture that year, a Louis XV ebony and tortoiseshell marquetry *commode à vantaux*, was sold on behalf of the late Lady Cholmondeley from Houghton and bought by the Getty Museum for £486,000.

Finally, to wrap up that remarkable year, there was Mrs Gould's jewellery sale which took place in New York and made $8.1 million. This would not have been the case had it not been for the quick-wittedness of my colleague, Humphrey Butler, who was attending the view in London when a gang of serious desperadoes came in to King Street. They were armed with shotguns and clubs with which they smashed the cabinets, looking for Mrs Gould's sapphire necklace. Humphrey, with considerable foresight and bravery, had slipped it into his pocket. They never got their hands on it. However, they did steal a diamond necklace, the property of another seller, the Countess of Iveagh. She was generously compensated by our insurance company but it was a tragic loss. It was one of the best diamond necklaces that the trade had ever seen, containing all 'old mined' stones of extraordinary quality. This I was told by a Hatton Garden friend who is no longer alive but his son, Andrew, is, so I will mention his name: Charlie Rothenberg. His advice enabled us to make a claim with the insurance company in their settlement with Lady Iveagh. It was particularly kind of him to give us this information and to ask for no reward whatsoever.

The year 1985 was in some ways the calm before the storm. The world was sloughing off the financial depressions of the early 1980s and good works of art were coming on to the market again. The year at Christie's was definitely dominated by the sale of the beautiful Mantegna belonging to Spenny, seventh Marquess of Northampton. I had known Spenny's father and used to stay frequently at Castle Ashby. Bim Northampton used to say that the Mantegna was the most valuable picture in England – well, he was right. When *The Adoration of the Magi* came up for sale it made £8.1 million, at that point the highest price ever paid for a work of art. Yet the sale had a sad twist: it was the last great one presided over by Patrick Lindsay, who, as the photograph of the sale shows, was not at all well. He was already suffering from the cancer that was to end his life the following year. During the previous two decades, he had been an inspirational auctioneer.

The year 1985 also marked the death of Peter Chance, who had become Chairman of Christie's in 1958 and with whom I had had my first dismally unsuccessful interview for a job. He had been a wonderful Chairman and was responsible as much as anybody else for the rise in the firm's fortunes. He would have been astonished by what was to happen to the art market in the next fifteen years. The $10.4 million record that year for the Mantegna would become, by the end of the decade, $82.5 million. It would, however, take another ten years for that $82.5 million to become $100 million.

Pablo Picasso. **Femme assise au chapeau**, *c.*1923

Peter's funeral took place at St Paul's, Deptford, the beautiful Thomas Archer church which he had helped to restore in his capacity as chairman of the Georgian Group. Peter, too, had succumbed to cancer, but not before he had bought his own piece of architectural history, Colby Lodge, Stepaside, Pembrokeshire. Colby Lodge is set in a beautiful valley and the house and grounds were eventually left to the National Trust. I shall always remember the funeral, because it was the last time that any of us would ever sing 'All Things Bright and Beautiful' including the third verse; 'the rich man in his castle' took a final bow.

Joseph Wright of Derby is an artist who occurs several times in this story and was particularly highly valued in France by Pierre Rosenberg, sometime director of the Louvre. His *Portrait of Mr and Mrs Thomas Coltman*, which came up for sale in the months following Peter Chance's death and was bought by the National Gallery for £1,404,000, was one of the best. Marginally less good than *The Old Man and Death*

at the Wadsworth Atheneum was *An Iron Forge*, sold by Sotheby's, which belonged to Edwina Mountbatten's father – a grand picture nonetheless. And, shortly before their own sale, the Edward James Foundation put up Picasso's *Femme assise au chapeau*, a picture dating to 1923, which made $4.29 million in New York. No less than three versions of Monet's *Haystacks* came up for sale in quick succession, making $2,090,000, $2,200,000 and $2,530,000.

Francisco de Goya. **Retrato de la Marquesa de Santa Cruz**, 1805

There was another sort of house sale which I was left to mastermind in the autumn of 1985 and which I enjoyed, as I think everyone else involved in it did. This was the recreation of Geoffrey Bennison's wonderful apartment in our rooms in King Street. John Richardson wrote a typically engaging foreword to the catalogue, starting with his meeting of Geoffrey at the Slade in 1941, where, according to John, he was 'the Slade's only star'. Anyone involved in the furniture trade or in decorating knew and loved Geoffrey. He was an inspiration to a generation of fellow decorators in England, in America and in France. His apartment at 4 South Audley Street was too small in which to hold a sale but much too charming to break up prior to one, so I got my old Coldstream friend, Jeremy Whitaker, to come and take photographs of the apartment and from them we recreated the rooms, using screens covered in Geoffrey's own fabric, just as they were in his flat. There was nothing of huge value but it looked wonderful and the prices fully justified the costs. This was a great farewell to a much-loved friend. The sale totalled £667,936 and, as someone wrote in Christie's *Review*, one could be certain that Geoffrey would have loved it all.

The 1985–6 season was again a successful one for Christie's. Towards the end of it I became Chairman of Christie, Manson & Woods. Yet towards the beginning of it I had been almost forced to resign because I had become involved in the sale of Goya's *Retrato de la Marquesa de Santa Cruz*.

Lord Wimborne was the owner of the Goya and his brother-in-law, Simon Dickinson, was a Director of Christie's Old Master Picture Department and had initially been involved in the sale. Simon, with whom I continue to work, has two amazing attributes: a very good eye for pictures and boundless enthusiasm. He has one disadvantage in that he does not always anticipate the consequences of what he gets involved in. I should have been more mindful of this when I became entangled in this story. In fact, one could say that it had started earlier for me than for anybody else because Ivor Wimborne had been a very close friend of mine at prep school. I still have his copy of *A Tale of Two Cities* which he won as a history prize and I swapped for another prize I had rather surprisingly won.

Théodore Géricault. **Buste de nègre**, c.1818-19

Ivor, to be honest, had shed the quiet charm he had as a nine-year-old and become a much more difficult character. He, first and foremost, should never have got involved with this picture. The problem was of course that it was very beautiful and obviously very valuable. I won't go into every twist and turn of the story but it became apparent, not before Christie's had spent a great deal of money on the project and a great deal more thereafter in legal fees to get out of it, that we would not be able to sell the picture, nor should we ever have tried. Through the considerable diplomatic skills of Jo Floyd, aided by Julian Agnew, we reached what was deemed an honourable settlement and the picture returned to the Prado.

At the end of 1985 there was a remarkable sale of works by Géricault from the Bühler Collection, the responsibility mainly of Noël Annesley. The sale was a triumph. The most expensive lot, *Buste de nègre*, sold for £145,800. The fact that it was such a success was in part due to Noël's patience since, during the bidding, somebody responsible for something decided to drill a hole in the pavement outside Christie's, severing our telephone communications with the outside world. Somehow we managed to carry on and the sale totalled nearly £5 million.

Chapter 17

The office in Monte Carlo; the Clore sale; the Edward James sale; the sale of Rysbrack's sculpture of Shakespeare; sculpture from Wentworth Woodhouse

In 1985, Guy Hannen had encouraged me to set up an office in Monte Carlo, which was fortuitous because it enabled us successfully to pitch for the estate of the late Sir Charles Clore who had died in 1979. Sir Charles Clore had been, since the end of the Second World War, one of the richest businessmen in Britain, with interests in retail, shoemaking and property. His Sears Holdings owned Selfridges, Mappin & Webb, and Garrards, as well as a large proportion of the British shoemaking industry under the banner of the British Shoe Corporation Ltd. The main engine of his considerable wealth, however, came from property, a world in which he excelled. He was supposed to have been the first to use the phrase 'Location, Location, Location' as a guide to buying property, which my daughter Kirstie has put to such good use. He was knighted in 1971 and remained extremely active up until his sudden death in 1979.

Sir Charles has always been credited with huge business acumen but his lasting legacy was the Clore Foundation, which made very generous contributions to charities in Britain and in Israel. Before his death he had already begun to work on a project to house the Turner Bequest. The gallery, designed by James Stirling and Michael Wilford, was eventually realised by his daughter, Dame Vivien Duffield, and opened in the presence of Her Majesty on 1 April 1987. The establishment of the Clore Galleries was very significant, but Charles Clore deserves more credit and recognition than he has ever received for being among the foremost post-war collectors of works of art in the country. The sales that I go on to describe were remarkable enough; but a large proportion of the paintings he had collected remain with the family and others were sold by his son, Alan Clore, at Christie's in 1989. He had also made donations to museums in his lifetime, most notably the magnificent Brancusi, illustrated on the back cover of the Royal Academy's catalogue of their 2012 Bronze exhibition.

After a long family dispute, Sir Charles Clore's will was finally settled in 1986 and we were asked to submit a proposal for the sale of the collection. With the help of a number of colleagues I produced the draft of the document for the executors and

OPPOSITE

Constantin Brancusi. **Danaïde**, c.1918

sent it to Patrick Lindsay to read through over the weekend. I asked him to let me know on Monday if he had any alterations he would like to make because we were to submit it in Jersey that following week. Patrick admitted to me that he could not come to Jersey and was not feeling up to reading the documents. He had finally realised how bad his cancer was and told me that he did not think he had long to live. This was very sad news as he was a close friend and colleague, and godfather to my son, Henry.

I tidied up the proposal and went to Jersey where, happily, the executors decided to entrust Christie's with the sale of the furniture, the Fabergé, silver and the miniatures. Some pictures were consigned to Sotheby's; others were retained by members of the family. The Fabergé formed its own sale in Geneva in November, which went extremely well, establishing a record for an individual piece, the figure of Catherine the Great borne by two liveried servants. This once formed a surprise for a lost egg and fetched £417,320. A replica of a Louis XVI secretaire made £197,712 and a very charming figure of John Bull sold for £50,326.

However, it was the furniture that was by far the most exciting part of the collection. We had proposed a sale in Monte Carlo which was to be our first sale there – this was something of a challenge, but it was not the only one. Almost all of the most expensive lots from the estate had been bought only seven years before from the collection of Akram Ojjeh. It should be remembered that the Ojjeh sale itself had an interesting history, which I include here.

In the early 1970s, Sotheby's had announced that they would be selling the collection of furniture formed by the Wildenstein family, drawn mainly from what the Wildensteins had been able to acquire from the Rothschild family in the early part of the twentieth century. Akram Ojjeh had persuaded Sotheby's to sell him the entire collection prior to the auction. It must be obvious that Monsieur Ojjeh had

One of a pair of Louis XIV commodes attributed to André-Charles Boulle

One of a pair of encoignures by Jean-Pierre Latz, 1597-8

Figure of John Bull by Carl Fabergé (workmaster Henrik Wigström), 1896-1908

offered a substantial premium to Sotheby's and to the Wildensteins to forgo the benefits of a public sale by auction.

Sotheby's, in turn, must have approached their sale in June 1979 with some apprehension, but they achieved very high (in some cases record) prices for the furniture, partly, rumour has it, because prior to the evening sale, that clever old fox Peter Wilson had asked Charles Clore and the great collector Stavros Niarchos to dine with him and had skilfully manufactured an argument between the two of them. After dinner they had taken up positions on opposite sides of the saleroom and bid against each other for almost all of the important lots. The prices in the Ojjeh sale had consequently been outstanding and bettering them was going to be difficult.

Our involvement in the upcoming Clore sale had an element of pass the parcel. When the music stopped, we would have to justify ourselves. This was going to be the more difficult because two crucial collectors were out of the market: Charles Clore was dead and his rival had got everything he wanted previously.

One of a pair of Sèvres blue lapis vases œufs, c.1768

As luck would have it, the sale in Monte Carlo was a great success and every lot with one exception sold: the impressive pair of Boulle commodes from James de Rothschild made £780,000; the lot which made the highest price, £1,073,000, was the magnificent Leleu commode which, according to tradition, was bought by King George III in one of the Revolutionary sales and in turn given by him to his doctor, Coningsby; a pair of Louis XV *encoignures* by Latz made £330,000 and the very stylish pair of Empire console tables by Jacob-Desmalter, rue Meslée, fetched £292,000.

But the real joy of the sale for me was a lot which Hugh Roberts and I did not even know existed as we unpacked the collection in the warehouse in Monte Carlo. It was a pair of Sèvres *bleu lapis* oviform vases and covers, *vases œufs*, most probably made for Marie Antoinette, which made £175,571 and were bought, after a bit of a struggle over their exit from France, by the Getty Museum in Malibu. I took the sale in my less-than-perfect French, and it was by far the most important sale up to that point that I had ever undertaken, totalling 50 million French francs (£4,400,000).

The following day we continued with a sale from various owners, which included an extraordinary pair of bronze statuettes by Barthélemy Prieur, of King Henri IV, naked, and his Queen, Marie de Médicis, naked to the waist, the King as Jupiter, the Queen as Juno, modelled in their lifetime.

If the Clore sale in December 1985 had been easy, the Edward James sale at West Dean in the summer of 1986 was not. Despite the beauty of West Dean and its surrounding countryside and the fascinating mishmash of the sale, which contained very good paintings and furniture, it was, unlike most house sales, not particularly well attended. Despite the fact that it was a great deal closer to London than Cullen House,

Pavel Tchelitchew. **Excelsior**, 1934

LEFT

Leonora Carrington. **The Guardian of the Egg**, 1947

Banffshire, the crowds of ladies shopping for damask tablecloths would have swamped the early arrivals at West Dean. Tony was in despair and I was ringing up friends in London to try and get them to come and see the sale, even if they weren't going to buy anything. The situation was not made any easier by the rather disagreeable correspondence in the papers about whether the sale should take place at all, West Dean being such an important shrine to surrealism. I do not think the British public as a whole particularly minded about surrealism, but the correspondence did not encourage them to come to the sale. In the end, those who wanted to come and buy did, and one should always point out that the summer of 1986 was not easy for financial reasons, being just over a year away from Black Monday.

Edward James had a colourful past including a marriage to Tilly Losch, later Lady Carnarvon. He was the leading advocate of surrealism in England and had befriended Salvador Dalí, Max Ernst and many other painters of that era. He had been particularly fond of the paintings of Max Ernst's lover, Leonora Carrington, and he was her most fervent patron. Her strange surrealist pictures and sculptures have an extraordinary charm which is appreciated more today than it was when these pictures appeared for sale. Lot 1656, *The Guardian of the Egg*, made £43,200 against an estimate of £20,000–£25,000. It was, needless to say, a record for her work at the time. Also represented in strength in the collection were forty-three works of that artist whose name I had had such difficulty spelling back in 1965: Pavel Tchelitchew. His *Excelsior* made £28,080 – another record. Although I had always been perplexed by Tchelitchew, I thought I had more or less sorted him out until I read the impenetrable note by Parker Tyler in the catalogue concerning one of the artist's interior landscapes:

> The underlying common identity is represented in the world body of myth formed by the voluminous hermetic tradition which descended from priestly and sectarian sources in Egypt and the Orient to mould Orphism Neo-Platonism and in the Christian era Agnosticism and Alchemy. Susceptible to every strain of mysticism by virtue of poetic intuition, Tchelitchew becomes a painter who portrayed hermetic eclecticism in a conscious series of real and ideal prisms.

The best of the Dalís had been sold in London but some still remained in the sale and a relatively early picture painted in 1935, *Paranoïc Face*, made £205,000. Among a quite considerable amount of interesting furniture, there was a pair of Italian painted commodes and a desk I would like to have owned myself, made in Italy at the end of the eighteenth century. The latter sold for £48,600 and there were some other impressive prices. For instance, from the main house came a set of four mid-Georgian armchairs upholstered in needlework, which made £129,000. In addition, there was a pair of Regency bookcases from Edward James's mauve-painted Petit Trianon, which reached £30,000.

Edouard Manet. **La Rue Mosnier aux paveurs**, 1878

I mentioned at the beginning of Chapter 5 my friendship with James West of Alscot Park. It was in the autumn of 1986 that he sold his wonderful Shakespeare bust by John Michael Rysbrack which fetched £291,600. In the same sale, the trustees of Olive, Countess Fitzwilliam (and I was one of them) sold a remarkable group of statues from Wentworth Woodhouse: four by Joseph Nollekens, totalling some £430,000; the Richard Wyatt of a huntress, which made £91,800; and the most impressive of the group, the huge Foggini of *Samson and the Philistines*, which fetched £345,600. Despite its unfortuitous start, the year had a triumphant ending!

In the last month of 1986, Christie's London offered as its principal lot in the impressionist sale one of the most beautiful paintings by douard Manet ever to come up for sale, his ravishing *La Rue Mosnier aux paveurs*, which fetched £7,700,000 ($10,987,900) – in pounds slightly less expensive but in dollars more than the Mantegna the year before. All this, though, was just the hors d'oeuvre for the main course in 1987. This was of course Van Gogh's *Sunflowers*.

Figure of Juno by Joseph Nollekens, 1776

Van Gogh's *Sunflowers* and *Pont de Trinquetaille*; sales of Francis Bacon, Rothko and Warhol; the death of Lord Bradford and subsequent sales; Renoir's *Place Clichy* goes to the nation; the Marbury Hall marbles; my trip to India with Nina Pillai; sale of Degas's two *Blanchisseuses*

In 1966, Andy Warhol wrote that 'in the future everyone will be famous for 15 minutes'. My fifteen minutes came in 1987 when the executors of the late Chester Beatty decided to sell their version of Van Gogh's *Sunflowers*.

Thousands upon thousands of words have been written about this painting by the most erudite Van Gogh scholars. I have but one thing to add on the art historical side concerning this picture, and that is that I have personally examined the hessian on which it is painted and also the hessian on which Gauguin painted *Le Ramassage du foin* (*Girl Harvesting*), which is dated November 1888 and was clearly started sometime earlier. Martin Bailey, in his excellent book on the subject, records Van Gogh and Gauguin living together at The Yellow House and using 'the same jute' rather than normal canvas. This is worth noting as, shortly after the sale, doubts were cast on certain aspects of the way the pictures were painted. Enough, though, about the picture. Any doubts about any particular aspect of it have been settled by Martin Bailey.

It was my luck to be in the rostrum to sell this remarkable work of art on the evening of 30 March 1987. Prior to this, depending on whether one uses dollars or pounds, the world's most expensive picture was either the Manet I have described in the preceding chapter, which sold in 1986, or the Mantegna sold from the same rostrum the year before that, which fetched $10.9 million and £8.1 million respectively. We had agreed to offer the *Sunflowers* with a reserve price of considerably more than that, which entailed a degree of risk. But the omens were good and about midday on the day of the sale, I received some encouraging news from my colleague in New York, Christopher Burge, who rang me to ask if, in the unlikely event of the bidding going above £20 million, I would accept an increment

OPPOSITE

Edgar Degas. **Blanchisseuses portant du linge**, c.1876

on the nation on condition that it would remain where it had always been, at Weston Park. This picture was described by John Evelyn as 'one of the best he ever painted', while Oliver Millar, in *Van Dyck: A Complete Catalogue of the Paintings*, describes 'the spirituality and technical brilliance of a portrait such as that of Sir Thomas Hanmer'.

I had had a lot to do with Weston's owner, the late Earl of Bradford, a most charming man, and a considerable expert on trees. He was, I believe, responsible for bringing the *Nothofagus* to Britain which grew extremely well on his large forestry holdings in Devon. Sadly, Gerald Bradford died far too young, and before arrangements could be made to hand over the estate to his son, Lord Newport, a great deal had to be sold or settled. The best picture in the house – *Christ Carrying the Cross on the Road to Calvary* by Jacopo Bassano – went to the National Gallery and the remainder of the pictures were allowed to remain at Weston Park. These included *Sir Thomas Hanmer* and five other pictures by Van Dyck.

I had quite a long connection with the Bridgeman family. Gerald Bradford's father was my grandfather's best man and, perhaps unsurprisingly, my father's godfather. I really enjoyed going to Weston and talking about the pictures. These conversations only had one drawback: Gerald's hearing was less than perfect. Conversations would typically to go along these lines:

LEFT TO RIGHT

Amedeo Modigliani. **Fillette au tablier noir**, 1918

Anthony Van Dyck. **Sir Thomas Hanmer**, *c.*1638

154

C.A. You know they now have accepted all the Van Dycks?

G.B Sorry, I didn't get that.

C.A. *(slightly louder)* You know they have accepted all the Van Dycks?

G.B. What?

C.A. *(slightly louder still)* All the Van Dycks have been accepted.

G.B. Charlie, you don't have to shout.

It is always sad when a great family house is broken up. The collection at Weston was very grand but at the same time quite intimate. Although no one lives in the big house any longer, it is obviously a plus that the vast majority of the pictures is still there and enjoyed by the public.

The second picture came from close friends of my mother's family and very old Christie's clients, the MacDonald Buchanans of Cottesbrooke. Constable's *Young Waltonians*, as it used to be called, was successfully negotiated to the National Gallery. It was always said to be Constable's favourite 'six-footer' and, hanging where it does in the same room as *Whistlejacket*, it looks magnificent.

The last of the trio of pictures we sold to the nation that year was Renoir's *La Place Clichy*, which now hangs in the Fitzwilliam Museum and came, needless to say, from a member of the Courtauld family. This is Renoir at his absolutely edible best. Samuel Courtauld built up a collection of impressionist and post-impressionist pictures which would stand up in any company, anywhere in the world. But it was

John Constable.
**Stratford Mill
(The Young
Waltonians)**, 1820

was one of the most alarming experiences of my life. We survived, but a lot of people we saw along the way did not fare so well. We arrived in Jaipur just in time to unpack and change for dinner with the Maharaja.

Roger and I were billeted in the Rambagh Palace. I had a large old-fashioned room, with a large old-fashioned bath, over which I hung the coat from my one tidy suit which had been nestling in the bottom of my rather inadequate suitcase. When I unpacked it, the coat was not in great shape. I had hoped that the steam would restore it to a state so that I would at least look presentable for the Maharaja and Maharani. I acquired a very old iron to try and get a crease in my trousers and whilst I was attempting this, I heard a splosh. The steam was probably helping my coat regain its shape but unfortunately it melted the glue on the coat hanger, which was just as old as everything else in the room, and my coat fell into the bath, into which I was hoping to get myself. We had about fifteen minutes before the car was due to arrive. I got the coat out of the bath, shook it, rang room service and asked for a hair dryer and got one which looked as though it had been fished out of a glass case in the Science Museum. It gave out a low whirring sound but very little else. I wrung out my coat again, shook it and, having had a very quick bath, I climbed into my trousers (not much of a crease), a shirt (still quite creased) and the coat. I immediately took it off again as it was soaking wet. The car arrived, slightly early. I put the coat over my arm and having met up with Roger, pointed out to the driver that he was early and suggested we go on a tour around the town. We did not want to appear for dinner before anybody else, I said. This was only partly true. I thought the longer we could drive with my coat hanging out of the window, the greater the chances were that it might at least be wearable. We made a lightning tour of Jaipur, dodging in and out of the traffic, to the glorious Amber Fort and back. We arrived in the town palace where there was a reception principally given for Nina Pillai but also including Roger and me. I put on my coat. It didn't look too bad in the ebbing light outdoors but, after half an hour, the Maharani asked me to accompany her into dinner. I was sitting next to her. She was charming and asked me if I liked hot food because, she said, they had very hot food in the palace. 'Yes,' I said, 'I really like hot food, the hotter the better.' 'You are sure?' 'Yes,' I replied. She also explained that they ate it principally with their fingers, with naan bread. Was that ok? Absolutely. We started dinner. It was delicious and I got stuck in with enthusiasm. 'You are so polite, you English, you don't really like the food, do you? It's too hot.' 'No,' I replied, 'I am really enjoying it.' I suddenly realised why she thought it was too hot for me. From the coat emerged clouds of vapour. I was forced to explain that it wasn't me that was on fire, but my coat. The Maharani snapped her fingers and a couple of regiments of men in white coats appeared, removed my coat and would have taken everything else off me, had they been able to. In about a quarter of an hour, it was returned, dry and beautifully pressed, but my embarrassment was not easily ironed out.

We returned the next day to Delhi, this time without any sartorial problems, and met yet more people, and I have to admit I thoroughly enjoyed my trip although no business resulted from it. I love India, I shall be going back again soon, but for pleasure, not for business, and I shall take a large suitcase.

Back in London we had to endure the stock market crash on Black Monday, 19 October 1987, which saw our shares plummet from 720p at the beginning of October to 270p at the end of the month, despite the fact that we had been trading extremely profitably since the beginning of the year.

In November 1987, our representative in Paris, Princesse Jeanne-Marie de Broglie, had persuaded Monsieur et Madame Philippe Durand-Ruel to include their important Degas, *Les Blanchisseuses*, which made a record price £7,480,000.

The market continued to boom in 1988, although it would not quite rival the previous year, and there were several wonderful individual lots, above all another Degas, *Blanchisseuses portant du linge*, a picture which had been sold before at Christie's and exhibited in our bicentennial exhibition. This picture came with a fascinating provenance, the Durand-Ruel family again, who had bought it from Bernheim-Jeune, and sold it to arguably the most important collector of Degas in Britain, Sir William Eden, father of the prime minister, who had at the time the money and the opportunity to buy almost anything he wanted.

It is inevitable that anyone with any profile at all in the art world is going to be asked who is their favourite painter. I cannot answer that question because I find it impossible to make up my mind. However, were I to be asked that question of all the things I have personally sold, from that much smaller shopping basket I think I would plump for Lot 16 on 28 March 1988, Degas's *Blanchisseuses portant du linge*. The artist signed the picture, which probably meant that he had finished it, although areas of the surface are clearly not fully painted in. But I suspect that, as with Picasso's *Acrobate et jeune Arlequin*, which came up for sale the following autumn and runs a close second in my affections, the artist thought, 'I can go no further.' The *Blanchisseuses* is really a sketch. It is painted *à l'essence*, that is to say in very thin, diluted oil, almost like watercolour, in shades of brown and purpley grey against a vivid yellow background, which perfectly sets off the white of the folded sheets. The pretty young laundry maids holding the basket strike almost provocative poses.

This is probably the moment to salute, in passing, the person who brought the picture in to us for sale, Robert Holden, who sadly died of cancer in 2015, which he had fought with enormous courage for at least ten years before finally succumbing. All of us in both auction houses waged many a battle with him and sometimes wondered why so many people used him to negotiate with us, but that is all in the past. He was involved with a lot of things in this book but I am particularly pleased that he wanted Christie's to sell this picture for his client in America.

Chapter 19

More Chatsworth drawings and George Lane Fox's Agasse; the sale of Stubbs's *Portrait of a Royal Tiger*; the Duke of Marlborough's papers; Modigliani's *Portrait of Marios Varvoglis*; Alan Clore's pictures; Gauguin's *Alyscamps*; the Goetz Collection in New York; Monet's *Pont du chemin de fer à Argenteuil*; Picasso's *Acrobate et jeune Arlequin*

The surprises, shocks and successes of 1987 gave way, as mentioned earlier, to a slightly less dramatic but steady stream of important sales and excellent pictures in 1988. Although I personally had a very soft spot for the Degas girls carrying the linen, it would not be the only highlight for this coming year. On 6 July Noël Annesley, who had been entrusted with the second tranche of the Chatsworth drawings, sold the Barocci *Madonna del popolo* for an extraordinary £1,760,000, more than the very beautiful Rembrandt *Ramparts* which fetched £1,375,000 – a record for a Rembrandt drawing.

From the 1960s to the 1980s, and I think this applies more to America than England, the auction houses relied to a very large extent on furnishing their sales with introductions from lawyers who dealt with deceased estates or with the general management of affairs. One of the leading firms of private client lawyers in England was Withers, with whom Christie's generally and I personally – as they were for years my own lawyers – had an extremely good relationship. In 1988 the senior partner, Brian Stevens, asked me if I would go to Yorkshire to see a client of his called George Lane Fox, who lived in a lovely house, Bramham Hall. I knew the family but had never met George, and I had never been to Bramham. My first impression was of the huge hall which, unusually, had rough, unrendered stones on the interior and had hanging on one of the walls a spectacularly beautiful picture by Jacques-Laurent Agasse. This Swiss animal painter, who had come over to England towards the end of the eighteenth century following in the footsteps of

George Stubbs, painted a large number of pictures for Lord Rivers, an ancestor of George Lane Fox.

George Lane Fox was quite a shy man but I got on well with him, and he decided to entrust us with the picture. It depicted two leopards happily playing in the sunshine in Lord Rivers's menagerie at Rushmore, Dorset. In the late eighteenth century it was the height of fashion for rich English lords to have their own zoo. Lord Rivers owned extensive tracts of land in Dorset and Wiltshire and had been an early patron of Agasse. His daughter, Marcia, married James Lane Fox in July 1789. Second only to Stubbs, Agasse was the best painter of animals in the eighteenth and nineteenth centuries and he never painted anything better than these leopards.

George Stubbs. **Portrait of the Royal Tiger**, *c.*1770

When the sale was announced it aroused enormous interest. It was due to be taken by my colleague, Noël Annesley, and on the day of the sale, 15 July 1988, I was free to look after the owner. I welcomed him into the building. He was extremely nervous. He was obviously desperate to sell the picture. I assured him that there was nothing to worry about and we sat in the hall at Christie's where I counted at least eight people who I knew were interested in buying it. During the sale I took George into my office and we watched, on closed-circuit television, almost incredulously, as the bidding rose. It was finally knocked down for just under £4 million, more, at the time, than any Stubbs had ever fetched at auction and certainly far more than any other Agasse. This was clearly going to solve a few problems back in Yorkshire and it is always enormously satisfying to sell something really well for a really nice client and to see them go away happy. The buyer of the picture was happy too. The underbidder was, of course, less happy, but he consoled himself by having a copy of the picture made and displaying it in his house overlooking Hyde Park, frequently failing to mention that it is not the real thing!

Sometimes referrals come in not from lawyers but from people's trustees. One such referral concerned my old friend, Evelyn de Rothschild, who had often told me that he was the trustee for the Portman family, by coincidence neighbours of the Pitt Rivers in Dorset. Lord Portman had no Agasse, but a near life-size portrait of a Bengal tiger by Stubbs, which to me was every bit as beautiful as Agasse's leopards and, being by the undisputed master of the genre, would, I thought, be more valuable. I was thrilled to have been asked to deal with this picture and we produced a first-class catalogue and promoted it with vigour.

To this day I have never been able to understand why *Portrait of the Royal Tiger* did not attract greater attention when it came up for sale. Noël Annesley sold it, no blame whatsoever attached to him, but the sale simply did not take off and this beautiful picture struggled to make its reserve. It was bought by a clever New York hedge fund manager and I think time will certainly prove that he made a really good investment with Stubbs's magnificent tiger. To me, though, it was one of the most disappointing results.

Business came in to Christie's in many ways and if the venerable firm of Withers, in the case of George Lane Fox and the Agasse, and Sir Evelyn de Rothschild, Viscount Portman's trustee, in the case of the Stubbs, were at the top of the food chain, this next story is about something that came in from the very bottom. Most people do not even know of the existence of licensed scavengers. These are, on the whole, energetic men who have applied to local authorities to be licensed literally to scavenge on council refuse tips. It was because of the efforts of one such person that I received a call from the Duke of Marlborough in 1995, when Fiona and I were living in a rented house in Kildare Terrace. I was just leaving for the office when I heard Fiona saying, 'Oh, yes, Sunny, here he is,' and she handed me the telephone. 'Sunny wants to talk to you.' I thought, good, he is going to ask me to shoot. He usually did, about that time of year, to fill in for somebody who had dropped out. But, by his tone of voice, I realised that he wasn't going to on this occasion. He said, 'I thought you were my friend?' I replied, 'Sunny, I hope I am.' 'Well, you're not behaving like one,' he continued and I asked what the problem was. He told me. 'Your wretched firm is selling a whole lot of stuff that belongs to me.' I realised it wasn't the moment to have a long conversation so I asked him where he would be at lunchtime and promised I would find out and ring him. By lunch I had ascertained that it was not King Street but Christie's South Kensington. There was, included in a sale on 29 November, a lot under the heading, 'Winston Spencer-Churchill (1874–1965) & Charles Richard John Spencer-Churchill, 9th Duke of Marlborough (1871–1934): An extensive collection of correspondence and legal documents relating to the separation on grounds of infidelity of the 9th Duke of Marlborough from his wife Consuelo'. This comprised, in fact, the entire correspondence regarding the divorce of the ninth Duke from Consuelo Vanderbilt, one of the most celebrated beauties of the Edwardian era – and probably of any era – who has made several appearances in these pages.

The papers included various letters, such as the one from Winston Churchill that caught Christie's eye; correspondence from Sir Edward Carson, the celebrated barrister, who would have been employed to represent the Duke; statements from private detectives and so on. How had these clearly very confidential papers got to Christie's? My telephone conversation with the eleventh Duke that morning made it quite clear that it was not on his instructions. It transpired that they had been consigned by a licensed scavenger. The papers had been dumped by the lawyers,

Lewis and Lewis, an eminently respectable firm who had closed down one of their offices in north London and thrown out all the documents before a certain date. At some stage, they would have almost certainly asked permission from their clients to do so, but there was no record of this. I had a lot of sympathy for Sunny who did not want his grandparents' divorce to be splashed all over the newspapers again but I also had considerable sympathy for the scavenger and, in the end, persuaded my colleagues to part with quite a bit of Christie's hard-earned cash to acquire the scavenger's interest in the papers and cancel the sale. Eventually, I sorted out the problem with Sunny and the papers are now in the archives at Blenheim.

Back to 1988, in March, in the same sale as the beautiful Degas, we sold a record-breaking and wonderful Modigliani of the artist's composer friend, Marios Varvoglis, which was probably the last picture he ever painted, and was, as James Roundell pointed out in the *Review*, still on his easel when he died. The picture is not signed. One would be suspicious if it was. Marios Varvoglis went on to have a distinguished musical career, ending up as co-director of the Hellenic Conservatory, and he put the finishing touches to the story of the picture in a certificate in 1958 in which he writes: '*mon portrait que mon ami Amédeo a fait les derniers mois de sa vie à son atelier de la rue de la grande Chaumière*'.

Van Gogh's *Adeline Ravoux* made another appearance in New York. The price rose from 150,000 guineas to $13,750,000. That summer we also sold a collection of pictures belonging to my friend Vivien Duffield's brother, Alan Clore, which included one of the best early Chagalls: *Paris, La Grande Roue*. This time the record £1.65 million did mean something. I have to confess to not usually liking Chagall's work but that picture had everything going for it. I worked hard to get these pictures for sale, not because Alan Clore was difficult to deal with, but because he was nocturnal and I could only see him in his Paris home between the hours of 10 pm and about 4 am. On several days one week I caught the plane at about six o'clock from City airport, landed in Paris, went to my hotel, had a bath, changed and went to have breakfast with Alan. We remained friends, I hope still are to this day, and the sale was generally considered to be a success. His Bazille, *Porte d'aigues-mortes*, that wonderful fortified town in the Camargue, made a record price, £715,000.

On the same day as the Alan Clore sale, there was another of those everlastingly seductive early Monets, from the early 1870s, when he was in Holland: *La Maison bleue, Zaandam*, made just under £4 million. In the same sale we sold a lovely Gauguin *Alyscamps*, painted in October 1888, when he was staying with Van Gogh, and when he probably cut off Van Gogh's ear. This picture joined the *Sunflowers* in Tokyo.

Paul Gauguin. **L'Allée des Alyscamps**, 1888

Noël Coward; Cecil Beaton; the Bugatti Royale; Renoir's *La Loge*; near death in pursuit of Cézanne's *Pommes et serviette*; New York sales for Paul Mellon, including Manet's *Rue Mosnier*; Boulle in Monte Carlo; 1990 success in New York with the Lehman Collection; Badminton Cabinet; Mrs Kramarsky's *Portrait du Dr Gachet*

As well as art history's great and good, there was a lighter side to the late 1980s, epitomised in two sales of drawings by Noël Coward and Cecil Beaton in 1988 and in the sale of the world's most expensive motor car in 1987.

Noël Coward was one of the greatest entertainers of the twentieth century. He was also an accomplished painter and, on his death, he left a considerable number of pictures and drawings which appeared in 1988 in a sale beautifully organised by John Lumley. I do not remember it particularly well since I was away at the time. But looking back at the photographs now, I am struck by what a really good artist Coward was. I have singled out *Jamaican Bay*, painted in gouache and watercolour, which fetched £46,000. Noël Coward's executor, secretary and friend, Graham Payn, wrote about the sale in the *Review* and included a photograph of himself, Noël Coward and Cecil Beaton in Jamaica.

By an amusing quirk of fate, Cecil Beaton's long-time friend and secretary, Eileen Hose, simultaneously asked me to sell her collection of Beaton's drawings. This sale was great fun and enjoyable to organise, but to be honest, talented though he was and a brilliant photographer, Beaton was no match for Coward as an artist. However, he designed costumes for that glorious Lerner and Loewe interpretation of Bernard Shaw's *Pygmalion*: *My Fair Lady*. We used Beaton's drawing for the Ascot scene as endpapers for the catalogues because

Fernand Léger. **Contraste de formes**, 1913

was rare and in superb condition; it fetched the enormous price of £9,350,000. The Picasso was an image so strong and so certain of itself that it stays with me forever. We turned over in London that week more than $100 million in value – the first time that had ever been achieved.

In a separate catalogue for 27 November 1989 was Picasso's quite disturbing *La Maternité*. When it had come up for sale in 1958 as the property of Arnold Kirkeby in Parke Bernet, it excited a great deal of interest with potential purchasers, curious as to why it was not included in the *Catalogue raisonné* of Picasso's work. Picasso cleared up the matter once and for all when he wrote that he was not surprised that it was not. It made at the time a record price for a work by the artist. It was bought by somebody I knew well, who kept the picture until eventually consigning it to us for sale. Together with the famous *Baigneuses*, it had been used to illustrate Picasso's work in *The Times* when they published his obituary. We produced an impressive catalogue, with a foreword by John Richardson, and the picture sold for just over £7 million which was, frankly, somewhat of a relief. It was a fascinating but controversial picture which clearly Picasso himself had struggled with.

Two weeks earlier in New York we sold a group of pictures for Paul Mellon which included Manet's other version of the Rue Mosnier, *La Rue Mosnier aux drapeaux*. I always preferred *La Rue Mosnier aux paveurs* but the *Drapeaux* was still a good picture and it did well, as did Van Gogh's *Le Vieil If*, and Picasso's *La Mort d'Arlequin*, last seen at Sotheby's in 1962 at the Somerset Maugham sale.

Before moving on to the New Year, I should mention a piece of furniture that was sold in the summer in Monte Carlo: an armoire consigned through our charming colleague in Paris, Laurent Prevost-Marcilhacy. This extraordinary, huge Louis XIV ebony and brass armoire, attributed to Boulle, made just a fraction under £1 million. It should have made a great deal more. This, and its *contrepartie* in Versailles, were almost certainly made for Louis XIV's son, the Grand Dauphin. The only comparable piece of furniture was the Badminton Cabinet which is discussed later in this chapter. Although that was, at the time, much more expensive, I would have preferred the Boulle armoire, which had been greatly admired by our most difficult client, now sadly no longer with us, Djahanguir Riahi, always known as 'Jinny'. He had two favourite expressions: one he applied to the Badminton Cabinet, '*Il manque le génie du création* [*sic*]' – he was Iranian, so his French was not perfect; the other was used to explain why he could not pay for something he had bought or just did not want to, '*Tu ne comprends pas, Charlie*' [which could have been either Charlie Cator or myself], '*je suis oriental*'. It was, in fact, neither

Pablo Picasso. **La Maternité**, 1901

Charlie Cator nor I who did not understand, it was Jinny who either could not or – which was more likely as he was highly intelligent – would not understand the simple principle that if you bid successfully on something in a sale, you have to pay for it, be you Oriental or not. Mercifully he bid on neither the Boulle armoire nor the Badminton Cabinet, possibly because the armoire was over 3 metres high and the cabinet nearly 4 metres high: the rooms in Jinny's apartment on the Quai Voltaire were no more than 2.5 metres in height.

Another item sold in Monte Carlo was one of the most attractive pieces of French porcelain that we handled: a Vincennes watering can from 1755, which made just under £56,000.

Christmas came and went. The old master sale in New York started well with a Veronese making a record price of just under $3 million. The subject was *Venus Disarmed by Cupid*. As yet there was little sign of any cracks in the market; these did not really appear until May.

By the beginning of 1990 a certain hesitation had crept into the market. We had not received many consignments for the spring impressionist sale in London and had to work hard to get a halfway decent sale for the summer. In New York, however, the May sale was, on the surface, a triumph, although not without some anxious moments. It contained a mixture of exceptional pictures: a Mondrian, *Tableau losangique II,* made $8.8 million; an early Chagall, *Au dessus de la ville,* just under $10 million; Mrs John Barry Ryan's Manet, *Le Banc,* always considered a gem, fetched a slightly disappointing $16.5 million; and, from the collection of the late Robert Lehman, Van Gogh's *Self-Portrait* reached $26,700,000.

Also from the Lehman Collection we sold Toulouse-Lautrec's *Girl with a Fur Stole: Mlle Jeanne Fontaine,* which was incidentally a picture we expected to get much more for, and Christopher Burge very cleverly dropped the hammer below the reserve. The purchaser, Marlborough Fine Art, took ten years to find a client for the picture. Lastly, and not a disappointment, we achieved $82.5 million – a world auction record – for Mrs Kramarsky's Van Gogh portrait of his doctor, *Portrait du Dr Gachet,* painted towards the end of both their lives in Auvers-sur-Oise.

Louis XIV Ebony and Brass Armoire
attributed to André-Charles Boulle,
c.1710-15

I was in New York bidding for this portrait, unsuccessfully, for a client and left to return to Monte Carlo via London to preside over our sale on 22 May, of very, very important and very, very unsaleable motor cars, and here the cracks really opened up. I forced my way into the rostrum through a pack of photographers, flashing away, and about two hours later had sold quite a lot of automobile memorabilia – hairbrushes, cufflinks and the like – but only one out of the collection of thirty-odd Formula 1 and racing sports cars, all with impeccable provenance and impeccable histories. Robert Brooks, who had masterminded the Bugatti sale, had left by this time and I had endeavoured, with the help of Colin Crabbe (who was then working for Christie's) and the rump of the Car Department, to put together a sale, but we would have been much better off not trying. There were several reasons for the sale result, but at the end of the day, with the absence of any Japanese buyers, the market for vintage cars had just gone. Summer in London, for the moment, continued the New York trend, with some very good sales, but with failures creeping in.

The impressionist sale was successful – just – and we managed to sell 70 per cent, with very strong prices for a number of pictures, the highest for Picasso's *Les Tuileries,* painted in 1901, which made £13,750,000 ($23,512,500). Selling *Les Tuileries* for that amount was a stroke of luck. But a bigger stroke of luck was that the bomb, which had been placed in the Carlton Club and went off coinciding with the end of the sale, did not kill anyone in Christie's, despite the shards of broken glass and splintered wood from the door of the club which hurtled down King Street. It was a miracle that nobody was even hurt. I think one person had a cut arm and had to be treated in the Press Office in Christie's – they were quite good at bandaging arms.

The next test of the market was a week later with the sale on 5 July 1990 of the Badminton Cabinet which in fact made a record for any piece of furniture, and for any piece of applied art, at £8,580,000. There was much muttering about the cabinet having been removed from Badminton and then the export licence was stopped, which was extremely unfair on the Duke of Beaufort's trustees, since they had tried to sell the cabinet to the nation for considerably less but, as with the Chatsworth drawings, the nation would not take the bait. In fact, the Chatsworth drawings were probably a greater loss to the national heritage than the Badminton Cabinet, which a number of people, including the Duke of Beaufort and myself, thought was a bit of a brute of a thing. It was about this that Riahi had said *il manque le génie du création*, maybe it did.

Selling the Badminton Cabinet, 5 July 1990

The day before the first sale, David Beaufort received a telephone call from a well-known member of the antique trade, who said: 'About the cabinet, David, it's not going to sell. He's a nice boy, Charlie, but he's out of his depth with this one. There's no interest in it, but I have a client who'll give you £3 million if you take it out of the sale.' David thanked him for his call and told him that he wanted to go ahead with the sale and thought I would be able to sell it. In the end, the dealer in question bid up to £6 million. François Curiel went on with his Italian client and eventually Barbara Johnson bid herself and came out the winner. The £8.5 million was a very good price and its pre-eminence as a piece of furniture was maintained when the Prince of Liechtenstein paid £19 million for it when it reappeared at auction on 11 December 2004.

Chapter 21

The market sinks; a new world with the odd success like Degas's *Chevaux de courses* and a beautiful Van Gogh drawing; George Embiricos and the sale of Van Gogh's *Sunflowers with Three Blooms*; a trip around the Western Isles; the Clanwilliam Commode; Holbein's *Lady with a Squirrel and a Starling* and the Tremaine Collection in America

The impressionist sale in London in autumn 1990 was a dismal affair. It had some quite good pictures in it, but there was no discernable interest in most of them. Almost every expensive lot was bought in and only about 20 per cent was sold. The singular exception was the rare Pissarro, *L'Hiver à Montfoucault (Effet de neige)*, which made £1,650,000. I remember hearing one colleague of mine telling a journalist, 'Trees don't grow to the skies'. True enough, the market had to halt somewhere before carrying on this inexorable upward path and although the old biblical cycle of seven fat years followed by seven lean years does not quite still apply, there are cycles. The middle of 1990 marked one and we had to get used to changed circumstances. However, while the total value of the market in 1991 was considerably less than it had been in the previous few years, there were some successes to lighten the gloom.

The impressionist sale in June contained one or two very good pictures; the best was a Degas, *Les Chevaux de courses*, which fetched just over £6 million, and probably would have made more the year before, but it was not a bad price. So enthralled was Degas by this picture, and by wanting to get it right, that he sold it and bought it back again to enable him to finish it better. When it came to us, it belonged to those admirable dealers, the Nathan brothers, and was a fitting tribute to their good taste as well as being a very good racing picture.

Vincent van Gogh. **Jardin de fleurs**, 1888

OPPOSITE

Hans Holbein the Younger. **A Lady with a Squirrel and a Starling (Anne Lovell?)**, 1526-8

Fiona and Mary Sabeti

mist was as heavy as the wind. It also transpired that the captain was quite new to *Astarte* and had never been outside the Mediterranean before.

Fiona, Maria Embiricos and the wife of the Swiss ambassador were all prone to seasickness and were not feeling particularly good by this time. And we had a problem. We could not actually find Staffa. It was a bit like looking for a needle in a haystack. Eventually we did find it and the crew got the recording equipment on deck and made one frankly futile attempt at getting the boat down to move this expensive equipment into the cave, which was occasionally visible through breaks in the rain and the mist. But it just was not going to work. So everything was stowed and we said goodbye to Staffa and any thoughts of Felix Mendelssohn.

The next port of call was to be Iona but we were having doubts about this when we sat down to lunch. Just as the first course had been served, there was a most terrible lurch and we were hit by a freak wave. I say freak, but on that particular day there were quite a few of them around, and the boat keeled over and hung – I believe the technical expression is – in the stays. Anyway, at that point it was either going to capsize or right itself. George went very white. Not a single piece of cutlery, glass, crockery or food was left on the table. Fiona screamed, Maria screamed, the wife of the Swiss ambassador screamed as well. Fortunately the boat did come upright. The captain then appeared, looking terrible, and George and I looked at the charts and decided that we would make for Tobermory in the lee of the Isle of Mull. We made it but I think it had been quite a close-run thing. *Astarte*'s previous owner, Brigadier Tim Landon, had had underwater escape hatches fitted to the bows of the boat. I know he had a bit of a thing about security because he lived in a house near me in Berkshire and I remember it being built. It had armour-plated walls and somebody told me that the escape hatches in the boughs of *Astarte* made it less seaworthy than it had been originally, and the waters off the west coast of Scotland can experience the worst weather in the world, when they set their mind to it.

We cowered in Tobermory and I hired the only bus on the island to take us to Iona. When the worst of the storm had abated and the skipper had got over the worst of

Francisco de Zurbarán. **David with the Head of Goliath**, 1650s

Bartolomé Esteban Murillo. **St Joseph and the Christ Child**, late 1660s

his breakdown, we headed south via Fort William and Oban. I would have loved the opportunity to take another Scottish tour with George, but he never again expressed a wish to go and see the Outer Hebrides.

Other than the excitement of the *Sunflowers with Three Blooms*, the season of 1991 had little to offer by way of impressionist pictures, except for the Degas and Cézanne mentioned above. The annual total amounted to approximately one-third of what had been sold the year before, which gives the reader some indication of how bad the situation had become. But, even in the desert, flowers grow. It is nice to be able to put on record that the best pictures in London came from the Bromley-Davenport family, the owners of Romney's *Portrait of Mrs Davenport*, the picture which had made so much money in the 1920s. This time they were selling something much more important: the Taddeo Gaddi *Altarpiece*, which was as rare as it was beautiful. It made just short of £2 million when it came up for sale on 24 May. In the same sale, bidding for a client, I paid £308,000 for the Bromley-Davenports' Master of the *Manchester Madonna*, a Mannerist painting close to Pontormo. Berenson apparently thought it was by Granacci, but whoever painted it did a good job.

In New York, Stephen Lash and our colleagues, after endless negotiations, secured Imelda Marcos's Collection, and found, among the pairs of shoes, a rare masterpiece: Francisco de Zurbarán's *David with the Head of Goliath*, which relates to the set of pictures of *Jacob and His Twelve Sons* in Auckland Castle, the ancient residence of the Prince Bishops of Durham. (Interestingly the Bishop of Durham was the only prince bishop in the Anglican Communion. The title, however, was repealed by an Act of Parliament in 1836.) The picture was bought for $825,000 by a discerning private collector in France and remains one of the best works by this fascinating painter to have appeared on the market in many years.

Winning a place yet again in the legion of Christie's most faithful clients was Julian Byng who, at the very end of 1990, sold his Murillo *St Joseph and the Christ Child* for £2,420,000. Noël Annesley was favoured by his old friend Ian Woodner with the sale of his beautiful old master drawings. Woodner himself was no mean artist: he could paint pots of flowers as well as Odilon Redon. Prominent in this sale was Primaticcio's red chalk drawing of *Ulysses Shooting through the Rings*. Another drawing from a different century caught the eye in June. Gainsborough's ravishing *Lady Walking in a Garden with a Child*, possibly a study for the *Richmond Water-Walk*, came from America and fetched £616,000.

There were two pieces of furniture that I particularly liked. The first was the Clanwilliam Commode by Johann Gottlob Fiedler. The commode was sent in for sale by the executors of Lord Clanwilliam, whose daughter Mary used to work for me. Their ancestor was a diplomat who attended the Congress of Vienna shortly after leaving Eton. A man of great good taste, he made a number of important purchases on the Continent but nothing finer than this commode, which is of rectangular form and decorated with ormolu of the highest possible quality representing classical figures. The parquetry on the front and sides is set with marquetry roundels of Roman goddesses, some dancing, some playing musical instruments. The whole is surmounted by a specimen marble slab. It is not so much the extraordinary craftsmanship in every element of the commode which makes it so attractive, but that it follows almost exactly the proportions of a Doric temple in its height, length and width. This, surely, is not an accident and it gives one the feeling of looking at a building of extreme elegance rather than a piece of furniture. It made just under £1.6 million, a record price for a piece of German furniture.

BELOW LEFT TO RIGHT

George II silver sideboard dish by Paul de Lamerie

The Clanwilliam Commode by Johann Gottlob Fiedler, c.1785

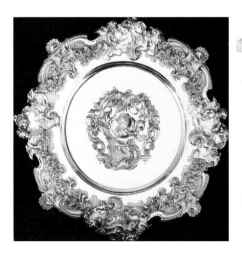

The other record-breaking lot of that year, the de Lamerie George II sideboard dish, was actually sent in for sale by the Government of Norway as part of the deal to settle the debts of Mr Hilmar Reksten. He started his career as captain of a fishing boat working out of the beautiful port of Bergen and ended up one of the world's leading owners of oil tankers, certainly the richest son of Bergen and the richest shipowner in Norway. He was hit, colossally hard, by the crash of the late 1980s. I made several visits to Norway and finally, at a meeting in June, which ran through the 'night' (of course at that time of the year in northern Norway, it does not get dark during the night), we agreed a contract for the sale of the dish. Fetching exactly £100,000 less than the Clanwilliam Commode, its sale price at £1,485,000 was still a record for any piece of silver.

All these works of art were wonderful and figured on the cover of our new slimline, soft-covered austerity *Review of the Season*. The large size of the cover was, as Francis Russell pointed out at the time, a mistake because the volume would not fit on to anybody's book shelf. I thought when he made the comment that it was irritating. It is much more irritating today now that I know it is true. Thank you, Francis!

The year 1992 was another when austerity gripped the art market – austerity only by comparison with the giddy days of the late 1980s. But, as in the year before, only more so, there were some stunning works of art. The frontispiece of the 1992 *Review* is Hans Holbein the Younger's *Lady with a Squirrel and a Starling* (1527). It does not need an adjective to describe it; it speaks for itself. No one is completely sure who the ermine-clad girl is, although she is probably Anne Lovell, wife of Sir Francis Lovell. Squirrels appear in the family coat of arms, echoing the squirrel in the picture, and the starling could refer to the family's seat at East Harling, Norfolk. The foliage in the background is the same as that in two paintings in oil on oak panels by Holbein in the collection of Her Majesty The Queen at Windsor Castle: *Portrait of a Young Man*, *Derich Born*, which is signed and dated 1533, and *Portrait of Sir Henry Guildford*, painted six years earlier. Susan Foister, in her catalogue *Holbein in England*, dates the latter to 1527 although stylistically it would appear closer to the portrait which is dated 1533. The starling has a knowing look. Most people are aware of the aerobatic skills of these birds, evidenced in their murmurations which one can see over the Somerset Levels. What fewer people know is that starlings are amazing mimics and can sing, not just birdsongs but also human songs. For years I was mocked for telling people that we had a starling at home that used to sing at least one Beatles' song, *I Want to Hold Your Hand* (it was very difficult not to listen to this song in 1964 when it came out). I realised that I was not making it up when I read that Mozart had a pet starling which used to accompany him while he was playing the piano.

TOP TO BOTTOM

El Greco. **El Expolio (The Disrobing of Christ)**, *c.*1577-8

Antonello da Messina. **Christ at the Column**, *c.*1475

The second picture to be negotiated in 1992 was the *Portrait of Lieutenant-General The Hon. Sir Charles Stewart, later third Marquess of Londonderry*, by Sir Thomas Lawrence, PRA, the very epitome of swagger. This picture, of the half-brother of Lord Castlereagh, then Foreign Secretary, was commissioned by the sitter's uncle, the

Marquess Camden. The earlier version now hangs in the National Gallery and, if possible, is even better than the present version. Both pictures are superb examples of Lawrence's work. He was the worthy successor to Sir Joshua Reynolds and, like Sir Joshua, a great collector as well a great artist.

Sold to the Louvre was this extraordinarily powerful Antonello da Messina, which came from the Cook Collection. We had attempted to sell it at auction a few years back when it had been inexplicably bought in. On this occasion, the National Gallery borrowed it but very graciously let it go when they discovered that the Louvre wished to buy it. Those who doubted the picture when it came up for sale the first time might like to know that Lucian Freud, who not surprisingly had a very good eye for other people's work, considered this to be the best painting ever to have come up for sale in an auction house in his lifetime. It certainly holds its head high in the distinguished company it keeps here.

Jasper Johns. **Device Circle**, 1959

The star at auction was a painting from the collection of the Earl of Malmesbury, Canaletto's *View of Horseguards*, which was sold on 15 April 1992 for £10,120,000. Noël was the auctioneer and the Andrew Lloyd Webber Foundation the buyer. This was no mean picture either. I must also mention El Greco's *Disrobing of Christ*, which sold later in May for £1,870,000. This picture is probably the preparatory study for the artist's great masterpiece in the Sacristy in Toledo. Along with the other pictures I have referred to, it makes up an impressive gallery in a time of famine. I mentioned Gainsborough's drawing of *Lady Walking in a Garden with a Child* from the year before. *A Peasant Family Going to Market*, the property of Lord Clark's Settlement Trust, was almost as good a drawing and it made £352,000.

There were some decent impressionists that year, even if the prices were depressed. However, what catches the eye looking back was a really good collection of more modern pictures from the Tremaine family in Connecticut. *Premier disque* by Robert Delaunay fetched $5,170,000. From the same collection, Jasper Johns's *Device Circle* made $4,400,000 and Willem de Kooning's *Villa Borghese* $2,090,000. Juan Gris's extraordinary cubist still life of 1913, *Poires et raisins sur une table*, made a record $3.3 million.

Leleu's bureau plat, which had last been bought in 1981 for £303,000 from Lord Lansdowne, was sold by Mrs Barbara Johnson, this time for £1,210,000. Sold by Lord Lansdowne from his de Flahaut connections came an exceptional pair of alabaster vases made originally by Pierre Gouthière for the Duc d'Aumont.

Sam Messer, the property magnate, with the help of John Partridge, had put together a collection of English furniture almost matching in quality anything produced in France. The most expensive lot in the sale was Chippendale's mahogany commode which made £935,000, followed by the Chippendale bookcase which made £374,000. A pair of George II armchairs of exceptional quality, coming from Anthony Ashley-Cooper, fourth Earl of Shaftesbury, made £275,000.

Claude Monet again made his way to the cover of the 1993 *Review of the Season* with *La Jetée du Havre*, but once more, the highlights were in the field of the applied arts. That is not to say we did not still hunger for paintings and, towards the end of 1993, I went to Switzerland with a group of my colleagues (Noël Annesley, John Lumley and Christopher Burge) to see various members of the Koerfer family.

Jacques and Christina Koerfer had put together a beautiful and wide-ranging collection of paintings, drawings and sculpture, principally encompassing the great names of impressionist and post-impressionist painting: Manet, Degas, Cézanne, Lautrec, Sisley, Gauguin, Vlaminck, Picasso, Modigliani, Braque, Matisse and Léger, together with the later masters Mondrian, Jasper Johns, Paul Klee (inevitably) and Giacometti. Jacques Koerfer had died, leaving his widow Christina and the children, of whom Patrick was a particular friend of mine. We had to compete fiercely with Sotheby's for the business, carrying out that alarming process of preparing our presentation in one room, knowing that they were doing exactly the same in another. We won, much to Sotheby's chagrin, as told in Michel Strauss's book about life at Sotheby's. We had discussed how to sell the collection as part of our proposal and then decided that the art market was not in a sufficiently strong state for us to offer the whole collection in one sale. This was obviously a tempting alternative as it would have been a sensation which might have breathed new life into the market, but those with wiser heads won the argument and it was probably the better answer for all concerned. The family, for various reasons of their own, had not particularly wanted a huge, headline-grabbing sale. One obvious advantage for Christie's was that we would have a considerable cache of pictures that we could feed on to the market, at various moments, over the next four or five years. The other advantage was that we gained considerable confidence from having won such a good collection in the face of the fiercest competition.

LEFT TO RIGHT

Louis XVI Egyptian alabaster vase with ormolu mounts, made for the Duc d'Aumont by Pierre Gouthière

Louis XVI bombé mahogany commode with ormolu mounts by Pierre Langlois *c.*1760-5

Peter Carrington retires and is replaced by Anthony Tennant; accusations of collusion with Sotheby's; Pictures by Cézanne from the Pellerin Collection in London; the Marquess of Anglesey's desk; sales from Wrotham; an Assyrian relief from Canford School; exceptional porcelain from Luton Hoo; the remarkable sale of the German computer

Peter Carrington, who had been Chairman of the International Company since Jo Floyd stepped down five years before, decided to retire in May 1993. Peter had been an exceptionally popular Chairman, a man of intelligence and humour, and, given his age and what he had already achieved, extraordinary industry. For me, who had always had an adjoining office to his, his greatest quality was an ability to make one laugh. He was going to be sorely missed. I don't think we realised when he told us all that he wished to go quite how much we would miss him, or how difficult we would find life without him. This was particularly true in the very difficult times we were facing. His replacement, Sir Anthony Tennant, was from a very different business background. Although he and Peter Carrington had a shared past – they had both been to Eton and trained with the Brigade of Guards – the two men could hardly have been more different. It would never have been easy for Anthony Tennant to succeed such a popular figure as Peter Carrington but the financial circumstances made it even more difficult.

We had already been discussing how best we could improve our financial position. As the preceding chapter indicates, we were still winning major business, and we were still able to sell it. The volume, however, had simply disappeared and try as we might we could not, overnight or even over a two- or three-year period, reduce the overheads without seriously damaging the core of the business. We had tentatively

OPPOSITE

André Derain. Le Port de Pêche à Collioure, 1905

Parmigianino portrait. He then consigned Murillo's *St Joseph and the Christ Child*, mentioned earlier, in 1990; a Pieter de Hooch, *The Courtyard of a House in Delft*, the following year; and in 1994, a particularly beautiful Giulio Romano *Holy Family* based on a design of Raphael. We had from the same client some of the finest ormolu-mounted porcelain to come on the market in England, including a pair of Louis XV celadon pot-pourri vases which sold in December 1992 for just short of £250,000 and a Louis XV powder blue pot-pourri vase and cover which fetched £117,000. There was also an important collection of Boulle furniture sold in June 1993, which included a Louis XIV side table that made £177,500, despite its dilapidated condition.

With the benefit of hindsight, Julian would have been better off having one sale of all the things which he drip-fed on to the market. It might have been painful but it would have produced better results. However he chose to organise his affairs, I have to be extremely grateful for his friendship and for the sales which, during my time alone, considerably exceeded £20 million. Julian's son, Robert, still lives at Wrotham which was where Julian Fellowes's *Gosford Park* was filmed, eventually leading to his production of *Downton Abbey*.

The Assyrian relief which came up for sale in July 1994 and fetched £7,701,500 was important then and has a charming story attached to it. It had been bought by Sir John Guest and was left by him and his successors in their house, Canford, near Wimborne. The house eventually became a school and the relief ended up in the tuck shop, where it was whitewashed over and used as a dartboard. This, though, was nothing compared with the fate that it would have suffered had it been left in Iraq, where it was made. Thank goodness for Sir Henry Layard who, under the patronage of Sir Stratford Canning, ambassador in Constantinople, excavated

Vincent van Gogh. **Self-Portrait**, 1889

Assyrian Relief, 883–859BC

Nimrud and Nineveh from whence the Assyrian came down like a wolf on the fold. Layard, who eventually married John Guest's daughter, became a successful politician and received a knighthood but he will always be remembered for his excavations. He removed many large reliefs from Nineveh which otherwise would have been destroyed and they do form a visual basis for our knowledge of that ancient civilisation.

The first of the Koerfer pictures were sold in 1994, including a beautiful cubist Picasso entitled *Violon, bouteille et verre*, which made $6,272,500. But by far the best sale was the final one that took place in New York in November 1998, where the last four pictures were offered and successfully sold: Van Gogh's *Self-Portrait* fetched a spectacular $71.5 million, making it the third highest price paid for a Van Gogh; Cézanne's *Le Château noir* made $11 million; Léger's *Composition (Le Typographe)* reached $6 million; and Miró's *Figure à la bougie* went for $2.3 million. The total for the collection amounted to $157.4 million.

In the spring of 1994 I was starting to work on the contents of Luton Hoo and I found in the strongroom, their existence unknown to the current owners, three of the most remarkable pieces of French mounted porcelain I have ever seen: a pair of aubergine ewers of Chinese origin mounted by Gouthière and a slightly earlier Chinese red and turquoise flambé-glazed vase and cover mounted in Louis XV ormolu. The aubergine ewers were a rival to Charles Clore's *vases œufs*. They made £1,046,500 for the pair, and the single vase just short of £300,000.

Soon after we sold the extraordinary Bronze Age sword, so different but also so beautiful, which is illustrated here. I think it is of quite extraordinary sophistication. The cleverest of modern designers would be hard put to do better than this. It came from Oxborough in Suffolk, and made £51,000.

But the sale which caught the public's imagination that season, and which was, I believe, to have a profound effect on Christie's immediate future, was that of the great couturier Hubert de Givenchy in Monte Carlo at the end of 1993. The *International Herald Tribune* claimed that it was an auction triumph and a historic sale. We travelled the collection from London to Paris and on to its eventual sale in Monte Carlo on 4 December. The most expensive lot was the Boulle Louis XIV ebony, brass and tortoiseshell bureau plat, which fetched £2,145,537. In fact the George II silver chandelier, designed by William Kent, did just better than the table at £2,271,745. We would not have been able to tackle this had we not first held the Clore sale in Monte Carlo the decade before. There was equally no doubt that Givenchy led the way to a series of sales that sustained us through the still doubtful market of the mid-1990s. What the public found intriguing about the Givenchy sale and what attracted other owners like David Cholmondeley (and indeed what has become the norm for what the auction houses now call collector sales) was the sheer diversity of items in the

The Oxborough Dirk, 1500–1300BC

BELOW

Chinese aubergine ewers with ormolu mounts by Pierre Gouthière c.1767

catalogue. It included ormolu and mounted porcelain; clocks; bibelots, like the beautiful pair of Louis XIV *médaillers*; bronzes, such as the Louis XIV group of Nessus and Deianira; splendid porphyry vases; books and bindings; antiquities, including a particularly good marble torso of Aphrodite after Praxiteles; and silver, such as a particularly fine German silver-gilt model of a blackamoor – almost needless to say, from a Rothschild collection. There were good pictures, too, such as a very fine Hoogstaten, *A Youth Reading on Stairs*, carpets and important furniture, including my favourite item, Lot 84, the seemingly ever-present Clore, Ojjeh, Wildenstein and Rothschild *bureau pupitre à écrire debout*. Hubert de Givenchy himself added to everything with his inimitable style, even organising the music for the publicised views, which set a new standard for presentation.

On 19 May 1993 I had been asked to take a sale of German and Austrian art. It was quite a long sale, not very exciting, but Lot 126 was interesting: a nineteenth-century German calculator, which we had been told by the experts was a forerunner to the most sophisticated of modern-day computers. As so often with things of great practical value, it was extremely handsome to look at, with its wheels and dials and stops, and certainly unlike anything else I had ever seen. It came from a client in Australia and we estimated it cautiously at £20,000. I was in a charitable mood so I asked my colleague, Dermot Chichester, whether he would like to sell this lot and I stopped the sale two or three lots beforehand and handed over to Dermot. I walked back to my office, did various things, and about ten minutes later returned to the saleroom to see how much the calculator had made. To my amazement, Dermot Chichester, who was normally a fast and competent auctioneer, was still intoning 'four million five hundred thousand, four million eight hundred thousand, five million'. I stayed, somewhat horror-struck, to watch. Eventually, the calculator was knocked down for £7,700,000. The purchaser was someone who was well known to the firm, having been a leading dealer in watches and instruments in Switzerland. Although the price was way beyond what he would normally have bid in a sale, there was no reason for us to doubt his bona fides. The underbidder, who was not so well known to us, had been checked out, and again there was no reason to doubt him. At the time we felt, although there was no way in which we could discover whether our hunch was correct or not, that one of the two bidders was acting for Bill Gates who, with his huge wealth and position in the field, and a known auction buyer, was an obvious candidate.

Bureau pupitre attributed to Joseph Baumhauer, *c.*1758

People do ask from time to time what happens if someone does not pay. In legal terms the answer to this is perfectly simple. If the auction house has not relinquished the object, or done some special deal to alter their normal terms of sale (as was the case over the calculator), they have no liability if the buyer defaults. We discovered quite soon after the sale that the buyer was suffering from severe and terminal cancer which had clouded his senses. If the blame must lie with someone, it must be with his wife, poor woman, who was with him at the time and who suspected that he did not know what he was doing. The underbidder has no responsibility to repeat his bid, nor does he have to justify his bidding. He made it clear in this case that he was not interested after the sale. This was hardly surprising. The successful bidder was not going to be the buyer.

We felt desperately sorry for the Australian owners who for a very few hours must have felt they had really hit the jackpot. We did compensate them, to a level they might have expected to get for the calculator had it not been for these two extraordinary bidders, but why two people should have behaved like this remains a mystery. I have never seen an auctioneer looking more unhappy at getting a record price for a lot when he finally knocked the calculator down. But, other than stopping the sale somewhere along the line, I cannot see what he could possibly have done. It was an extraordinarily unfortunate incident but one, as I think this story shows, where there were no villains, just victims.

In October 1993, a picture by Thomas Gainsborough, *Peasants Going to Market*, came up for sale but was sold privately by its owners, the Council of Royal Holloway College, for £3.5 million. This was the culmination, and small reward, for the number of years that I had been closely involved with Royal Holloway College.

I had always been intrigued by this institution because, as a boy at Eton, one of the places we were allowed to visit with our parents was the Savill Garden at Windsor, the entrance to which is almost opposite that of Holloway College, housed in a vast red-brick pastiche of Chambord, built from 1879 by the architect William Crossland, a pupil of Sir George Gilbert Scott. Crossland had spent three months in 1873 sketching Chambord with a view to building the college. The deeds of foundation were drawn up in 1876. Holloway College was 'to afford the best education suitable for women of the middle and upper classes'. It was the first institution for higher education exclusively for women founded in this country. Holloway had determined that the college should have a gallery where the students could appreciate great works of art. He set about acquiring what he considered to be masterpieces: Gainsborough's *Peasants Going to Market* from the late eighteenth century was certainly one; another, from the early nineteenth century, was one of Constable's famous six-footers, a *Sketch for a View on the Stour*; from the mid-nineteenth century, Turner's *Van Tromp Going About to Please His Masters* was a third.

Holloway also possessed an earlier masterpiece, *St Francis in the Desert* by Giovanni Bellini. He had bought it, not at auction, but with his house near Egham, which he used when supervising the work on the college. He obviously did not like the picture. He had no recorded interest in old master paintings and he only acquired it with the house from a Mr Dingwall, who had previously bought it at Christie's on 19 June 1852 when, as Lot 48, it fetched 700 guineas. Holloway never moved the picture into the college and it remained in the house until his death, when it passed to his sister-in-law, Miss Mary Ann Driver. Colnaghi's bought it from her trustees in 1912 and then, with Knoedler, it was sold to Henry Clay Frick in 1915. At the time of its acquisition by Colnaghi's, Mrs Bernard Berenson, who had seen it in London, had written to Isabella Stewart Gardner to tell her that it was 'the most beautiful Bellini in existence, the most profound and spiritual picture ever painted in the Renaissance'.

Thomas Gainsborough. **Peasants Going to Market**, 1770

It is strange that a collector as resolute as Thomas Holloway should have allowed something quite as good as the Frick Bellini to pass through his hands, so to speak, unremarked. His pursuit of Victorian masterpieces was much more resolute and successful. This is not the place to review exhaustively the collection. As I wrote earlier, we sold the Gainsborough privately and the Turner was, very cleverly, sold by the college itself to the Getty Museum, saving any commission, for what were then, I think, record prices.

However, these pictures did not form the core of the collection, which was represented by Millais's *The Princes in the Tower*, Luke Fildes's *Applicants for Admission to the Casual Ward* and Frank Holl's *Newgate Committed for Trial*. Even more important was Frith's wonderful *Railway Station* – a masterpiece in the artist's oeuvre rivalled only by *Derby Day*.

Two other pictures need special mention and they were both bought at Christie's. Landseer's *Man Proposes, God Disposes*, first sold on 28 May 1881, fetched £6,615, an auction record for any work of art. It depicts the destruction by two polar bears of the remains of Franklin's ill-fated effort to navigate the North-West Passage. It is of interest to me personally as my family brewery was asked to provide unfreezable beer for the expedition. The gallery in which it hangs was used by the middle-class lady students to take their exams and, during this period, the Landseer was always covered by a Union flag as it was felt it would bring back luck. It remained his most expensive work until the appearance at auction some years later of the *Monarch of the Glen* which made £7,245.

The other picture, which coincidentally made the same price as *Man Proposes, God Disposes* when it came up for sale on 13 May 1882, was Edwin Long's *The Babylonian Marriage Market*. The idea for this popular subject came from Herodotus, the great Greek historian, who wrote that the first ever auctions took place in Babylonian villages for the dispersal of maidens into marriage. George C. Swayne, in his *History of Herodotus*, goes on to say that the convention of Babylonians was to auction off the young women in an order judged on their appearance, so that the prettiest girl would be auctioned first and so on until even the plainest was got rid of to some cynical worthy who decidedly preferred lucre to looks. This is beautifully portrayed in the picture, with the prettiest girl sitting on the right gazing at her own image in the mirror and the poor old girl on the left waiting her luck with an air of resignation. Edwin Long used James Christie III as a model for his auctioneer, except that his face was covered in a large, black beard, and he used Christie's room and rostrum for the setting of this splendid scene.

Edwin Long. **The Babylonian Marriage Market**, 1875

What is perplexing is how this subject should ever have been thought suitable for Holloway College, but popular it was, and when it was sold at Christie's, the sale was received with a round of applause and, when the hammer fell, loud cheering! The sum Holloway paid was thought to be quite exceptional and was, I have stated earlier, a saleroom record until 1892. The subject is less popular today and I was warned when giving lectures in America never to use my slide of Long's masterpiece, nor to mention the custom it depicted.

Chapter 23

The Houghton sale; Monet's *Cathédrale de Rouen*; George Dawe and his *Portrait of Mrs White*; Donald Trump; Joseph Hazen's pictures; Bermejo's *St Michael Triumphant*; *Whistlejacket*

It was as a direct result of the Givenchy sale, organised so beautifully by Charles Cator and his team in the Furniture Department, that Lord Cholmondeley, worn down by trying to deal with the government over the contents of Houghton, came to us and asked if we could do something like that sale for him.

The Houghton sale at the very end of 1994 was, like its precursor the Givenchy sale, a showstopper. Lord Cholmondeley – David from here on in – had inherited Houghton on his father's death. He realised that he had to spend a great deal of money on it. For those who don't know the house, it was built for Sir Robert Walpole, prime minister of Great Britain under Georges I and II. It is said of Walpole that he had a greater knowledge and control of the realm than any other monarch or politician, with the exception of Thomas Cromwell in the reign of Henry VIII. But as well as being a hugely successful prime minister, although at moments controversial, he was also a great builder.

Most of the outside of the house was the work of James Gibbs and Colen Campbell, and William Kent was responsible for the inside (and parts of the outside). Other architects are also said to have been involved in the project, in particular Thomas Ripley and Isaac Ware, but it is safe to say that the majority of the work was shared between Gibb, Campbell and Kent and it is hard to think of three better practitioners. The house was built by Sir Robert for the dual purpose of hunting and politics, two pastimes that were not indulged in by the fair sex then – not in England in any case. And no woman, not even his wife, to whom he was happily married, spent more than the odd day at Houghton.

What is more extraordinary, and in some ways surprising, is that Sir Robert, while being noted as a collector and a buyer of pictures, also received most in the form of gifts and profited considerably from his position as paymaster general, which entitled him to sell commissions. *Plus ça change* … The thing which distinguished him from latter-day practitioners of these dark arts was his taste.

The chimneypiece in the stone hall at Houghton Hall

OPPOSITE

George Stubbs. **Whistlejacket**, 1762

201

While prime minister, he ran the country extremely well. He ran his own affairs, however, with a reckless disregard as to who would pay the bills. He died in debt and his son was similarly impoverished. The estate passed from his son Robert, second Lord Orford, to his son, George, third Lord Orford, to Sir Robert's third son, Horace Walpole, fourth Lord Orford and finally to Horace's sister, Mary, who married the third Earl of Cholmondeley. The house then suffered a hundred years of neglect by the eventual heirs, the Cholmondeleys – not only neglect but also attempts to sell the house, in some cases with its contents. But nobody was prepared to take on the house, from which the majority of the pictures had been removed and sold to Catherine the Great of Russia on a valuation done by James Christie. Interestingly it was also Christie, wearing not an auctioneer's hat but that of a retired naval officer, who supervised their passage up the Baltic to St Petersburg.

Houghton Hall

The house was revived by David's grandparents, Sybil Sassoon and the fifth Marquess of Cholmondeley. They both loved Houghton and, armed with Sassoon money and Sassoon taste, set about restoring it to its former glory with some success. But, even so,

Jean-François de Troy. **La Lecture de Molière**, *c.*1730

when David inherited, a great deal needed to be done. Having discussed a number of options with David himself, Charlie Cator and I went round the house trying to select a group of works of art which reflected the historic Houghton of Sir Robert Walpole and the restored Houghton of David's grandmother, Sybil, and her brother, Philip Sassoon who, to a great extent, had helped her. I hope we succeeded, partly because it is what we set out to do, and partly because I think Houghton is the most beautiful house I have ever known, both inside and out. The unique combination of beauty and history makes it imperative that it should survive.

The Boulle *coffres de toilette ou mariage* made just over £1.5 million. The beautiful Rubens sketch, *The Marriage by Proxy of Princess Marie de' Medici and King Henri IV of France*, which came in fact from the Cholmondeley family, made £1.7 million. The most expensive lot, *La Lecture de Molière* by Jean-François de Troy, had originally belonged to King Frederick the Great of Prussia, and passed from Sir Philip Sassoon to his sister; it made £3.9 million.

The Houghton Louis XVI Sèvres pair of pot-pourri vases

Anyway, going round the house today does not (I am of course biased) feel as if one is in an empty shell and, in any case, the majority of lots in the sale came not from historic Houghton but from the no-less-beautiful additions made by Lady Cholmondeley. The sale took place in London on the evening of 8 December 1994 and we had arranged a prior view of the collection in Paris, which was extremely well attended. When I climbed out of the rostrum nearly three hours later, David Cholmondeley was £21 million better off.

The sale was not quite as easy as some had imagined. One particular lot, the pair of porphyry and gilt-bronze two-handled lion vases, was returned sometime after the sale and subjected to long litigation, ending in Christie's being exonerated, but I always felt sorry for the purchaser. She was wrongly advised to attack Christie's and she eventually resold the vases, not for what she had paid for them but in fact for exactly the original saleroom estimate. But the litigation had cost her a very great deal of money and to an extent it removed the gilt from the gingerbread, in what was otherwise a spectacularly successful sale.

In late 1993, when David Cholmondeley and I were discussing the early details of the sale, he asked if I would like to stay for a weekend in December to shoot. I accepted with alacrity. Sadly, Fiona could not come due to some commitment with the children but David's other weekend guests were highly entertaining. David was at the time seeing Lisa B, the ravishingly beautiful actress, now Mrs Anton Bilton.

As well as Lisa B, there was an old friend of mine, Sabrina Guinness, now married to the playwright Tom Stoppard, and happily living in Dorset; another old friend and sometime colleague Christopher Balfour, whom I always call 'Curly'; and lastly, the legendary Debo Devonshire and her then teenage grandson, Billy Burlington. It was a wonderful group and we had a really enjoyable evening on the first night.

In those days, I used to run a lot and I went out for half an hour before breakfast the next morning. On my return, the butler greeted me and said, 'Mr Allsopp, please would you call your wife, it is rather urgent.' I got into my car to use the old black brick-like telephone and called Fiona. 'My darling,' she said. I sensed the foreboding in her voice, 'Are you having a lovely time?' 'Yes,' I said, 'I think I am in love with Lisa B!' 'I'm so sorry but you must call your mother.' I was devoted to my mother but I had a foreboding about this particular conversation. 'Must I?' I said, rather feebly. 'Yes, I think you must call her.' You can guess why. I could. My father had been ill for some time and had been, for several years, in a rather forbidding home at Amesbury. In Dad's mediumly lucid moments, he thought he was back at Hindlip. The two houses had a certain faded nineteenth-century grandeur, as did the inmates. I steeled myself and rang my mother, feeling the weekend slipping away. 'Oh darling, you've heard?' 'Yes, Mum, I really am so sorry.' 'I want you to meet me at the undertakers in Amesbury at twelve o'clock.' 'That's going to be difficult,' I said; 'I am in Norfolk and I have just come in from a run, I don't think you want me in my very old shorts and trainers at the undertakers.' We compromised at 2 pm. I went back into the house and bumped into Debo. 'Come on Charlie, we're off in five minutes, aren't you coming shooting?', she asked. 'I don't think so, Debo,' I replied. 'But you know about these things. You can tell me what I ought to do.' 'Why?', she asked. 'Dad's just died.' 'No,' said Debo, 'you are not coming shooting.' She was right. I thanked David, tipped the butler – it wasn't his fault – and set off on the long drive to Amesbury. Like so many fathers and sons, my relationship with Dad was complicated but I couldn't let my mother deal with a particularly gloomy undertaker all by herself. As I wove my way through the Saturday traffic of most of southern England I mused about the extraordinary lengths some people have gone to to acquire a title. During the next few hours, I was not amongst them.

This story has a rather good postscript. Leaving David Cholmondeley one gun down for his best shoot fortunately did not mean we lost the sale. The plans proceeded apace and at the reception in Paris, hosted the following June by 'The Chairman of Christie's Europe, Lord Hindlip', I was accosted by Philippine de Rothschild. 'Charlie, I thought I knew everyone at Christie's but I don't know this Lord Hindlip. Would you introduce me?' When I finally explained it to her, she said 'I never understand the English.'

Claude Monet. **La Cathédrale de Rouen**, **effet d'après-midi (Le portail, plein soleil)**, 1892-4

There were, in 1995, some signs that the market was recovering and none clearer than the sale on 26 June of Monet's *La Cathédrale de Rouen, effet d'après-midi*. The picture sold for £7.6 million (just over $12 million) and was the object of spirited bidding. In 1965, when I was in New York with John Richardson, there was an exhibition of Monet, organised by the late Alfred Barr, then director of the Museum of Modern Art. The exhibition catalogue claimed that Monet was the father of modern art. John strongly contested this and also tried to instil in me a belief that the early paintings like *La Terrasse à Sainte-Adresse*, which I, like many others, was so attached to, were not his best things and that the series paintings from the 1880s and 1890s, were so much more interesting. This picture, executed in 1894, is a prime example of the latter. I now agree with John. This and pictures like it, with their shimmering light and sometimes almost fuzzy outlines, are Monet's real contribution to the history of art, but they are not the precursors of modern painting.

ABOVE LEFT TO RIGHT

Andy Warhol. **Shot Red Marilyn**, 1964

Roy Lichtenstein. **Kiss II**, 1962

However, modern art was well represented that year with two great images: Andy Warhol's *Shot Red Marilyn* which sold for $3.6 million in November 1994 and Lichtenstein's *Kiss II* which made just over $2.5 million in May 1995. I hesitate to say this but if you don't like the Warhol I think you have a problem.

Mrs White, *née* Watford – not as pretty as Marilyn Monroe but hardly a bad-looking lady – was painted in 1809 by one of Sir Thomas Lawrence's pupils, George Dawe, RA. The portrait was sent in for sale by Valentine Abdy, who worked for a time for Sotheby's, on behalf of the executors of his father Sir Robert Abdy's estate. The picture made £177,500, a very good price in those days. But what really intrigued me was that it reminded me of one of my favourite novels, Evelyn Waugh's *A Handful of Dust*.

I went to Hatchards recently and they were running a competition where everyone had to vote for their favourite novel. I rather hoped that Evelyn Waugh would win. The people's favourite was *The Warden* by Trollope which, I have to admit, is a very good book. But what did George Dawe have to do with *A Handful of Dust*? He shared a similar fate with its hero, the luckless Tony Last, who ended his life having to read *Little Dorrit* time and again to his captor on a remote stretch of the River Amazon. George Dawe, immediately after the Congress of Vienna in 1815, had to go to Russia and paint, at the instigation of Tsar Alexander I, all 329 of the Russian generals who had distinguished themselves in the Napoleonic Wars. I don't think poor Dawe ever returned from St Petersburg. Tony Last certainly never made it back from the Amazon.

Picasso's *Le Miroir*, which I think (a matter of opinion of course) to be the most successful of all the Boisgeloup paintings, made $20,022,500 on 7 November 1995.

George Dawe. **Portrait of Mrs White (née Watford), full-length in a White Silk Dress**, 1809

Just over a year later, also in New York, Willem de Kooning's *Woman, 1949* fetched $15,622,500, which was the highest price for a work of art sold at auction in 1996. The last time a work by a living artist had been the most expensive picture sold during the year was 1882, with the sale of Edwin Long's *Babylonian Marriage Market*. I suspect that time will treat de Kooning more kindly than it has Edwin Long, but you never know.

Going back to 1995, I was asked by my colleague in New York, Stephen Lash, if I would go to Palm Beach to meet the property tycoon Donald Trump, who had just acquired Mar-a-Lago, the legendary home of Marjorie Merriweather Post, the founder of General Foods. The name gives away the near unique situation of the property, which stretches from the ocean to the lake or, as it is otherwise known, the inland waterway, which runs the whole length of Florida from north to south. I had always been intrigued about the house because of another story John Richardson told me, about a conversation which took place there between the bedridden Marjorie Merriweather Post and her equally famous niece, Barbara Hutton. Miss Hutton had just divorced her sixth husband and, sitting at the end of Mrs Post's huge bed, she was given some unsolicited advice about keeping a man by her four-times-married aunt. Now, I suppose, all this pales into insignificance compared with the fame of the current owner (who, by the time this book is published, may be the president of the United States) for whom I was asked to undertake the valuation and whom I found extremely straightforward to deal with; although he did not sell any great works of art, we had a successful sale of the things in Mar-a-Lago which he did not want.

New York had the whip hand over London in the year in question. The collection of Joseph Hazen contained two special pictures: Juan Gris's *Le Jacquet*, which made $3.4 million, and a very composed Degas, entitled *Femme au tub*, which sold for $5,447,500.

Old masters sold at auction were slightly thin on the ground in 1996. There was, however, an English picture by Richard Wilson, RA, *An Extensive Welsh Landscape*, one of the most beautiful by the artist I have ever seen, which fetched £210,500 – not a huge price but English landscape painting at its best. In 1979, I commented that I would like to have bought a Pietro da Cortona drawing, *Head of an Angel*. That came up again in 1996 and its price had risen from £7,000 to £111,500.

The painting of *St Michael Triumphant* by Bartolomé de Cárdenas, called 'Bermejo', which was the best picture without any doubt, was sold by private treaty to the National Gallery. I did the negotiation for this picture and I know the gross price was around £18 million. It came yet again from that great treasure house Luton Hoo, and was reunited with its old bedfellow, Altdorfer's *The Agony in the Garden*.

Luton Hoo was writ large that year because it was, during the eighteenth century, the home of the Marquesses of Bute, who coincidentally had a whole sale in Christie's on 3 July. The enormous Maggiolini desk, which made £1,651,000, had probably not been at Luton Hoo but many of the other things in the sale certainly had, and the most desirable lots were a series of Paul Sandbys, exquisite watercolours of Luton Hoo itself. The most expensive sold for £375,500.

The 1997 season was one where the biblical feast replaced any lingering thoughts of famine or lean cows. Wherever one looked, one could find exciting works of art being traded for huge sums of money. First, though, a warning for the overhasty into which category I, and many others, fell, over the Bellinter tables. In that year's *Review*, there is a large colour photograph of one of them which states that, according to a family tradition, these magnificent marble-slab side tables were supplied in about 1740 to John Preston (who died in 1753) for the Hall at Bellinter House, Co. Meath. Bellinter House was destroyed by a fire, as were many of the houses in the Republic. Along with the tables came a rather faded, smudgy photograph purporting to depict the tables in situ at Bellinter. They were sold on 17 April – I am almost sure I was the auctioneer – for £600,000, and bought by a discerning collector from the Far East. He was thrilled. We were thrilled. The owners were obviously thrilled. We were only slightly suspicious when two others of quite similar date and decoration, which, like the Bellinter tables, had interesting provenances, were sent in a few months afterwards. We catalogued and sold them. But, before they could be collected and paid for, yet another similar pair of tables appeared with an even more 'interesting' provenance. This time, we asked the help of the leading furniture restorer in London, who came along with his boy scout knife and scratched off several layers of almost completely new paint. All the tables were of recent manufacture. We wrote to the nice man in the Far East who was terribly upset and initially refused to accept any payment from us but in the end it was agreed that he would take a refund but keep the tables on the understanding he had them stamped to say they were made *c*.1995. Those who had brought in the other two tables fled before Miss Marple, Hercule Poirot or that nice Christopher Foyle could lay their hands on them.

But it does just go to show that if you can invent a good enough story to persuade somebody to suspend their critical faculties, you can fool most of the people most of the time. Of course, when you look at these tables with the knowledge that they are fakes, you can find fault with them, but when you are confronted with a photograph claiming to show them in the nineteenth century in their original eighteenth-century setting, it is not so easy. I don't think that there were many other fakes sold that year.

Stubbs's portrait of *Whistlejacket* certainly was not. This majestic picture, now in the National Gallery, was by family tradition (and a family tradition a good deal more reliable than that surrounding the Bellinter tables) intended to have been a monumental equestrian portrait of King George III. *Whistlejacket*'s owner and Stubbs's patron, Charles, second Marquess of Rockingham, fell out with his sovereign over the American War of Independence. I have, from

The Rockingham Silver Ewer and Dish by David Willaume, 1726

OPPOSITE

Bartolomé de Cardenas (Bermejo). **Saint Michael Triumphant over the Devil with the Donor Antonio Juan**, 1468

time to time in this book, mentioned both my gratitude and affection for Juliet Tadgell (*née* Fitzwilliam) from whose family this picture came. I have not, however, done justice to the second Marquess of Rockingham, who was the patron of Stubbs, served twice as prime minister and was a man of considerable intelligence, aided by Edmund Burke, his secretary, one of the most influential political thinkers of his time. Both Rockingham and Burke were informed, wise and far-sighted enough to have supported the independence of the American colonies.

Lord Rockingham's taste was as exceptional as that of his father, Thomas Watson Wentworth, the builder of the magnificent Wentworth Woodhouse and prodigious patron of the arts, who, amongst much else, commissioned David Willaume to make the Rockingham ewer and dish illustrated here. The dish was one of the most beautiful pieces of silver I ever handled, and can be compared with de Lamerie's sideboard dish illustrated on page 186. *Whistlejacket* was to have formed a pair to the other life-sized portrait of one of Lord Rockingham's stallions, *Scrub*, now in the collection of the Earl of Halifax. But Lord Rockingham changed his mind again; he did not really like the picture of Scrub and did not think it was a fitting pair for *Whistlejacket*. Whatever the reasons, *Whistlejacket* lived in solitary splendour at Wentworth Woodhouse, spent a short time at St Osyth's Priory and then moved to the National Gallery which acquired it for a gross price of £15,750,000. Every time I see it, I become more and more convinced that it is the greatest picture ever painted by an Englishman and will almost certainly remain so.

Chapter 24

Michelangelo's *Risen Christ*; sales for the Loeb family and for Victor and Sally Ganz; Diana, Princess of Wales and the sale of her dresses; the estate of Marilyn Monroe and the sale of her sequinned 'Happy Birthday' dress; the Sensation exhibition; my interview with Ali G; reality in 1998; Van Gogh's drawing; the Wentworth sale

There were two collections we secured in New York which certainly reinforced our position vis-à-vis Sotheby's. More important than that, in retrospect, they defined clearly how the market was changing. One can always argue whether or not the crash of 1990 had a direct bearing on this change of direction; I suspect it did. Tastes were changing. One of the factors that drives change in the art market is the rarity of the particular works of art one is trying to sell. Many people think that if something is rare it has to be valuable. In reality the reverse is true. You cannot create a market in rare works of art because the market requires a plentiful supply. Occasionally something really exceptional comes up for sale like, for example, Michelangelo's drawing of *The Risen Christ*, which appeared on 4 July 2000 and fetched over £8 million – a huge price because everyone has heard of Michelangelo. But, by and large, it is the people who collect works of art who create the market because they want to buy what their peers do. There is nothing wrong with wanting to keep up with the Joneses – it is the natural competitive urge of successful men and women. It is the reason why, after the event, we discovered there were at least six people all prepared to bid more than £20 million for Van Gogh's *Sunflowers*. But this sort of popularity is only sustainable when there is a supply which enables the Joneses to keep up with each other. In the 1970s and the 1980s there was still, as I hope this book shows, a plentiful source of really good impressionist and post-impressionist

Henri de Toulouse-Lautrec.
Danseuse assise aux bas roses, 1890

OPPOSITE

Pablo Picasso. **Femme assise dans un fauteuil (Eva)**, 1913 pictures. By the later 1990s, this was becoming less true. Two collections show this clearly: the first, that of the late John and Peter Loeb, was primarily of impressionist and post-impressionist masterpieces; the second, that of Victor and Sally Ganz, dealt exclusively with the twentieth century. Both these collections were known to me, in the first case very well.

I visited the Loebs with Jo Floyd within my first few days of working at Christie's in New York. It was the first major collection of impressionist pictures I ever saw there and it made a lasting impression on me with its Monets, Cézannes, Van Gogh's *Oleanders* above the fireplace and a portrait of *Madame Cézanne* and Picasso's 1901 *Arlequin assis* in the same room.

Peter Loeb was a niece of Governor Lehman and her husband was the very successful senior partner of Loeb Rhoades. Their eldest daughter, Judy, was a close friend of mine and had been married to a very good-looking American fighter pilot, Dick Beaty, who was one of those volunteers who fought with the Allies in Europe before America had even entered the war. Her brother, John, also an old friend, became US ambassador to Denmark after a career in the family firm. Judy's younger sister, Ann, married Edgar Bronfman. Her younger brother Arthur, a bachelor, was the most popular rare book dealer in New York and the youngest child, Debbie, was married first to one friend of mine, David Davies, and then to another, James Brice.

On either side of the war, this family represented the aristocracy of New York and their collecting and philanthropy reflected this. No description of the Loeb family should omit a reference to Peter's elder sister, Helen Buttenwieser, who was a barrister. It was she who, in the interests of justice and when no one else would, defended the Communist spy Alger Hiss in the Cold War America of Senator McCarthy. This was an incredibly brave thing to do.

I do not want to claim undue credit. I played only a small part in acquiring the business for Christie's. Stephen Lash, then head of the Estates Department in New York, was married to Wendy Lehman, a cousin, who was also a close friend of the family, as was Christopher Burge. The sale took place on 12 May 1997 and did well, reaching the third highest total for a private collection. Cézanne's portrait of his wife made $23,102,500 and his *Les Toits de l'Estaque*, $12.6 million. *Portrait de Manet par lui-même, en buste (Manet à la palette)* fetched $18,702,500 and, regarded by many as the most desirable lot in the sale, Toulouse-Lautrec's *Danseuse assise aux bas roses* sold for $14.5 million. For the record, the Van Gogh and the Picasso had already been pledged to the Metropolitan Museum. The sale, as successful as it was, did not quite generate the huge excitement the Ganz sale did that autumn.

John Richardson had taken me to see Victor and Sally Ganz shortly after he arrived in New York in January 1967. They were old friends from his days of

Pablo Picasso. **Nu couché**, 1942

living with Douglas Cooper, next door to Picasso in the south of France. I have to admit to being less than blown away by the collection when I first saw it, with its fierce late Picassos, magnificent Rauschenbergs and Jasper Johns, but these were hardly familiar to me in the 1970s, although I subsequently grew to love them, as did the enormous number of people who came to view the sale in New York in November 1997.

The sale, conducted by Christopher Burge with his usual aplomb, was an absolute triumph, and everything made way above expectations, with the possible exception, strangely, of the earliest of the Picassos, the great cubist *Femme assise dans un fauteuil*. This only just exceeded its estimate and was bought by that most discerning of cubist collectors Leonard Lauder, who, with the generosity for which he is famous, has now given the picture, along with much of the rest of his cubist collection, to the Metropolitan Museum.

The prices were amazing, but an exception was Jasper Johns's strange variant of Picasso's equally strange 1936 *Chapeau de paille*. It did not really work, and it did not sell. I had a personal disappointment in the fact that I expected to buy Lot 49, Picasso's fantastic *Nu couché* of 30 September 1942, but was outbid by Heinz Berggruen for his museum in Berlin at $14.5 million. There was a top price of $31.9 million for one of Picasso's *Femmes d'Alger* series and the highest price in the sale was for his *Le Rêve*, which made $48.4 million. But no two juxtaposed collections ever showed this shift in taste more clearly. As a personal footnote to this, when I first saw Picasso's *Chat à l'oiseau*, I found it disturbing. I now actually love this picture and wish I could own it myself.

By the time the last Ganz pictures were sold it was already fairly clear that the market as a whole had recovered and, although nothing at the time made as much as Van Gogh's *Portrait du Dr Gachet*, in quite a short time two of the Ganz pictures had become the world's most expensive – a testament to the Ganzes' extraordinary taste and the fact that, by now, buyers preferred works from the twentieth and twenty-first centuries.

In June 1997, I had to make one more trip to New York to conduct a sale not of pictures, nor furniture, nor silver, but frocks. It all started a long time ago.

In the hall at Althorp, home of the Spencer family, there is a small picture of the Empress Elizabeth, Archduchess of Austria, jumping a fence and accompanied by a young man,

Leaving a reception at Christie's, King Street, with Princess Diana

both of them suitably mounted. In 1875, the Empress, most certainly bored with her life, had enquired of Queen Victoria whether she might be able to hunt in England and Ireland. The Queen eventually decided to ask Lord Spencer, recently returned from Ireland where he had been viceroy, to entertain her and find a suitable pilot. Lord Spencer by this time was old and had given up hunting. However, while viceroy, his ADC, a fellow officer in the 12th Lancers, had been my great-grandfather, Bay Middleton, whom he knew to ride well. At first Lord Spencer's entreaties were met with a stern refusal. Bay had just become engaged to a well-off Scottish lady and was planning to settle down. He was not interested, he is recorded as having said, in being a nanny.

However, on meeting the Empress, he put his matrimonial plans on hold and for the next eight years he squired the Empress over the huge fences of the Pytchley and elsewhere in Leicestershire and Cheshire and latterly in Ireland. He even went to stay with the Empress to hunt in Hungary where he received a mixed reception. He had no title, but the fact that he rode well and had been in a good regiment made him socially acceptable in England in the second half of the nineteenth century. The same was not universally true in the archduchy. Some, the keener horsemen, accepted him on face value as a good sport and a chap, while others did not.

However, this was immaterial because at some stage he would have to give up what was in all probability a platonic relationship with the Empress and return to his would-be bride, who was fast and unsurprisingly getting bored of waiting.

All this I discussed with the Princess of Wales when I first met her, early in her courtship with Prince Charles. She was not overly impressed, not being particularly fond of hunting, but I liked her and saw her again from time to time. She came once or twice to Christie's for charity events and there is a very nice photograph of us leaving the building together which I have always been fond of. After the sad break-up of her marriage I occasionally saw her but it was not to me that Princess Diana made her initial approach about possibly selling her dresses for charity, but to my colleague and friend, Christopher Balfour. He had been our adviser when he worked at Hambros Bank, and what a good adviser he had been. When he left the bank, we offered him a position at Christie's. Although he was not really interested in works of art, he was a superb ambassador for the firm and his involvement in securing the sale of the dresses was only one of a number of important jobs he did for Christie's.

I confess I know next to nothing about haute couture or indeed any couture. My wife was famously economical and normally acquired her clothes at Marks and Spencer 'in the sale', so I could contribute next to nothing to the sales plan. But I did suggest in the early stages that perhaps some of the proceeds of the sale should go to the Royal Marsden Hospital, one of the hospitals which treated my wife through her long illness. The remainder of the proceeds of the sale was to go to the London Lighthouse, an admirable charity with which Curly was involved, and which did excellent work for those suffering from the curse of HIV. The other person who has to be mentioned in the context of the dress sale was the redoubtable Meredith Etherington-Smith, who masterminded the photographs, the production of the catalogue and much of the ensuing sale in New York. I was only brought in as the auctioneer.

I had seen Diana on occasions in the run-up to the sale which, although attracting huge publicity, I always felt might be difficult. But, come the day before the auction, Princess Diana was to attend a reception at Christie's and Curly, Meredith and I, along with various other luminaries from the charities involved, lined up outside our premises on Park Avenue. The limousine arrived and I stepped forward to greet the Princess. In the flash of seemingly thousands of cameras and to guide her through the throng of journalists, paparazzi and well-wishers, I placed a perfunctory hand on her shoulder. I was appalled when I awoke the next morning to see that I had been accused of putting my hand on a quite different part of her anatomy. I rang my old friend, Princess Margaret, to apologise to her and all her relations and repeated my denials. She told me not to be so silly. 'Surely you know how they made that photograph', she said, and she explained how it had been done. I suppose that, with her considerable experience of photography, she should have known. I did not, but it took some of the sting out of what I found a thoroughly unpleasant situation, although I have to confess to a sense-of-humour failure on the subject.

The reception itself went off extremely well and Princess Diana was quite remarkable. She seemed to know everyone in the room, irrespective of the fact that she had never met any of them before in her life, and she was charming to them all. Princess Diana left for England that evening. I talked to her after the sale and made a date to have dinner to discuss it. I never saw her again.

The sale was, I suppose, a great success. It was also extremely difficult as publicity does not (as every auctioneer knows) always turn into bids at the sale. Some things went well, others were very sticky, and the much-photographed hoorah that I gave at the end of the sale was as much out of relief as exultation. That was another fifteen minutes of Andy Warhol's fame, but it was nothing like as satisfying as the *Sunflowers*.

I did experience something to equal that satisfaction two years later, again in New York, although I was suffering from the most appalling cold bordering on flu. This was the sale of Marilyn Monroe's 'Happy Birthday Mr President' sequinned dress, into which that greatest and most glamorous of film stars had been sewn with, so the story goes, absolutely nothing on underneath, to give her great rendition of the well-known song for JFK in Madison Square Garden. Somehow the dress retained some of the magic of Marilyn Monroe whom sadly I had never met. The sale as a whole on 27 October 1999 was a huge success, especially the wonderful sequinned dress, which made $1,267,500. That really was quite something.

The 'Happy Birthday Mr President' sequinned dress worn by Marilyn Monroe

Prior to his arrival at Christie's, Anthony Tennant had had a fundraising role with the Royal Academy and had been quite a serious collector of British painting. This led to his suggestion that we sponsor the Sensation exhibition, in effect the public exhibition of the Saatchi Collection. At best, this was a dubious undertaking. One discerning French friend dismissed it with some justification as puerile and boring. I had worries about the exhibition, misplaced as it turned out, but I missed the picture which caused serious offence and had to be withdrawn from the London show, Marcus Harvey's *Portrait of Myra Hindley*. My mother-in-law, of whom I was extremely fond, was a magistrate and committed prison visitor. She visited Myra Hindley and always said she was one of the very few truly evil people she had ever met. Others clearly agreed and the picture caused not a sensation but an outrage.

The piece which worried me was the Chapman Brothers' *Zygotic Acceleration,*   With Ali G, the 'Art' interview
Biogenetic, De-sublimated Libidinal Model (enlarged x 1000). I thought I would test this on
my daughter Natasha, who was at the time about eleven. She showed none of the
shock or horror that I was anticipating but a very dismissive 'Why have they got
such cheap trainers on, Dad?' Natasha *dix points*, Chapman Brothers *nul point*. Chris
Ofili's Turner Prize *The Holy Virgin Mary*, mixed media with elephant dung, caused
a politically fuelled outrage when the show went to New York's Brooklyn Museum.
Despite the fact that the show had nothing whatsoever to do with Christie's New
York, the then mayor, Rudy Giuliani, closed down our street as a gesture of distaste.

The Sensation show had another spin-off and gave me my third and quite
unexpected fifteen minutes of fame. About six months or so after it had closed and
moved to Brooklyn, where it so upset the delicate sensibilities of the Republican
voters of New York, I received a call in my office in King Street asking me if
Christie's was still interested in cutting-edge contemporary art and in promoting
culture to young people of different ethnicities etc. I said, 'Yes, of course.' The lady
from Channel 4, as that she was, went on about a television interview and again I
said, 'Yes, of course', but would they check with our Press Office because they had
the final say in such matters. Our temporary Press Office eventually called me back
and outraged my liberal prejudices by asking me if I minded talking to a black
interviewer. 'Who on earth do you think I am?' I replied, genuinely quite cross.

Anyway, the plot was being laid for my once famous interview with that legend from 'de Staines massive', the lycra-clad, blinged-up, bearded, beshaded but in fact very white, Ali G! He began by introducing me: 'Wicked! I is here with Lord Hindlip, he be da head of Christie's and he knows everything about art and ting [...] Tell us, Lord Hindlip, is all da guys in de art world batty boys?' I had never heard this particular expression before but its meaning was fairly clear and I laughingly said this was not true.

Before ending the year 1997 I cannot help but illustrate *Mademoiselle Pogany II* by Constantin Brancusi, which made $7 million. It was an extraordinarily beautiful object.

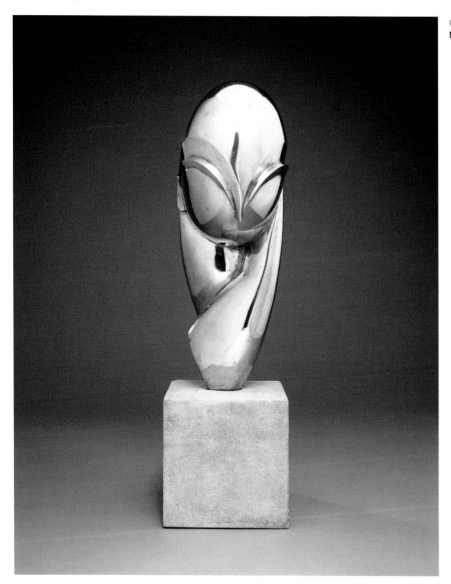

Constantin Brancusi.
Mademoiselle Pogany II, 1920-5

George Stubbs. **Portrait of Thomas Smith the Banksman**, *c.*1765-6

The following year was the last in which Christie's were located on Madison Avenue before moving to their prestigious new home on Rockefeller Plaza. But on the whole, with one notable exception, wherever the sales took place, they were successful. May in New York saw the sale of a particularly important Van Gogh drawing depicting fishing boats pulled up on the shore, *Bâteaux de pêche sur la plage à Saintes-Maries-de-la-Mer*; it made $5 million.

Back in England we had several notable house sales. One of these was Hackwood, for the heirs of Lord Camrose, which included in its £7 million total a group of the finest carved giltwood mirrors designed by John Vardy – a better quality I have never seen. The best of them sold for £106,000. Every lot sold and 7,000 people attended the view. Country house sales had lost none of their glamour.

George II mahogany and fretwork
secrétaire-cabinet by Wright and Elwick

The sale of the contents of Wentworth had perforce to take place in the London rooms but nevertheless was a resounding success with record prices paid in almost every category. The cover lot, a splendid Van Dyck portrait of *Lady Lucy Percy, Countess of Carlisle*, was withdrawn because the Tate Gallery expressed a wish to buy it. They were not as good as their word, but the nation's loss was of enormous value to the family because the picture is now worth very considerably more than the £3 million for which the trustees would have sold it to the Tate.

From the very first lot, the first book printed in the English language, records fell: Lot 2, the Rockingham Chaucer, *The Canterbury Tales*, made £4,621,500; George Stubbs's *Bay Malton* fetched just over £3 million; and the discovery amongst the pictures, *grâce aux* sharp eyes of Francis Russell, of the same artist's *Portrait of Thomas Smith the Banksman* (which is what the colliery supervisor was called), made £771,500. The best price in the furniture section was for Lady Rockingham's George II *secrétaire-cabinet*, made by the northern firm Wright and Elwick, which sold for £507,500, and the majestic Rockingham wine cistern by David Willaume, which reached £1,431,500.

I wrote above that all the sales with one exception were a success. The one sale which was not a success was that of the stock of French & Company, the property of the Zimet family. I have a long association with Martin Zimet which goes back to the early 1960s, and, despite the fact that he is a very difficult man to deal with, I like him and found him quite compelling to draw. Here he is talking to a pelican, which was taken from a Hondecoeter that was on someone else's stand at the Maastricht art fair..

What was included in the sale was by and large of very high quality. The estimates were admittedly what could be described as challenging, indicating challenging reserves. But this was only a contributory factor to the failure of the sale which

LEFT

An ormolu-mounted Japanese lacquer bureau en pente by Bernard II van Risenburgh, c.1750-5

BELOW

Charles Hindlip. **Martin Zimet talking to a pelican**

we unfortunately heavily underwrote. The real problem was that most of the furniture trade did not share my affection for Martin and, without their support, the sale was very unlikely to succeed. It opened well, the first fifteen lots all sold, culminating in a very good price indeed for the Duc d'Aumont's alabaster vases which made just over $2 million. Unfortunately, only two other subsequent lots sold in the sale: the Louis XV black lacquer *bureau en pente* by Bernard II van Risenburgh made the same price as the vases and the Pierre Langlois ormolu-mounted rosewood commode made a record price for a piece of English furniture, selling at $2,532,500. I was forced to ring up Christie's relatively new owner, François Pinault, and tell him that we had just lost potentially about £10 million of his money. Although much of this was recouped through aftersales, it was still an unpleasant experience for all concerned. Fortunately, the next year we were able to make spectacular amends.

Mr "French" and his funny bird

ÆTAT SVÆ 36
ANᵒ 1634

Chapter 25

Three Rothschild sales

Among the many interesting people John Richardson introduced me to during the five years we worked together in New York, was the writer Alan Pryce-Jones, and it was while dining with Alan that I met Baronne Alphonse de Rothschild (born Clarice Sebag-Montefiore). She was the most elegant lady. She lived in a stylish apartment in New York which seemed to me full of fascinating things, particularly black lacquer furniture, although she explained that she had recently sold a great deal to the old-established firm of Rosenberg and Stiebel and before that, at the time of the Anschluss, most of her husband's possessions had been lost.

I saw her two or three times while I was in New York and each time I was impressed by her charm, style and friendliness. When, in 1994, a delightful, slightly shy American, who introduced himself to me as Mr Looram, came into Christie's, I did not immediately put two and two together and he did not talk about his wife and their Rothschild connections. But he showed me an extraordinary French Empire box which looked to me as if it could have been made by Martin-Guillaume Biennais, who specialised in small boxes, pistol cases and similar objects for important clients at the end of the eighteenth and beginning of the nineteenth centuries. I asked if I could keep the box overnight and think about it and, more by luck than good judgement, I identified the contents as dental instruments, and deduced from the motifs on the box that it had almost certainly been made for Napoleon. Mr Looram entrusted us to sell the box, which made £62,000, on 9 June 1994. After the sale he wrote to say how grateful he was, and that appeared to be the end of the story.

However, about four years later, my friend Eric de Rothschild contacted me to ask if his cousin, Betty, had been in touch with me. At the time she had not. He said she was going to and he thought it would be rather exciting. It turned out that his cousin Betty was Mrs Looram, the daughter of the charming lady in New York and the last Austrian Rothschild, Baron Alphonse. Until the Anschluss, Baron Alphonse, his wife Clarice, and their children Albert, Betty and Gwendoline, had been living in enormous style in a palace in Vienna on Theresianumgasse and another large house which was to be snatched by Hitler for his country residence. They suspected something, Betty told me, of the dire state of Jews in Germany but their life in Austria until the Anschluss, though uncomfortable, had been relatively unimpaired.

Flemish Gilt-Brass Astrolabe, *c.*1570

OPPOSITE

Frans Hals. **Portrait of Tieleman Roosterman**, 1634

They still owned the largest steelworks in in the country. Shortly after the Anschluss, the entire family was arrested and it was only after the intervention of the Americans and their threat never to buy steel from Austria that part of the family was released and allowed to emigrate. Baron Alphonse himself remained a captive in Austria throughout the war. Some of their works of art had presumably been taken to New York before the Anschluss but, apart from those, their many possessions throughout Austria were confiscated and, at the end of the war, remained there as the property of the State. It was only in 1998 that Betty Looram happed on a scheme which led to the entire collection being restituted, but this followed a great deal of preparatory work going back as far as 1947. It was immediately after this that she got in touch with me and asked me to go and look at some photographs. What photographs!

It really was Aladdin's Cave and I could barely either believe my eyes or conceal my delight when she said that the family wanted to sell the collection. She accepted the terms that I suggested for the sale and I should make it clear at this moment that it was not entirely due to me that we achieved this, because Betty also had another friend in Christie's, Elizabeth Lane, whose husband had at one time been married to Miriam Rothschild. Despite their divorce, Elizabeth was a good friend of the Rothschild family, had met various relations and had become a particular friend of Betty Looram.

One of the reasons for mentioning all this is the fact that the story of Napoleon's toothpicks etc. did, I think, have a material effect and proves that, if you pay attention to something relatively unimportant, the results can sometimes turn out to great advantage. I am not sure that Christie's today is aware that out of little acorns mighty oak trees grow.

By 1999, clients normally insisted on long, complex contracts, going into endless detail and complicated financial terms. In this case, no contract was asked for. Betty signed the letter I wrote to her suggesting that Christie's would charge 5 per cent to sell the collection, which would cover expenses. It was a really nice way to do business and the incredible results justified the Rothschild family's faith. The sale, when it finally took place on 8 July 1999, made $100 million, the highest total we had ever achieved for a collection that did not include modern pictures. Every single lot was sold.

After we had agreed the details of the sale, I went to Austria to discuss the logistics and to see the objects themselves, which were scattered among museums in Vienna. I had to look at a few things in the Albertina, not very many, and the curator asked me if there was anything else I would like to see. In for a penny, in for a pound I thought, and I asked if I might possibly have a look at the Dürer drawings. I was allowed to handle the amazing *Das große Rasenstück* (Great Grass), which was almost as remarkable an experience as anything that happened in the ultimate sale.

The sale of the Rothschild collection coincided with the opening of our new premises in New York and the works of art went on view there for a fortnight. It was

The Rothschild Prayer Book,
*c.*1505–10

wonderful to be able to show off so many marvellous things in the Rockefeller Center. What did this remarkable collection consist of? Fine musical instruments, not a subject about which I know anything, but one could not fail to be impressed by the beauty of an object like Lot 18, the seventeenth-century French guitar, which made £17,250. Another category about which I know very little is arms and armour, but here again, there were things of extraordinary rarity and beauty, such as the sixteenth-century French combined *coutelas* and wheel-lock pistol of blue and gold damascene steel with gold inlays, and a quite amazing firing mechanism, similar to one designed by Leonardo da Vinci, which sold for £84,000.

The Rothschild family had always collected beautiful illustrated books. The second lot in the sale's evening session was the Rothschild Prayer Book, a book of hours from Ghent, *c.*1505, illustrated by, among others, Simon Bening, and including a small group of miniatures, probably by Gerard David – things of such exquisite beauty. It made £8,581,500.

Then there were the coins and medals, including a remarkable gold 20-*excelentes* of Ferdinand and Isabella, which sold for £221,500. There were some good boxes and very good silver, foremost among which were a Swiss silver-gilt cup and cover with the arms of the cities of Basel, Schaffhausen, Bern and St Gallen which made £463,500. There was also an extraordinarily beautiful German silver-gilt enamel-covered beaker from Augsburg, dating from 1729, which sold for £474,500.

Royal Louis XVI commode by Jean-Henri Riesener

Louis XVI longcase clock

The porcelain and glass section included an extremely rare example of Medici porcelain, the earliest successful European porcelain that was ever made: an oil and vinegar bottle mounted in silver-gilt, from about 1575, which sold for £287,500. One of my favourite lots, and something I had never seen before or since, was a pair of very large lead bas-reliefs of Venus and Adonis, attributed to Jakob Molinarolo, which made £194,000.

Then there were the most fantastic mathematical instruments. I could easily have stolen Lot 158 (sold for £144,500), a pair of sixteenth-century German gilt-brass compasses, which actually made one want to return to geometry lessons. No wonder the Rothschilds were so good at maths! The sixteenth-century astrolabe from Louvain, c.1570, fetched £265,500. A Mamluk gilt-brass mosque lamp from the fourteenth century came just before a group of stunning Persian rugs and carpets and made £771,500. The Tabriz sixteenth-century medallion carpet made £1,596,500.

The suite of Louis XV chair covers mounted on later seats was interesting insofar as the covers were photographed in the Régence salon in the Vienna residence, along with a piece of furniture which had made its last appearance in the Ojjeh sale, which I discussed earlier. When sold by Mr Ojjeh, the *encoignure* made a world record for a piece of French furniture. That price was to be beaten that night by Lot 201, the commode made by Jean-Henri Riesener, which was bought by the Château de Versailles, from whence it came, having originally been made for Fontainebleau, and it sold for just over £7 million.

I would like to have kept the Louis XV bureau plat made by Jacques Dubois, and the absolutely wonderfully extravagant Louis XV ormolu-mounted black, gold and

David Teniers the Younger. **Archduke Leopold's Picture Gallery in Brussels**, 1653

red lacquer commode. Another real highlight of the sale was the Duc de Choiseul's longcase clock, the movement by Ferdinand Berthoud, the case by Balthazar Lieutaud and the mounts by Philippe Caffieri, which made a modest £1,926,500.

Even the Rothschilds make mistakes: their Cuyp, Lot 217, was by Calraet, as are so many others. There were no doubts about Lot 218, the Wynants, which made a record for the artist (although he had had a bit of help from Adriaen van de Velde). And Lot 219, Frans Hals's *Portrait of Tieleman Roosterman*, made £8.2 million – a record for Hals – and went to Cleveland, Ohio. But I would rather have owned the following item, Lot 220, Hals's *Portrait of a Gentleman*, described in a sale in Brussels in November 1868 by an auctioneer who knew a thing or two about promotion as *Un magnifique portrait d'homme dans lequel Frans Hals, le Vieux, a déployé toutes les ressources de son génie*.

The market did not quite agree. The picture made only £2.2 million but all was put right again when the final lot in the sale, the Teniers depicting Archduke Leopold Wilhelm's picture gallery in Brussels (which was bought by a friend of mine who sometimes asks me to shoot), set yet another record when it sold for £2,971,500. What a lovely picture! What a lovely sale! What a lovely collection and what an incredibly nice family to deal with!

I took this sale myself except for the first section, which was beautifully done by my friend Noël Annesley who knows so much about music and who really appreciates the lute, and it was equalled only by the sale of the *Sunflowers* as the high point of my career at Christie's. That career had two or three years more to go and did include several more remarkable sales, but nothing quite like the collection of the Barons Nathaniel and Albert von Rothschild.

Christie's during the 1990s and early part of the next millennium held two other sales for the family. The first in 1995, which I have taken out of chronological order, for Baron Alphonse, came to me through the same friendships. I was asked by Edmond de Rothschild, the head of the Neapolitan branch of the family, now living in Switzerland, to go and talk to him. After telling me he thought I looked like his cousin, Eric, which was rather flattering, we got down to the point. He did not want to sell his bureau plat which my old mentor, Jo Floyd, had said was the most beautiful and valuable piece of French furniture in the world: the desk by Bernard II van Risenburgh of completely unusual and asymmetrical form. He wanted to discuss the sale of his rare collection of paintings by Giovanni Boldini, fifteen in all, which had been acquired by his father, a substantial number of them showing ladies with whom his father had been romantically attached.

Rembrandt van Rijn. **Portrait of a Lady, aged 62**, 1632

I have always been particularly impressed by the work of Giovanni Boldini, whose favourite sitter was said to have been Consuelo Vanderbilt, wife of the ninth Duke of Marlborough. However, judging from the pictures, Boldini had had a good time painting a number of Baron Maurice de Rothschild's friends, particularly the famous Marchesa Luisa Casati, here shown wearing a large black hat with ostrich feathers, an expensive fur stole which almost exactly matches her brown and black greyhound (who wears a silver and jewelled collar, which might just as easily have been worn by the Marchesa herself), and white gloves, with a lot of purple orchids. The picture represents the very essence of the turn of the century.

Count Robert de Montesquiou wrote of the Marchesa's picture in the Salon:

> *Madame Casati devant elle a sa grâce*
> *Son mystère, ses chiens, son énorme chapeau*
> *Et son bouquet de fleurs qu'un seul coup d'œil embrasse*
> *Lorsque le temps est clair et que le jour est beau.*

One cannot argue with this description. She was the most beautiful of all the ladies. She was a great friend of Boldini and captivated turn-of-the-century society. The art critic for *Le Figaro* wrote of the same Salon exhibition that '[Boldini's] talent has reached its climax […] Mme. La Marquise Casati is the most beautiful piece of pure painting in the whole Salon.' He goes on to compare the picture with Tintoretto and Goya. Lot 12, Boldini's portrait of Donna Franca Florio, also in black, was almost as attractive.

All the pictures were extremely appealing and if the sale, which took place in New York on 1 November 1995, was not quite as successful as it might have been, it may have been that I overestimated their charm; though many of them had been compared with the work of Sargent, this they were not. It may have been a mistake to have sent the Boldinis to New York. Although in Christopher Burge one could not find a better auctioneer and although Boldini had been hugely popular in America, the sale would probably have done better in London where today Boldini is perhaps more revered. But, who knows? It was not a failure but it was not the runaway success that I had hoped for.

The third Rothschild sale, which came to London through the good offices of Stephen Lash, was for the heirs of the Late Baroness Batsheva de Rothschild, who had gone to live in Tel Aviv. It included twelve old master pictures which were sold on 13 December 2000, followed by a sale the next day of works of art from her collection. The pictures made very high prices. The little Watteau *Le Conteur* sold for £2.4 million ($3.5 million) and the beautiful Rembrandt *Old Lady*, in its quiet way as good as Rembrandt gets, made £19,803,750 ($28,675,830).

The three sales were under the Rothschild name. But there were two others which also owed much to Rothschild taste and collecting which I shall consider in the next chapter.

Giovanni Boldini. **Portrait of the Marchesa Luisa Casati, with a greyhound**, 1908

The Akram Ojjeh collection; sale from Luton Hoo; the former property of Djahanguir Riahi; a sale from Longleat

The first collection, formed by Akram and Nahed Ojjeh, was sold on 11 and 12 December 1999 in Monte Carlo. The name Ojjeh, if for no other reason, will be familiar because it was under his name that Sotheby's presented, in June 1979, the magnificent collection which they had first intended to sell a few years earlier as the collection of Georges Wildenstein. Three of the most important lots came from Wildenstein, and, before that, Baron Alphonse, and there were ten other named Rothschild provenances, but the feel and the style of the collection was entirely what you would expect from a member of the Rothschild family.

The most magnificent of the lots, though, in the Ojjeh sale, was the suite of gold and black lacquer furniture by Riesener, which made FF38,512,500 ($6,893,234). This came from Queen Hortense, King Louis of Holland, Prince Demidoff and, after Baron Alphonse, his cousin, Madame Batsheva de Rothschild. That, of course, is not to play down the extraordinary enthusiasm of Akram Ojjeh as a collector. His widow, Nahed, also had wonderful taste, and it was a particular pleasure for me and François Curiel, who steered this project, to deal with her. I still treasure the fountain pen she gave me which I used to take her sale; this included our old friend, the magnificent commode by Leleu, which, as noted previously, came from King George III, and made FF41,812,500 ($6,482,054), an increase on what it had previously made when it appeared in our rooms as the property of Hubert de Givenchy and from the estate of Charles Clore. Finally, I should mention a picture that I have always liked from the collection, Fragonard's beautiful ésquisse for the picture in the Louvre, *Le Verrou*, which sold for $8,534,904.

On 5 July 2000 we had a sale in London from Luton Hoo which, were you to be shown the works of art with the possible exception of the pictures (although there were even overlaps there), you might be tempted to believe was another great Rothschild collection from the nineteenth century, albeit one with a particularly strong Christian input. In fact, what you would be looking at had nothing at all to do with the Rothschild family, and had no pieces in it with grand Rothschild names.

It had all belonged to, and been put together by, Sir Julius Wernher, a German who had emigrated first from Saxony to South Africa where he teamed up with a group of 'entrepreneurs' (not a French word), amongst whom several were Jewish. The taste which informed the collection, and which I suppose one could say ran exactly parallel to that of Baron Alphonse in Vienna, was completely German. It had been housed first in London, at Bath House, the residence of that great collector Alexander Baring, and thereafter at Luton Hoo, among whose various owners were Lord Bute, the prime minister, and then the Leigh family.

LEFT TO RIGHT

Reliquary figure of Saint Sebastian from a design by Hans Holbein the Elder, 1497

A pair of ivory panels from a polyptych forming the Annunciation, *c.*1270-90

The collection contained very fine silver from Spain, Italy, Germany and Holland, including two of the Aldobrandini tazze, which fetched £1,140,500. There were originally twelve of these magnificent tazze. Other than the two in the present collection, there is one in the Victoria and Albert Museum, two in museums in Portugal, one in Madrid, one in Minneapolis, Minnesota, one in the Bruno Schroder collection, and four more in private collections. The ones in the July 2000 sale fetched £1,140,500.

The most remarkable individual lots of silver (and there was a great deal to choose from) were the Kaiserheim reliquaries taken from designs by Hans Holbein the Elder and other contemporary German printmakers. They came from the Abbey of Kaiserheim in Saxony and truly deserved the description 'magnificent'. They aroused considerable interest. The clocks and scientific instruments were almost as fine.

The Wernher ivories were of particularly high quality. Lot 59, a pair of panels depicting the Annunciation, made £289,750. The bronzes were equally fine, with our friend Saturn or Cronus portrayed again, this time munching away at his son's ankle. I am not sure that I would have used the term 'chocolate brown' in the description, but anyway this time it was cast by Pietro Francavilla, bearing a French Royal inventory mark. Saturn made over £1 million. The next lot was attributed to

Sansovino and was of St John the Baptist and had once belonged to Sir Julius's partner, Alfred Beit.

The best piece of furniture was the Louis XV ormolu-mounted *secrétaire en armoire* by Riesener but stamped Oeben, a wonderful thing; it fetched £1,213,750. I don't want to labour the Rothschild similarities but there is an identical secretaire at Waddesdon, from the collection of James de Rothschild. The tapestries at Luton Hoo were as fine as any, such as Lot 77, from the royal workshops at Gobelins.

Lastly, I turn to the pictures: the beautiful Rubens sketch of a stag hunt – in fact *Diana and Her Nymphs* – fetched £3,083,750, and Titian's *Portrait of the Doge Giacomo Doria* was bought for £2.4 million by the Ashmolean Museum and I believe has cleaned very well. In all, the sale totalled $30 million.

The considerable majority of the sales about which I have written and with which I was most involved were great fun. I am not trying to give my colleagues who worked with me or myself too much credit but I am convinced that what we achieved with these sales not only made a substantial amount of money, but also enhanced Christie's reputation.

Obviously in selling a Picasso for £20 million, however much you spend on the promotion, you are going to make more money than if you sell part of the contents of a great house like, for instance, Longleat, for £20 million; but Christie's or Sotheby's would not be what they were without house sales and single-owner collections. They bring, if not an equal profit, then an equal glamour to the business and most, as I said, are profitable.

I have confessed to the one that was most spectacularly unprofitable, the French & Company sale, so it was with some trepidation that, the following year, Charles Cator and various other Directors on both sides of the Atlantic embarked on the sale of the collection formerly the property of Monsieur and Madame Djahanguir Riahi; and, just in case he thinks he is going to get away with it, I would like to record the fact that it was originally John Lumley who introduced me to Jinny Riahi, as he owned not only *L'Hiver à Montfoucault (Effet de neige)* but also a number of other paintings.

TOP TO BOTTOM

Royal Louis XV commode attributed to Jean-Pierre Latz and Jean-François Oeben, c.1757

Commode from the suite of Louis XVI furniture by Jean-Henri Riesener

Riahi was, though, not really interested in pictures. For him the *génie du création* rested in the art of the eighteenth-century *ébénistes* and *ciseleurs*. I genuinely think that money played a very secondary part in Riahi's thinking. He did not live extravagantly, surrounded though he was with some of the grandest furniture ever made. When he ate, he ate off the finest silver, but he didn't eat very often! He was a real collector: ownership, not profit, was what drove him. It is also what drove Charlie Cator, Hugh Roberts before him, myself and the Accounts Department, close to demented. In our backward Western ways, ownership only passes when money changes hands. Potentially, this could have had a very debilitating effect on the firm's owner, François Pinault, who always asked us to keep a close eye on cashflow. Had the sale in New York not been a success, it would have been an ugly post-mortem because, when it took place, the whole collection was effectively owned, not by the Riahi Family but by Christie's – thus, in turn, François Pinault. Some of the works of art included in the sale had never even got to the Riahi apartment on the Quai Voltaire but lived behind bars in the Ports Francs in Geneva.

With our almost 100 per-cent ownership in mind, we decided we would sell the whole collection without reserve and publicise the fact to make sure that members of the furniture trade (all of whom knew and had sold things to Riahi) did not behave as they had with French & Company and boycott the sale. We went to see them first, told them what wonderful things (which was largely true) they had sold to Riahi, that we very much hoped that they would support the sale and that we would like to write, in the introduction, a brief description of them as dealers. It worked. Not a single lot was bought in. Well, it could not be really because there were no reserves. But every lot made its estimate or more and after taking out all the expenses for the sale for which we had received many plaudits, and the envy of the opposition, we came away almost exactly where we would have been had we never met Jinny Riahi.

He is now sadly no longer with us. To say that I miss him is probably not completely true. To say that I bear him no ill will whatsoever and have affectionate memories of him is true. This is a brief description of the sale's highlights. I illustrate the magnificent Savonnerie carpet and the Latz commode made for *la chambre de la Dauphine*, which Jinny felt was the high-water mark of Louis XV furniture. Who am I to disagree? *Je ne comprends pas. Je ne suis pas oriental*.

In my teens and early twenties, if I was lucky enough to have a girlfriend I would take her to look at buildings within striking distance of my parents' house in Wiltshire. Lacock Abbey was a favourite destination, only about 5 miles from home and romantic. Much more romantic was Wells Cathedral with its sublime scissor arch supporting the tower. More romantic still was Longleat, as fine as any house in Britain, with the added advantage of being owned by a cousin, albeit a rather distant one (my grandmother was Agatha Thynne, a great-granddaughter of the second Marquess of Bath). I never ventured inside Longleat in those days nor visited the fledgling safari park – the view of the house from Heaven's Gate was enough and if a girl was not moved by that view, she wasn't going to be a longtime fixture.

In 1988, as I remember, David Beaufort asked me to have lunch with his father-in-law, Henry Bath, whom I knew slightly but who, as a result of David's introduction, I got to know a great deal better and grew to like very much indeed. Lord Bath had done a great deal for the house and contents but houses like Longleat swallow money. Sales were inevitable, although the majority took place after Henry's death and during the tenure of his son, the current Marquess, Alexander. The Thynne family had always been bibliophiles and by the eighteenth century there was a good original library at Longleat. This was considerably added to by the first Viscount Weymouth with Bishop Ken of Bath and Wells, who, after being deprived of his see by

Meissen turkey modelled by J.J. Kändler, c.1733

William and Mary, took up his tenure at Longleat and virtually lived in the library, bringing his collection with him. The library was further added to in the nineteenth century by the eccentric Beriah Botfield, who claimed to be descended from the original Thynnes, and who had amassed a substantial collection of illustrated books of a very high order. There were subsequently, in the collection, significant overlaps between the three libraries, which meant that the early sales were relatively uncontentious. Later, selecting lots for sale which would not destroy the historic feel of the house and collection became more difficult, but my colleague Charles Cator and I, with a great deal of help from the librarian at Longleat, Kate Harris, put together what was a successful sale on 13–14 June 2002. It included a number of Dutch seventeenth-century pictures collected by Botfield, more books, and very fine French and Italian eighteenth-century furniture.

In the early days of the nineteenth century, three names constantly appear in Christie's catalogues: Hertford, Rothschild and Bath. The second Marquess of Bath, from whom I am descended, was a voracious collector and the fact that we could remove £20 million worth of works of art from the house and leave it, to all intents and purposes, still fully furnished, attests to this. Among the most expensive lots in the catalogue of Printed Books and Manuscripts on 13 June was Lot 2, Jean du Quesne's beautiful secular illuminated manuscript of the *Commentaires de César* and *Cronique habregie*, which made £611,650. That evening in the sale of Furniture,

Longleat

Porcelain and Silver, Lot 330, a wonderful pair of ormolu-mounted Japanese black and gold lacquer cabinets, made just over £1 million. Lot 351, a magnificent Meissen turkey, modelled by J.J. Kändler, sold for £831,650. One of the finest desks by David Roentgen, Lot 400, made £545,650. Lot 422, the rare and unusual serpentine commode by Pietro Piffetti, sold for £204,650.

The icing on the cake, as far as Longleat was concerned, was supplied by my colleague Edward Manisty who managed to surrender, in lieu of the tax due from the sale, Wootton's masterpieces in the Hall, for a net figure of around £10 million, on condition that the pictures remained in the house.

RIGHT

Roll-top desk by David Roentgen
c.1776-9

Magnificent French furniture sold on behalf of a friend – my last sale; a farewell to Christie's; some thoughts on modern painting; the London Group – Lucian Freud, Francis Bacon, Frank Auerbach and Michael Andrews; Rodrigo Moynihan; Freud's portrait of Her Majesty The Queen; an expensive Bacon

Louis XVI table de café mounted with Sèvres porcelain by Adam Weisweiler

The last time I climbed into the rostrum in King Street was at eleven o'clock on Thursday 12 December 2002 to sell a collection described in the catalogue as 'Magnificent French Furniture and Works of Art'. It was the property of a father and son, both of whose friendship I greatly valued. The sale, impressive though it was, was only a small fraction of a very great collection, although it contained some extraordinarily good things. The Harewood House Carlin Sèvres-mounted *console desserte* sold for £2,646,650. The Louis XV ormolu-mounted bureau plat by Pierre Garnier, which had belonged to Alfred Farquhar, the eighteenth-century banker and collector, fetched £303,650. The pair of grey painted and gilt chairs which were made for Madame du Barry fetched £732,650 and the last lot, the Louis XV ormolu and Sèvres-mounted *table de café* by Adam Weisweiler, apparently given to Marie Antoinette by the Marquis de Baldi-Piovera, sold for £2,371,650.

Quite a lot of people, I think, guessed who owned the collection, although he had chosen to remain anonymous. When I started all those years ago at the Front Counter, I would have been thrilled, but slightly incredulous, to think that this would be the last sale I would ever take. It was a wonderful way to end my career at Christie's.

Before, so to speak, closing the book on Christie's, I would like to pay a tribute to Maryvonne Pinault, who was always extremely nice to me and my wife Fiona. She came to our house on a number of occasions and we went to hers in France; and I know that Charlie Cator particularly valued and values still her support. As well as being a significant collector, she has been an important benefactor to Versailles.

I have acknowledged my debt to Christie's and so many of the past and present staff and I would like to thank them again for all the help I have received while working on this book. It must be obvious that it would not have been possible to write it without that help and friendliness. I hope everything continues to go well for them and I am sure it will. There are, however, two things which I could suggest that might help.

Firstly, Christie's friendly and helpful experts are sometimes a little bit difficult to access. The switchboard at Christie's is, I am afraid, the least good of the four main auction houses. It is too much to hope that we could ever get back to the wonderful days of Jean, who presided over the exchange in the 1960s and 1970s and who knew every detail (probably too many in fact) of the lives of the people who worked in the firm and often quite a lot about the people who worked outside and rang in.

Today, the opposite is true. Recently I wanted to talk to my old colleague, Noël Annesley. I rang the main number and requested Mr Annesley. 'How are you spelling that?', I was asked. 'I am not spelling it. I want to talk to him.' The operator then said, 'There is no Mr Annersley [*sic*]'. I said, 'No, Annesley, he is the Deputy Chairman!' There was a long pause during which a lot of triumphalist music burst on my ear. The most attractive music can become unattractive if it keeps on going round and round and then stops and nothing happens, and you have to ring again. I don't think I am the first person this has happened to.

One other thing, and this applies to all the major auction houses: do they really need such vast catalogues? I have a friend who came back from holiday and was unable to open the door because there were so many catalogues lying on the floor that he had to take it off its hinges to get in. I don't get so many but, when I have fought my way through the wrapping and got to grips with the catalogue, the endless comparisons with other works make it difficult to see what is actually being sold. These comparisons usually demonstrate that what is being offered is considerably less impressive than a great many other things that the particular artist has painted. Slimmer, simpler catalogues would be easier to read, easier to handle, save money and do their bit to prevent deforestation.

These two niggles apart, things at King Street look pretty good. What is in store for the market for the next fifty years? It would be difficult to think of anything that I could write that would turn out to be quite as inaccurate as what that much-respected journalist A.C.R. Carter wrote in 1928 when he predicted the continuing dominance of Christie's.

The old firm has, however, managed to rise, Lazarus-like, from what looked like almost certain death. This book, if nothing else, in charting its rise back to the top, shows that Christie's succeeded not because of a fixation on the new but because it concentrated on strengthening its position in the areas where it had always done best. It consciously employed better-qualified experts who, in turn, improved the knowledge and capabilities of existing staff, particularly younger members of the firm like me.

The most important part of the recovery was Christie's ability, in the early 1960s, to hold on to its old clients, to keep them and their families faithful; not, as some of our colleagues believed, because Christie's had a God-given right to sell certain families' works of art, but to ensure that Christie's would at least still be consulted. My old colleagues succeeded in hanging on to old clients and gaining new ones. This was not done overnight, nor were we in a position to buy business or expensive PR. Nor were we keen on slogans. Our recovery was achieved, to a very large extent, by being nice to clients; by the clients liking and trusting Christie's and the people who worked there, who maintained a degree of professionalism and, from that, achieved good sales results. Success came also by encouraging a sense of fun and enjoyment.

I do not want to speculate on where the art world is going. I will never be one to worship at Marcel Duchamp's urinal. However, as Edmund Burke wrote in a letter to Fanny Burney, 'the arrogance of age must submit to be taught by youth', and my son, Henry, organised an exhibition in New York, ten years or so ago, entitled 'Aftershock: The Legacy of the Ready-Made', which strongly supported the Duchamp legacy. Time will tell whether arrogant old age or youthful enthusiasm is right, but I hold one truth to be self-evident: if Michael Craig-Martin thinks that a glass of water is a tree, he needs to go as quickly as he can to Specsavers. I doubt that I will survive to see the day when some great pin pricks Koone's balloon, but we all have to have something to look forward to and there is a world for the optimist 'outside of a dog'.

There are some great artists today who I am sure will leave a legacy. Gerhard Richter is certainly one. There is almost nothing he cannot do and do well. Peter Doig is impressive too and he has hopefully got many miles left on the clock. About art in this country, I am less certain. I have often hoped that Damien Hirst might somehow become an English rival to Andy Warhol. He has not made it yet. But there are British stars. David Hockney has produced drawings which rate with the very best and his Californian paintings are a joy; he is also an extremely nice man and his anarchic passion to chain-smoke to the end cocks a splendid snook to the ogre of political correctness. Hockney, despite the Woodbines, is still with us. Sadly, all but one of the member of the London group who were his friends, and in one case mine, too, are not.

If anyone has any doubts about the survival of art in Britain, they need to look no further than to this group: Lucian Freud, Francis Bacon, Frank Auerbach and Michael Andrews. Although Freud and Auerbach were both born in Berlin, Bacon was Irish and born in Dublin, and only Michael Andrews was born in England (in Norwich), but is buried in Scotland. They chose to live and work in London, and all were great figurative painters and shared a passionate relationship with their subjects, be it their still lifes, landscapes, or human or animal forms. Mike Andrews is the least well known of the four, despite the fact that he had a very well curated exhibition at Tate Britain in 2001; his works seldom appear on the market. They are still almost all owned by a devoted group of admirers, coincidentally almost all friends of mine, who are lucky enough never to need to sell the pictures. I have another friend with whom I used to work, who loves Andrews's pictures. She could never have afforded one and asked if I would copy one of his landscapes for her. I did, and I think that Andrews's genius shows through even this 'rotten copy'.

Frank Auerbach is now very well known. He draws and paints quite beautifully and again was recently exhibited, also at Tate Britain. Some ten years ago, when his prices were less than they are now, I thought I had bought one of his pictures at the Maastricht Fair. But when at the end, I went to collect it and pay, the dealer in question had sold it to someone else, saying he did not think I was serious. I could have killed him.

Lucian Freud was my friend and, again, is sadly no longer with us. I never asked him whether he thought of himself as an English painter. I did once suggest to him that he was influenced by Klimt. He was absolutely furious and threatened never to speak to me again. I was also brave enough to tell him that I thought the best thing he ever painted was his *Portrait of John Minton*. Lucian, with his characteristic modesty, said yes, he did think it was a good picture and that John Minton had asked him to paint it as a memorial, as he had already decided that he was going to kill himself. I asked the same question of another artist whom I knew and liked, Rodrigo Moynihan: why had he painted John Minton set apart from all the other painters in his great picture *Portrait Group*? Rodrigo, who really was modest, said it was almost unconscious: 'He seemed to have drifted away.' Rodrigo's picture was painted in 1951 and Lucian's in 1952. Minton died in 1957. I never knew Minton, but you can see

Charles Hindlip, **copy of Michael Andrews's Running with the Deer.**

BELOW

Lucian Freud. **Portrait of John Minton**, 1952

from Lucian's brilliant picture that he was deeply troubled, and equally so in Rodrigo's group portrait.

I have another postscript to my friendship with Lucian. John Richardson was kind enough to record the following in his foreword, entitled 'Remembering Lucian', in the National Portrait Gallery's exhibition catalogue, just after Lucian had died:

> A week or two before Lucian died, I flew to London to see him for what was destined to be the last time. By chance, I had the perfect present for him. An old friend of Lucian's and mine, Charlie Hindlip, had had a brilliant idea. To demonstrate the accuracy of Lucian's controversial portrait of the Queen, he had taken a reproduction of the image and a same-size press photograph of her wearing the same diadem, cut them in two and pasted the differing halves together. The match was so perfect you had to get close to spot which half was which.

> Lucian was dozing when I handed this collage to him, but as soon as he saw what it was, he shot up in bed and brandished it at us. 'That's it! That's it!' he cried, and sank back on to his pillows, all too evidently vindicated. Mindless fuddy-duddies who had condemned the likeness had finally got their

Rodrigo Moynihan. **Portrait Group**, 1951

comeuppance. Instead of opting for a bland effigy of a waxwork monarch, Lucian had had the guts to depict Her Majesty as a very human being, wearing a royal diadem as comfortably as if it were a hat. Thanks to a shared passion for horses, painter and sitter got along extremely well. Let us not forget that, while King Charles I had knighted his court painter, Anthony Van Dyck, and Queen Victoria had given Frederic Leighton a peerage, the present Queen, years before he painted her, had accorded Lucian two of the greatest honours in the land – the Companion of Honour and the Order of Merit.

I am really grateful to John for having written this, and here is the collage about which he writes.

Francis Bacon needs no introduction from me. En passant, I have to admit that it took me some years of looking to realise his especial genius, but this true story answers the question many people, who are not always interested in pictures for their own sake, ask: 'What has gone up in value most?' Here, I think, is the answer.

Her Majesty The Queen - collage

In the spring of 1965, David Bathurst, the head of Christie's Modern Picture Department, asked me one morning if I had seen a note he had made about a picture by Bacon. Had he left it on my desk? 'No.' Had he talked to me about it? Again 'No.' 'Damn,' he said, 'you were my last hope. I got a call on Monday from a lady who wants to sell a Bacon. It sounded rather good and I made a note of her name and address. I've lost it. I think she said she lived in Abbotsbury Road; I can't remember the house number or her name, but I'm fairly sure I had to go this afternoon to see her. I will just have to walk up and down the street and hope I can see the picture.' This was an unlikely hope, given the net curtains at the windows and the hedges and trees in the gardens of the distinctly leafy edge of Holland Park.

But, as luck would have it, and it certainly was David's lucky day, he caught a glimpse of what could be the picture, just visible in the stairwell of number 43. Taking his luck and courage in both hands, he pressed the bell. It was answered by the picture's owner who said, yes, she was expecting him. The picture illustrated here made 5,500 guineas ($16,170) in a sale that June. The owners, none the wiser about the missing note, were pleased, and the picture was bought by a client of Leslie Waddington who gave it to me to sell in 1989. I sent it to America where, on 7 November, it made $5,720,000 (£3,360,000), only a small fraction of the $85 million (£50 million) that I am assured it is worth today; in other words, it has gone up in pounds by close to ten thousand times. This is not a bad return and for something which would give many people lasting pleasure.

This should encourage both painting and collecting and that is my last word on the subject of records. Although I have mentioned them time and again, they are merely milestones showing how far the market has travelled. What is incontrovertible is that there will be thousands more, all as meaningless as the thousands that precede them, but they will all have their fifteen minutes of fame.

Francis Bacon. **Study for a Pope**, 1955

Chapter 28

A lecture to the World Food Forum; Fiona and I visit Ascoli Piceno and admire Crivelli's altarpiece and a carabinieri bride; last word left to Hilaire Belloc

I had left Christie's before I did my copy of Michael Andrews, before Lucian's portrait of the Queen, before the Bacon was worth what it is today, and before I had unsuccessfully tried to buy the picture by Frank Auerbach.

Christie's held a farewell dinner for me and, overcome by both emotion and some rather good wine, I made what Fiona said was one of my worst ever speeches. I did look forward to life after Christie's but I approached it with a certain apprehension, as they insisted that I should do nothing for the six months after I left. This was because I had arranged, on my leaving, to join Agnew's. That firm had long associations with Christie's and I felt that there was little serious danger of a conflict of interest – none as it turned out. But my luck was in, and, during my enforced idleness, a kind friend asked me if I would consider giving a lecture in Rome to the annual conference of the World Food Forum. I was to be paid quite a decent amount of money for doing so and was told I could choose my subject as long as it involved works of art.

I have always held the view that painting gives away a great deal about national characteristics. I wanted to explore this idea and talking about it would give me an opportunity to use quite a considerable number of my favourite works of art to illustrate the talk. This in itself would be fun, and I was also given fairly generous expenses, certainly enough to enable Fiona and me to fly to Rome business class and to stay in a perfectly adequate hotel. I worked hard on the talk, and got together a good lot of illustrations – about fifty, approximately one a minute – which would leave a short time at the end for questions. Fiona and I arrived in Rome and noticed that the large conference centre was surrounded by Italian police looking less than welcoming. We were told by the organisers that there had been serious protests from various Green groups. I am not a fervent Green myself but I was more in favour of the protesters than I was of the World Food Forum, as it transpired that this organisation is chiefly responsible for filling everything on supermarket shelves with as much sugar and other chemicals as can possibly be stuffed into a packet for the maximum profit and the maximum increase in the girth of the consumer.

Dinner at White's for John Richardson, 2009

L-R: David Hockney, John Richardson and Lucian Freud

245

Andy Warhol. **210 Coca-Cola Bottles**, 1962

Unsurprisingly Coca-Cola was sponsoring the forum, and fortuitously I was intending to end the talk with an illustration of one of Andy Warhol's *Coca-Cola Bottles*.

I have a certain ambivalence about Coca-Cola as a drink but none whatever about Andy Warhol as an artist. I am not quite sure how many people came to the talk – perhaps several hundred – nor do I really know what they expected to hear, but one soon gets a sense of the audience, and the sense that I got on this particular occasion was that they were not interested in the link between painting and nationality. I think they had heard of France, Spain, Germany, Italy, Great Britain, America; they were less sure of themselves when it came to the Low Countries and Flanders and I sympathise with them over Belgium. I was also uncertain whether they had ever visited the Vatican, which was less than a quarter of a mile from the auditorium. They did not seem to grasp the significance of the Pope and they did not seem to be familiar with the works of Raphael, nor did they seem particularly excited by Botticelli's *Birth of Venus*, nor the great Bronzino in the National Gallery, *An Allegory*

Sandro Botticelli. **The Birth of Venus,** c.1485

with Venus and Cupid. I have always found this last picture to be a popular one, but it was not so with members of the World Food Forum and I don't think that whatever love they probably had practised on each other, they understood much about either Venus or Cupid. From the look of most of them, it had not been much fun either.

I got through the fifty minutes, received a ripple of applause for the slide of the *210 Coca-Cola Bottles* and then there was a mad rush for the exits because in the adjacent hall there was a demonstration of synchronised swimming in which the onlookers, to a man and a woman, were clearly keenly interested. They obviously preferred the sight of pirouetting bikini-clad figures underwater to my overview of Western Art!

I gathered up Fiona, preparing to leave to go into Rome and have a good dinner, when a very nice, tall Englishman accosted me and said he did not think I knew him but he had seen me. I did recognise him. He was called Percy Weatherall and he was a member of the Keswick family and had just come back from Hong Kong. He said he had thoroughly enjoyed the talk but thought he was the only one who had. He was particularly interested in *Eton College* by Canaletto, which I had slipped in as a bridge between Italy and England. It was really nice to know that somebody had enjoyed it – it had been quite hard work!

Fiona and I left the next day and by lunchtime got to Tivoli, which I had never really explored before. It was wonderful. We carried on eastwards of Rome, quite a long day's drive, to a town called Ascoli Piceno, where that beautiful painter Carlo Crivelli made his home and eventually died. At about noon the next day we reached the cathedral to look at the great Crivelli altarpiece, but we had a certain amount of trouble getting to it because the cathedral was full to bursting with members of the carabinieri in ceremonial uniform. The local general (the carabinieri have military ranks) was giving away his daughter into marriage and the participants were starting to line up for the service. The bride, whom at this stage we could see only from the rear, had a splendid veil, dress and train, and was escorted by at least a dozen small people in carabinieri uniform with another dozen small people dressed seemingly similarly to the bride.

We took in the Crivelli while the service was going on and sneaked round behind the altar to get a look at the bride from the front, which was rather a remarkable sight. The demure appearance of the dress from the back was in sharp contrast to the dress in the front which was split to the navel and exposed quite a lot of what one would normally only expect to be revealed at some time after the marriage ceremony, certainly not during it. But it was a wonderful Mass, very colourful, and there were a lot of plumed helmets to go with the splendidly exposed front of the bride. The bridegroom, who was clearly marrying the boss's daughter, was not quite so splendidly attired as the bride's father but he was obviously well on the way up what I imagine is a bit of a greasy pole, if my dealings with the carabinieri are anything to go by. I hope they were very happy. They certainly seemed to enjoy the occasion.

We left both Crivelli and the carabinieri and the next day explored the highlands of the Marche, where I was thrilled to find on the snowline something which I had never seen before and probably never will again – a magnificent wild peony growing literally through the snow. We wended our way north, taking in some new sights and some old, stopping for longer than I have ever done before in Spoleto. The Filippo Lippi altarpiece in the cathedral must be one of Italy's very best sights.

It was a good trip and I got back just in time to accompany my new boss, Julian Agnew, to the Maastricht Art Fair. I had been to Maastricht before but never for very long and I had never worn a smart badge with 'exhibitor' on it, which I probably wasn't meant to, because I had not served my six months of purdah. I half-wished I had because the hotel that Julian had put me in (not the one he was staying in himself) had a problem which is quite rare in Holland – the drains. There is an old French expression, *fosse septique*, which has rather fortunately gone out of common usage but it certainly came back to mind every time one either left or re-entered the hotel.

Later that spring, or as it was early summer, the six months were up and I started working full-time in that venerable establishment in Bond Street. I was able to bring one quite important picture to be sold by Agnew's, a masterpiece by John Martin, an artist sometimes confused with his brother who was mad. Mad John was not, inventive and eccentric he was. The picture in question was entitled *Joshua Commanding the Sun to Stand Still upon Gibeon*. It belonged to the United Grand Lodge of England and was introduced to me by my old friend, Spenny Northampton, who

TOP TO BOTTOM

Carlo Crivelli. **Polyptych depicting the Madonna and Child with Saints (detail)**, 1473

Charles Hindlip. **Carabinieri Wedding**

Filippo Lippi. **Detail from The Life of the Virgin Cycle**, 1466-9

was the Grand Master. The picture was taken to Maastricht the next year, when I was staying in better accommodation, and was bought quite quickly by the National Gallery in Washington for £3 million.

John Martin was an artist who has always interested me. Not only did he paint beautifully, but he was also an engineer and inventor and in 1834 produced what I believe was a viable plan to make the Thames semi-tidal and hugely improve the traffic flow along the embankment. Before totally clogging up the traffic, our ex-Mayor, Boris, could have done a lot worse than study Martin's plan from 1834. Part of it contained drawings for the improvement of the sewerage system, which could also have been studied with effect by the designers of the hotel I stayed in during my first working trip to Maastricht.

After about a year with Agnew's, Julian's brother Jonathan, who, not having wanted to join his family firm, had been a leading figure in the City of London, suggested a possible merger of Agnew's with a company with which I associated myself somewhat later, Simon Dickinson. We made considerable progress with plans for a merger which, even with the benefit of hindsight, might have been a success, but we were never able to resolve final details. We did, however, have a meeting in the hopes of doing so at the Carlton Tower Hotel where, after a very good dinner, when discussions had gone quite well, Julian Agnew turned to Simon Dickinson and said, 'I know, Simon, that you would like your firm to continue, as mine has, for many generations.' Julian was, I think, the fifth generation to be chairman of his family firm. Simon nodded vigorously. When the same remark was addressed to his partner, David Ker, the response was not so enthusiastic. 'I am the first member of my family to be in trade. I very much hope I shall be the last.' That was not the end of the discussions but it pointed the way.

After eighteen months I did, with some reluctance, leave Agnew's, to set up on my own in a small office I rented from Dickinson. My early days as an independent art dealer were really rather successful. I made quite a decent profit participating with Dickinson in the sale of a Canaletto, and bought from Christie's Paris a picture entitled *Vue des jardins de la Villa Médicis* by Michel-Martin Drölling, a little-known but very appealing plein-air painter who had worked first with Ingres in Rome and then with Corot.

I paid four times Christie's estimate to buy the picture in a 50 per-cent share with Dickinson. We then sold it a couple of years later to the Rijksmuseum, for double what we paid for it. Dealing was beginning to look dangerously easy. Whether it had been beginner's luck or the market or, more likely, a combination of the two, things were better then than they ever were subsequently. However, I have sold a few beautiful works of art as a dealer.

I was particularly attached to the small *Portrait of Queen Mary* by Hans Eworth, the most Holbeinesque of painters. It was a lovely thing and, as so often and so happily seems to be the case, the best pictures belong to the nicest people. This came to me through the good offices of Richard Stanley, who was the trustee at Longleat, with whom I had so many dealings, and the picture belonged to his in-laws, the Wynne Finch family. I was also very pleased to be given a Matisse bronze, *Vénus à la coquille,* which again I sold jointly with Dickinson for what I think at the time was a record.

These were successes – they could not perhaps be described as triumphs, although the Rijksmuseum picture was certainly a triumph when comparing its price with Christie's original estimate for it. Commercial common sense prevents my giving a list of the various works of art in which I still have an interest, and which remain unsold. Regrettably, this is a slightly longer list than that of the successes. One can still make money selling old master pictures, but it sometimes takes a very long time and requires both patience and a degree of optimism which some, like Simon Dickinson, seem to possess in almost inexhaustible quantities. I sometimes run out of it. I have, though, over the past fourteen years, which seems a terrifyingly long period, relished the freedom to take my own decisions, enjoyed the successes and had only myself to blame for my mistakes.

I hope I live long enough to sell a few more pictures and to help a few more friends with their valuations. But even if I never have another client and never deal with another picture, I will count myself extremely lucky to have spent my working life in the world's last great unregulated market. As all other markets, it has had its ups and downs but, unregulated though it is, the clients, the dealers, those in the auction houses, have been good friends and have inflicted far fewer wounds on their fellow mortals than those in most other professions. The vast majority of them have been bound by a love of works of art and a love of beauty which transcends almost everything else, and I hope I have been able to show that, in a strange, sometimes jealous, often competitive, almost always beautiful world, we have had a great deal of fun. I will leave the last words to my great hero Hilaire Belloc:

> From quiet homes and first beginning,
> Out to the undiscovered ends,
> There's nothing worth the wear of winning,
> But laughter and the love of friends.

Michel-Martin Drölling. **Vue des jardins de la Villa Médicis**, 1811–16

Index

Page numbers in *italics*
refer to the illustrations

253

Picture Credits

Chapter 1 p.8 Accepted by the HM Government in lieu of Inheritance Tax and allocated to the National Gallery, 1999 © The National Gallery, London; p.9t Charles Hindlip/© Matthew Hollow Photography; p.9b Charles Hindlip/© Matthew Hollow Photography; p.10 National Gallery, London UK/Bridgeman Images; p.11 © Christie's Images Limited; p.12 Private Collection/Piccadilly Gallery, London UK/Bridgeman Images Chapter 2 p.14 Strasbourg, Musée des Beaux-Arts, photo Musées de Strasbourg, M. Bertola; p.15 Private Collection; p.18 Courtesy National Gallery of Art, Washington; p.19t Hamburger Kunsthalle, Hamburg, Germany/Bridgeman Images; p.19b © Christie's Images Limited; p.20 Museo Thyssen-Bornemisza, Madrid, Spain/De Agostini Picture Library/G.Nimatallah/Bridgeman Images Chapter 3 p.22 Courtesy National Gallery of Art, Washington; p.24l The Ella Gallup Sumner and Mary Catlin Sumner Collection Fund, 1953.15, Wadsworth Atheneum Museum of Art, Hartford, Connecticut, photo Allen Phillips/Wadsworth Atheneum; p.24r Private Collection/Bridgeman Images; p.25l Museum of Fine Arts, Boston, Massachusetts, USA/1931 Purchase Fund/Bridgeman Images; p.25r Harvard Art Museums/Fogg Museum, Bequest of Grenville L. Winthrop, 1943.248, Imaging Department © President and Fellows of Harvard College; p.27 The Barnes Foundation, Philadelphia, Pennsylvania, USA/Bridgeman Images/© Succession H. Matisse/DACS 2016; p.28t Frick Collection, New York, USA/Bridgeman Images; p.28b Metropolitan Museum of Art, New York, USA/Bridgeman Images Chapter 4 p.30 National Gallery, London, UK/Bridgeman Images; p.34l The Norton Simon Foundation, Portrait of a Boy, 1655–60, Rembrandt van Rijn, Dutch, 1606–1669, oil on canvas, 25-1/2 x 22 in. (64.8 x 55.9 cm); p.34r National Gallery, London, UK/Bridgeman Images; p.35 © Scottish National Gallery, Edinburgh/Bridgeman Images; p.40 National Gallery of Canada, Ottawa, photo © NGC, Lot and his Daughters, 1622, Orazio Gentileschi, oil on canvas, 157.5 x 195.6 cm; p.41t © 2016. Image copyright The Metropolitan Museum of Art/Art Resource/Scala, Florence © photo SCALA, Florence; p.41b The Jack and Belle Linsky Collection, 1982. Acc.n.: 1982.60.17. © 2016. Image copyright The Metropolitan Museum of Art/Art Resource/Scala, Florence © photo SCALA, Florence; p.42 Detroit Institute of Arts, USA/Founders Society Purchase/Bridgeman Images Chapter 5 p.44 Private Collection/Bridgeman Images; p.46 Birmingham Museum and Art Gallery/Bridgeman Images; p.50 Gift of Consuelo Vanderbilt Balsan, 1946. Acc.n.: 47.71 ©2016. Image copyright The Metropolitan Museum of Art/Art Resource/Scala, Florence © photo SCALA, Florence; p.51 Private Collection/photo © Christie's Images/Bridgeman Images Chapter 6 p.52 J. Paul Getty Museum, Los Angeles, USA/Bridgeman Images; p.54 © American Illustrators Gallery, NYC/ www.asapworldwide.com /Bridgeman Images © Maxfield Parrish Family, LLC/VAGA, NY/DACS, London 2016; p.56 State Hermitage Museum, St Petersburg, Russia/Peter Willi/Bridgeman Images; p.57 Musée d'Orsay, Paris, France/Bridgeman Images; p.58l The Jack and Belle Linsky Collection, 1982. Acc.n.: 1982.60.20 © 2016. Image copyright The Metropolitan Museum of Art/Art Resource/Scala, Florence © photo SCALA, Florence; p.58r Private Collection/Bridgeman Images; p.59 The Metropolitan Museum of Art, New York, USA/Bridgeman Images; p.61 Norton Simon Art Foundation, Vincent van Gogh, Dutch, 1853–1890 Portrait of the Artist's Mother, October 1888 Oil on canvas, 16 x 12-3/4 in. (40.6 x 32.4 cm) Chapter 7 p.62 Private Collection/photo © Christie's Images/Bridgeman Images; p.66 © National Portrait Gallery, London; p.67 photo Ralph J. Kueppers 08/1977, Maryland Historical Trust; p.68 East Falls Historical Society Chapter 8 p.70 Private Collection © Succession Picasso/DACS, London 2016; p.71 National Gallery, London, UK/Bridgeman Images; p.72t Norton Simon Art Foundation, The Flight into Egypt, c.1544–5, Jacopo Bassano (Jacopo da Ponte), Italian, 1510–1592, oil on canvas, framed: 60 5/8 x 90 in. (154.0 x 228.6 cm); canvas: 48 ½ x 77 ¼ in. (123.2 x 196.2 cm); p72b Private Collection/Bridgeman Images; p.73 Private Collection/photo © Christie's Images/Bridgeman Images; p.74 © Guildhall Art Gallery, City of London/Harold Samuel Collection/Bridgeman Images; p.75 Iris & B. Gerald Cantor Center for Visual Arts at Stanford University; Lent by V. Scott Borison Chapter 9 p.76 Metropolitan Museum of Art, New York, USA/photo © Christie's Images/Bridgeman Images; p.77 © Christie's Images 2016/Mark Boxer Estate; p.79l© Christie's Images Limited; p.79r Private Collection/photo © Christie's Images/Bridgeman Images; p.80 National Gallery, London, UK/Bridgeman Images; p.81 Private Collection/photo © Christie's Images/Bridgeman Images Chapter 10 p.82 © The National Gallery, London; p.84 Private Collection/photo © Christie's Images/Bridgeman Images; p.85 Private Collection, on loan to the Scottish National Gallery, Edinburgh, since 1973; p.86t © Bristol Museum and Art Gallery, UK/Accepted by Her Majesty's Government in lieu of tax and presented, 1988/Bridgeman Images; p.86b Private Collection/photo © Agnew's, London/Bridgeman Images; p.87t Yale Center for British Art, Paul Mellon Collection; p.87b © Christie's Images Limited Chapter 11 p.88 Private Collection; p.89l photo © Christie's Images/Bridgeman Images; p.89r © Christie's Images Limited; p.90t The Norton Simon Foundation, Portrait of a Lady, 1641, Johannes Corneliszoon Verspronk, Dutch, 1606/9–1662, oil on canvas, 31 1/8 x 26 1/8 in. (79.1 x 66.4 cm); p.90b Private Collection/photo © Agnew's, London/Bridgeman Images; p.91 © Walker Art Gallery, National Museums Liverpool/Bridgeman Images; p.93t Private Collection/photo © Mark Fiennes/Bridgeman Images; p.93b Private Collection/photo © Christie's Images/Bridgeman Images; p.94t Private Collection/Bridgeman Images; p.94b Private Collection/photo © Christie's Images/Bridgeman Images; p.96l © The National Gallery, London; p.96r Manchester Art Gallery, UK/Bridgeman Images; p.97 Courtesy National Gallery of Art, Washington Chapter 12 p.98 Purchased with assistance from the Friends of the Tate Gallery 1975 © Tate, London 2016, Giovanna Baccelli, Exhibited 1782, Thomas Gainsborough, 1727–1788; p.101 © Christie's Images Limited; p.102 © Victoria and Albert Museum, London; p.103 Photograph courtesy of Sotheby's Picture Library; p.105 © Christie's Images Limited; p.106 © 2016 The Andy Warhol Foundation for the Visual Arts, Inc./Artists Rights Society (ARS), New York and DACS, London; p.107l photo © Christie's Images/Bridgeman Images; p.107r © Christie's Images Limited Chapter 13 p.108 © The National Gallery, London; p.110 Birmingham Museums and Art Gallery/Bridgeman Images; p.111 Private Collection/photo © Christie's Images/Bridgeman Images; p.112 © Christie's Images Limited; p.113l Private Collection; p.113r Private Collection/photo © Christie's Images/Bridgeman Images; p.114 © Christie's Images Limited; p.116 Manchester Art Gallery, UK/Bridgeman Images Chapter 14 p.118 Cincinnati Art Museum, Ohio, USA/Mr and Mrs Harry S. Leyman Endowment/Bridgeman Images; p.119 Private Collection/photo © Christie's Images/Bridgeman Images; p.120l Private Collection/Bridgeman Images; p.120r Private Collection/photo © Christie's Images/Bridgeman Images; p.121 © Christie's Images Limited; p.123 Charles Hindlip/© Matthew Hollow Photography; p.124 Private Collection/Bridgeman Images; p.125t Private Collection/De Agostini Picture Library/Bridgeman Images; p.125b Staatsgalerie Moderner Kunst, Munich, Germany/Bridgeman Images © Salvador Dali, Fundació Gala-Salvador Dali, DACS 2016 Chapter 15 p.126 Private Collection/Bridgeman Images 2016 © 2016 Mondrian/Holtzman Trust; p.127 © The Trustees of the British Museum; p.128t © Charles Hindlip; p.128m Private Collection/photo © Christie's Images/Bridgeman Images; p.128b The J. Paul Getty Museum, Los Angeles, Digital image courtesy of the Getty's Open Content Program; p.129 Photograph courtesy of Sotheby's Picture Library; p.130 © Christie's Images Limited; p.131t © Christie's Images Limited; p.131b Private Collection/photo © Christie's Images/Bridgeman Images; p.132 Belton House, Grantham, Lincolnshire, UK/National Trust Photographic Library/Andrew Butler/Bridgeman Images; p.133 Belton House, Grantham, Lincolnshire, UK/National Trust Photographic Library/Andreas von Einsiedel/Bridgeman Images; p.134l Private Collection/photo © Christie's Images/Bridgeman Images; p.134r © The National Gallery, London; p.135t © Christie's Images Limited; p.135b Los Angeles County Museum of Art, CA, USA/Bridgeman Images Chapter 16 p.136 © Christie's Images Limited; p.139 Private Collection © Succession Picasso/DACS, London 2016; p.140 Prado, Madrid, Spain/Bridgeman Images; p.141 Private Collection/photo © Christie's Images/Bridgeman Images Chapter 17 p.142 Presented by Sir Charles Clore 1959 © Tate, London 2016 © Succession Brancusi – All rights reserved. ADAGP, Paris and DACS, London 2016; p.144tl © Christie's Images Limited; p.144tr © Christie's Images Limited; p.144b Private Collection/photo © Christie's Images/Bridgeman Images; p.145 Private Collection/photo © Christie's Images/Bridgeman Images; p.146l Private Collection/Bridgeman Images; p.146r Photograph courtesy of Sotheby's Picture Library; p.148 Private Collection/photo © Christie's Images/Bridgeman Images; p.149 J. Paul Getty Museum, Los Angeles, USA/Bridgeman Images Chapter 18 p.150 Private Collection/photo © Christie's Images/Bridgeman Images; p.152 Seiji Togo Memorial Sompo Japan Nipponkoa Museum of Art, Tokyo, Japan/Bridgeman Images; p.154l Private Collection/photo © Christie's Images/Bridgeman Images; p.154r © The Trustees of the Weston Park Foundation, UK/Bridgeman Images; p.155 Presented to the National Gallery under the acceptance-in-lieu procedure, 1987 © The National Gallery, London; p.156 Fitzwilliam Museum, University of Cambridge, UK/Bridgeman Images; p.157t Birmingham Museums and Art Gallery/Bridgeman Images; p.157b Photograph courtesy of Sotheby's Picture Library Chapter 19 p.160 Private Collection/photo © Christie's Images/Bridgeman Images; p.162 Private Collection/photo © Christie's Images/Bridgeman Images; p.164l Private Collection/photo © Christie's Images/Bridgeman Images; p.164r Private Collection/photo © Lefevre Fine Art Ltd, London/Bridgeman Images/© Chagall ®/© ADAGP, Paris and DACS, London 2016; p.165t Private Collection/photo © Christie's Images/Bridgeman Images; p.165b Private Collection/photo © Christie's Images/Bridgeman Images; p.166 Private Collection © Succession Picasso/DACS, London 2016; p.168 The J. Paul Getty Museum, Los Angeles, Digital image courtesy of the Getty's Open Content Program Chapter 20 p.170 Private Collection/photo © Christie's Images/Bridgeman Images; p.171t Private Collection/photo © Christie's Images/Bridgeman Images; p.171b © The Cecil Beaton Studio Archive at Sotheby's; p.172 Private Collection/photo © Christie's Images/Bridgeman Images; p.173 Private Collection/photo © Christie's Images/Bridgeman Images; p.174 Private Collection/photo © Christie's Images/Bridgeman Images/© ADAGP, Paris and DACS, London 2016; p.175 Private Collection © Succession Picasso/DACS, London 2016; p.176 © Christie's Images Limited; p.177 © Christie's Images Limited; p.178l Private Collection/photo © Christie's Images/Bridgeman Images; p.178r Private Collection/photo © Christie's Images/Bridgeman Images; p.179l Private Collection/Bridgeman Images; p.179r © The National Gallery, London Chapter 21: p.180 Bought with contributions from the National Heritage Memorial Fund and The Art Fund and Mr J. Paul Getty Jnr (through the American Friends of the National Gallery), 1992 © The National Gallery, London; p.181 Private Collection/photo © Christie's Images/Bridgeman Images; p.182t Private Collection/photo © Christie's Images/Bridgeman Images; p.182b © Christie's Images Limited; p.184 Charles Hindlip; p.185l Private Collection; p.185r © Christie's Images Limited; p.186l © Christie's Images Limited; p.186r Prussian Palaces and Gardens Foundation Berlin-Brandenburg/Photographer Roland Handrick; p.187t Upton House, Warwickshire, UK/National Trust Photographic Library/John Hammond/Bridgeman Images; p.187b Musée du Louvre, Paris, France/Bridgeman Images; p.188 Private Collection/Bridgeman Images © Jasper Johns/VAGA, New York/DACS, London 2016; p.189l Private Collection/photo © Christie's Images/Bridgeman Images; p.189r Private Collection/photo © Christie's Images/Bridgeman Images Chapter 22 p.190 Private Collection/photo © Christie's Images/Bridgeman Images © ADAGP, Paris and DACS, London 2016; p.192 De Agostini Picture Library/Bridgeman Images; p.194t Private Collection/Bridgeman Images; p.194b © Miho Museum; p.195t © The Trustees of the British Museum; p.195b Private Collection/photo © Christie's Images/Bridgeman Images; p.196 photo Pascal Hinous/© Christie's Images Limited; p.198 Ex-Royal Holloway and Bedford New College, Surrey, UK/Bridgeman Images; p.199 © Royal Holloway and Bedford New College, Surrey, UK/Bridgeman Images Chapter 23 p.200 Bought with the support of the Heritage Lottery Fund, 1997 © The National Gallery, London; p.201 © Country Life/Bridgeman Images; p.202t photo © Neil Holmes/Bridgeman Images; p.202b Private Collection/Bridgeman Images; p.203 © Christie's Images Limited; p.204 Private Collection/photo © Christie's Images/Bridgeman Images; p.205l Private Collection © 2016 The Andy Warhol Foundation for the Visual Arts, Inc./Artists' Rights Society (ARS), New York and DACS, London; p.205r Private Collection © Estate of Roy Lichtenstein/DACS 2016; p.206 Private Collection/Bridgeman Images; p.208 Bought by Private Treaty Sale with a grant from the American Friends of the National Gallery, London, made possible by Mr J. Paul Getty Jnr's Endowment Fund, 1995 © The National Gallery, London; p.209 © Christie's Images Limited Chapter 24 p.210 Private Collection/photo © Christie's Images/Bridgeman Images © Succession Picasso/DACS, London 2016; p.211 Private Collection/Bridgeman Images; p.213 Private Collection/photo © Christie's Images/Bridgeman Images © Succession Picasso/DACS, London 2016; p.214 © Christie's Images Limited; p.216 © Christie's Images Limited; p.217 Channel 4; p.218 Private Collection/photo © Christie's Images/Bridgeman Images © Succession Brancusi – All rights Reserved, ADAGP, Paris and DACS, London 2016; p.219 Private Collection/photo © Christie's Images/Bridgeman Images; p.220 Private Collection/photo © Christie's Images/Bridgeman Images; p.221t Private Collection/photo © Christie's Images/Bridgeman Images; p.221b Charles Hindlip Chapter 25 p.222 Cleveland Museum of Art, Ohio, USA/Leonard C. Hanna Jr Fund/Bridgeman Images; p.223 Private Collection/photo © Christie's Images/Bridgeman Images; p.225 Private Collection/photo © Christie's Images/Bridgeman Images; p.226l Private Collection/photo © Christie's Images/Bridgeman Images; p.226r Private Collection/photo © Christie's Images/Bridgeman Images; p.227 Private Collection/photo © Christie's Images/Bridgeman Images; p.228 Private Collection/photo © Christie's Images/Bridgeman Images; p.229 Private Collection/photo © Christie's Images/Bridgeman Images Chapter 26 p.230 Private Collection/photo © Christie's Images/Bridgeman Images; p.232l © Victoria and Albert Museum, London; p.232r Courtauld Institute of Art, London, UK/photo © Christie's Images/Bridgeman Images; p.233t Private Collection/photo © Christie's Images/Bridgeman Images; p.233b © Christie's Images Limited; p.235 Private Collection/photo © Christie's Images/Bridgeman Images; p.236t Tim Firkins; p.236b © Christie's Images Limited Chapter 27 p.237 © Christie's Images Limited; p.240t Private Collection/© Matthew Hollow Photography; p.240b © The Lucian Freud Archive/Bridgeman Images; p.241 Presented by the Trustees of the Chantrey Bequest 1952 © Tate, London 2016, Portrait Group, 1951, Rodrigo Moynihan, 1910–1990; p.242 Royal Collection Trust 2016 © The Lucian Freud Archive/original photo © Ian Gavan; p.243 Private Collection/photo © Christie's Images/Bridgeman Images © The Estate of Francis Bacon, All Rights Reserved, DACS 2016 Chapter 28 p.244 © David Dawson; p.246 Private Collection/photo © Christie's Images/Bridgeman Images © 2016 The Andy Warhol Foundation for the Visual Arts, Inc./Artists' Rights Society (ARS), New York and DACS, London; p.247 Galleria degli Uffizi, Florence, Italy/Bridgeman Images; p.248t Sant'Emidio, Ascoli Piceno, Italy/Bridgeman Images; p.248b Charles Hindlip/© Matthew Hollow Photography; p.249 Cathedral of Santa Maria Assunta apse, Spoleto/De Agostini Picture Library/A. Dagli Orti/Bridgeman Images; p.251 Photo courtesy of the Rijksmuseum, Amsterdam